ROGER MARTIN DU GARD

Roger Martin du Gard

ROGER MARTIN DU GARD

BY

DENIS BOAK

LECTURER IN MODERN LANGUAGES
IN THE UNIVERSITY OF HONG KONG

CLARENDON PRESS · OXFORD

1963

Oxford University Press, Amen House, London E.C.4

GLASGOW   NEW YORK   TORONTO   MELBOURNE   WELLINGTON
BOMBAY   CALCUTTA   MADRAS   KARACHI   LAHORE   DACCA
CAPE TOWN   SALISBURY   NAIROBI   IBADAN   ACCRA
KUALA LUMPUR   HONG KONG

Printed in Great Britain by the Villafield Press, Bishopbriggs, Glasgow

PREFACE

Despite his Nobel Prize, Roger Martin du Gard in his lifetime attracted much less critical attention than other modern French novelists such as Duhamel, Romains or Mauriac. This has to some extent been redressed after his death, but there is still no full-length study, although the monographs by Lalou, Daix, Borgal, Brenner and Gibson contain much interesting material, together with Mme Alméras's medical thesis. Since I began work on Martin du Gard, two major documentary sources have become available: the *Souvenirs*—his literary autobiography —in 1955; and copious extracts from his correspondence in the special memorial edition of the *Nouvelle Nouvelle Revue Française* in December 1958. Since then, there has been a fairly steady stream of minor *inédits* in various journals, not all of which I have yet had the opportunity of consulting. I was fortunate enough to have a two-hour conversation with Martin du Gard in June 1955, when he was engaged upon his *Souvenirs*, and I have drawn extensively on this latter work for biographical material, even where sources are not expressly quoted.

The bibliography is not intended to be exhaustive: indeed, since new items appear almost monthly, any attempt of this kind would be premature. I have included in it: first, works by Martin du Gard (quotations in the text are taken from the two-volume *Pléiade* edition); second, other books, and third, articles, which at some stage of the work I found helpful. Novels to which I may refer are not included. The most important critical work on Martin du Gard, besides the books mentioned above, is, I think, to be found in Camus's preface to the *Pléiade* edition, in Ikor's article, and in the relevant chapters by Peyre and Magny. An important letter, probably to the late Jean Prévost, is quoted by Claude Roy in *Descriptions critiques*.

The critical viewpoint from which this book is written should perhaps be clearly stated. It appears to me that all critical judgments, at all levels from the aptitude of the individual word or image, to the problem of the value of a writer's work as a whole, are ultimately subjective or relative. There can be no final criterion of any such term as 'plausibility', 'objectivity', and so on, which will satisfy more than the individual reader or critic. All critical arguments must be persuasive, not conclusive; and the critic can do no more than make judgments, from the widest possible information available, and then explain why he makes them. This is the method which I have tried to follow in this book.

For typographical reasons I have suppressed the exclamation mark when referring to *Devenir!* in the text, and similarly the definite article in the case of *L'Eté 1914*. The study is chronological except for Martin du Gard's drama, which I have grouped together in the penultimate chapter, and is a shortened version of a Cambridge Ph.D. dissertation. I should like to thank the Master and Fellows of Clare College, the French Government, and the Ministry of Education for the grants and scholarships which made it possible; *Librairie Gallimard* for permission to reproduce the frontispiece and quotations from Martin du Gard's works; and Professors O. Nadal, J.-B. Barrère, and especially I. D. McFarlane for valuable suggestions and advice in the course of my research. I should also like to thank Mr. David Schalk for his criticisms of the dissertation, Mrs. Dorothy Tanfield and Mr. Louis M. C. Yung for preparing the typescript, Miss Estelle Bok for the index; and the Clarendon Press for prompt co-operation in publication.

D. B.

Hong Kong,
March 1962.

CONTENTS

I

EARLY YEARS

OF ALL leading modern French novelists, Roger Martin du Gard is probably the least well-known in Britain. Even in his own country, despite his 1937 Nobel Prize, he was never a prominent literary figure to the man in the street. This was intentional: throughout his life he consistently shunned all publicity, from newspaper interviews to the attempts of friends to coax him into the *Académie française*. He devoted himself single-mindedly to his art, never hesitating to abandon or destroy what failed to come up to his rigorous standards, rarely using his pen for any but purely literary purposes.

Only the First World War interrupted a modest and retiring life, lacking incident and adventure except for his occasional travels—to North Africa for his honeymoon, in 1906; to England, with the troupe of the *Vieux-Colombier*, in 1914; to the Rhineland, with the French Army of Occupation, in 1919; to Italy, in 1936 and 1937; to Sweden, to receive the Nobel Prize, in 1937, returning via Denmark, Germany and Austria; to the Antilles for a cruise, in 1939, which war interrupted, forcing a hasty return via the United States. His working life was mainly spent in steady, methodical work away from Paris with its paralysing distractions, usually in some peaceful refuge in the countryside, or, towards the end of his life, on the *Côte d'Azur*. Yet this very modesty conceals a surprising paradox: his ambitions were perhaps greater than those of any other modern French writer except Proust. He saw Tolstoy as the *unique* master of the novel, and deliberately set out to emulate him; and if physical immortality was impossible, he would strive for literary survival. Fame as a man did not interest him; but fame as a writer was a constant preoccupation. Only time will show how far he was successful.

Martin du Gard was born at Neuilly-sur-Seine on March 23rd, 1881. His father was an *avoué* in Paris, and there was a fairly long legal tradition on both sides of his family, which had certainly never before produced an artist. Indeed, it is not altogether fanciful to perceive a similarity between his methods of work and those of a patient, steady solicitor, and in view of his firm belief in hereditary characteristics, he himself would probably not have disclaimed this. His childhood passed without incident until he met, at nine or ten, a boy a little older than himself, one Jean, who fired him with the desire to write verse tragedies on the Classical model. Although he had little success, unlike Jean, who copied out his final versions into an impressive exercise-book, in violet ink, rather like the youthful André Mazerelles in *Devenir*, it is from this time that he dated his firm intention to become a writer.

At the age of eleven, he began to attend the *Ecole Fénelon*, a Catholic school, also following classes at the *Lycée Condorcet*. He by no means distinguished himself there, but was lazy, he claims, rather than stupid, spending much of his time on surreptitious reading.

On the staff of the *Ecole Fénelon* at that time was Abbé Marcel Hébert, who became its *Directeur* in 1895. Hébert, although unable to prevent his pupil's steady and untroubled progress away from the bosom of the Church, nevertheless exercised considerable influence upon him. Hébert was one of the leading members of the Catholic Modernist movement in the late nineteenth century, and his ideas were to form the basis of the *Compromis symboliste* section of *Jean Barois*. (William James, among others, was an admirer of his writings.) Born in 1851, he had been ordained in 1876 after outstanding studies; after 1882, his reading of Kant, Biblical exegesis and scientific work had led him away from literal acceptance of Catholic dogma to the conception of their symbolical truth. By 1895 this development was complete, and about 1898 Hébert began to take an interest in Jaurès and the ideals of Socialism. Then, in 1901, he met the same fate as other leading Modernists such as Loisy and Houtin: he was accused of heresy, some of his private papers being stolen to support the accusation, and forced to resign his post. His attempts to remain within the Church despite this setback proved unsuccessful, and in 1903 he moved to Brussels, where he lived by lecturing in a popular university and by contributing to the Left-wing Press. Returning to Paris in 1907, he continued his journalism, but otherwise lived in semi-retirement until his death in 1916.

Hébert greatly influenced Martin du Gard, who made a generous tribute to him after his death.[1] On having to choose a confessor from the priests at the *Ecole*, Martin du Gard immediately decided upon Hébert, although he admits that he had, 'par nature, aucun sentiment de piété'.[2] His contact with Hébert in the confessional, however, was fruitful, despite his own lack of zeal, since he admired Hébert both for his spiritual and his intellectual purity. Although he left the *Ecole Fénelon* in 1895, he continued to visit Hébert, and later began a correspondence lasting until his death; *Barois* is dedicated to Hébert, and he was probably the model both for the hero of *Une Vie de Saint* and Abbé Vécard in *Les Thibault*.

By this time Martin du Gard had begun to write in greater earnest:

J'avais toujours sur moi un petit dictionnaire de rimes, un cahier où j'écrivais des poèmes sentimentaux et je composais aussi de brèves nouvelles, d'inspiration exclusivement 'réaliste',—et d'un mauvais goût inimaginable . . .[3]

—the 'mauvais goût' no doubt being the somewhat scabrous subject-matter; a taste which as we shall see recurs throughout his career. Yet this writing was scarcely aiding his progress at school, and in January 1896, his father, alarmed by his apparent backwardness, put him *en pension* at Passy with a former *normalien*, Professor Mellerio of the *Lycée Janson de Sailly*. Martin du Gard later used this experience in *Devenir*, transferring

---

[1] *In Memoriam*, Paris, 1916; reprinted in A. Houtin, *Un prêtre symboliste: Marcel Hébert*, Paris, 1925, and in the *Pléiade* edition.
[2] *In Memoriam*, p. 564.   [3] *Souvenirs*, p. xliii.

it to Bernard Grosdidier, and he bears abundant testimony in his *Souvenirs* to the excellent formative effect of the months spent with Mellerio. This took several forms. In the first place, it was the first time that he had been separated from his parents, and he now began to look more objectively at his former environment. This is no doubt the origin of the social irony, tending towards satire, which permeates *Devenir*, and also of his acute observation of the external details of social behaviour. Secondly, Mellerio and his wife took an interest in people as human beings, distinct personalities, and this too influenced Martin du Gard, who was later to claim that in the last analysis a novelist stands or falls by the number of individual characters he has succeeded in creating. Thirdly, he was allowed, indeed encouraged, to read widely, whatever he wanted, with no parental censorship, as previously, over what he read. (We may note, in this context, the sharp contrast in *Le Cahier gris* between the strict supervision of Jacques's reading matter and the complete freedom enjoyed by the Protestant Daniel de Fontanin.) This was doubly valuable because it was supplemented by intelligent discussion with the Mellerios. The range of books available was extensive: 'De Chateaubriand à Paul Bourget, à Anatole France, je crois qu'aucun écrivain du XIX siècle ne manquait à l'appel.'[1] In addition to this literary initiation, he was undergoing a full course of coaching, which succeeded so well that in October 1897 he was able to join the *classe de rhétorique*, as a day-student, at the *Lycée Janson de Sailly*.

A further benefit, arising more directly from the coaching, was that he learned the value of 'la dure et fructueuse expérience du travail'—of planning and perseverance. His wide reading meant that he became one of the best-read French novelists, and was thus free to select from a wide variety of ideas, themes and techniques; planning and steady work provided him with the means of execution after the original creative act of conception had taken place, permitting him to curb excessive enthusiasm and stimulate flagging inspiration. The planning, which preceded actual composition, is of the utmost importance in his work,

---

[1] Ibid., p. xliii.

largely accounting for its solidity. Even *Devenir*, dashed off in a few weeks, was written to a careful plan; the later novels even more so. The relevant passage in the *Souvenirs* pays ample tribute to Mellerio's insistence on 'le sens de la composition,' the feeling for the construction of the work which is so characteristic of Martin du Gard.[1]

Martin du Gard went on to take his two *Baccalauréats* at the *Lycée Janson de Sailly*, and in November 1898 entered the *Sorbonne*, to prepare for the *Licence ès Lettres*. About this time he discovered Tolstoy, when Hébert lent him a copy of *War and Peace:* the influence of Tolstoy has since been paramount in his work, as he has readily acknowledged.[2] At the *Sorbonne* he became a pupil of Faguet, who began to take an interest in him, encouraging him and recommending him to gain practice and experience by writing for the Press. He did not take this advice, and, although he has incidentally shown considerable critical talents, has always avoided journalistic work, which he regarded as the needless frittering away of creative material in an impermanent medium.[3]

In any case, his stay at the *Sorbonne* was brief, since he failed his *Licence* in July 1899. Unwilling to spend another year grinding at Latin and Greek compositions, he decided to attempt the entrance examination of the *Ecole des Chartes*. He has claimed that he did not know why he took this step, but the reasons seem fairly clear. Above all, he wished to escape the dullness of a legal career; at the same time, he had to appear to be usefully occupied, as his cousin has put it, 'pour ne plus s'entendre reprocher par son père de n'être pas encore avoué, notaire, inspecteur des finances ou lieutenant de hussards comme les camarades de son milieu et de son âge'.[4] To realize his literary ambitions, he had to mark time somehow, and the lengthy course at the *Ecole des Chartes* combined this with a means of

---

[1] Ibid., pp. xlv–xlvi.　　[2] Ibid., p. xlvi.

[3] Cf. a remark in a letter to André Maurois: 'le romancier impénitent qui demeure en moi souffre de vous voir jeter dans des "essais" tant de beaux sujets de romans', quoted by Maurois in the *Nouvelle N.R.F.*, 12/58, p. 1035.

[4] Maurice Martin du Gard in *Revue des Deux Mondes*, 1/10/58, p. 464. (François Mauriac, too, a few years later, was a student at the *Ecole des Chartes*.)

profiting from the *volontariat*, which would reduce the period of his military service to a single year. According to his cousin, he was also deeply dissatisfied with his social background, and his desire to write, to establish himself in a field of his own choosing, was closely connected with this, since it would permit him to 'se faire prendre au sérieux par ses parents et (..) inquiéter un peu les consciences trop tranquilles.'[1] And in addition to his feeling at his fortunate station in life, a certain physical ugliness made him feel still more at odds with the bourgeois society of his birth.

Whatever his motives, his years at the *Ecole des Chartes*, where he remained until 1905, with the exception of a year's military service in 1902–3, were clearly not wasted. Like most of the *Ecoles Spéciales*, the *Ecole des Chartes* has no exact English equivalent. It is intended primarily for the training of palæographers and archivists in the handling of historical sources, both documentary and archaeological. Although at first sight this appears remote from creative writing, Martin du Gard has paid tribute to what he learnt;

... l'attention qu'il m'a fallu accorder aux siècles passés, m'a donné du goût pour l'histoire en général, et a fait naître en moi une curiosité toute nouvelle pour les événements contemporains. Jusque-là, je m'en étais fort peu soucié ... (..) Cet intérêt pour l'histoire (..) m'a fréquemment amené à faire, dans mes livres, une place aux faits politiques dont mes personnages se trouvaient être les témoins. Il m'était devenu impossible de concevoir un personnage moderne détaché de son temps; de la société, de l'histoire de son temps.[2]

But more important than the content of his studies was the rigid scientific discipline of the *Ecole*, the meticulous regard for accuracy, the painstaking investigation, powerfully reinforcing the respect for planning and hard work already instilled by Mellerio. This intellectual integrity remained with him: three times he abandoned work on which he had spent years, and twice he destroyed it, to make his decision irrevocable (*Marise* and *L'Appareillage*). It is of course arguable, to quote Robert Mallet, that 'l'enseignement de l'*Ecole des Chartes* avait agi sur un tempérament prédisposé à l'accueillir, car "on n'est jamais

---

[1] Ibid., p. 463.   [2] *Souvenirs*, pp. xlviii–xlix.

influencé que par ceux qui vont dans votre sens" '[1]; but it appears from the correspondence with Margaritis that the method of the *Ecole* radically changed his literary technique, which had previously suffered from excessive 'facilité', and, one may suspect, the inability to follow through inspiration by execution which so characterizes André Mazerelles:

... après la discipline des Chartes, sous l'influence de Coppet à qui ma grande facilité faisait une peur effroyable—j'ai renoncé à cette façon de travailler dans la rue; j'ai affirmé que l'inspiration venait aussi bien dans la turne, avec l'application et la régularité de vie; et j'ai adopté cette méthode cul de chaise.[2]

In December 1905 he graduated from the *Ecole* with his thesis for the *Diplôme d'archiviste-paléographe*. This thesis, at the time the only monograph on the Abbaye de Jumièges near Rouen (now ruined, but formerly one of the largest Benedictine monasteries in France), was published in 1909, and substantially reprinted in 1927. It necessarily contains little sign of literary ability, but illustrates clearly the rigorous scientific methods and standards practised at the *Ecole*.

In the following February 1906, Martin du Gard married Hélène Foucault, the daughter of a Paris lawyer. The couple spent an extended honeymoon of four months in North Africa before returning to settle down in Paris, and during this time Martin du Gard was at last able to devote himself to full-time writing. His first novel was to be a long work in three parts, on the Tolstoyan model: the story of a country priest, to be entitled *Une Vie de Saint*:

C'était la minutieuse biographie d'un prêtre du diocèse de Sées: je le prenais à sa naissance et le conduisais pas à pas, à travers les étapes de son évolution religieuse, à travers toutes les expériences de sa vie et de son œuvre paroissiale, jusqu'à sa mort, à un âge avancé, dans un humble presbytère de campagne. (Je n'imaginais pas que mon entrée dans la littérature pût se faire autrement que par un long roman dialogué, s'étendant sur plusieurs tomes, et où je comptais mettre en scène tout un monde . . .[3]

But the attempt finally came to nothing: after eighteen months of hard work, after Martin du Gard had written the length of two small volumes, he was obliged to abandon the attempt. It is not difficult to see why he failed. His ambition and self-confidence evidently exceeded his ability; instead of making his literary *début* with a short novel, largely autobiographical, in the conventional manner, or with a slim volume of verse, like Romains, Duhamel or Mauriac, he embarked upon an enormous epic in several volumes, which most novelists would be content to make the crowning achievement of their maturity. Then, as if to make matters more difficult, he chose as his subject the life of a country priest. Now, however well he knew Hébert, he was scarcely in a position to write his biography; and there was a world of difference between the life of a scholar and teacher like Hébert, and a simple country priest. He would therefore be forced to rely on imagination or second-hand knowledge. Also, since the priest was to die at an advanced age, he would have had to be born about the 1830s, which would involve considerable historical reconstruction, if only of environment. The technical problems were immense, to say nothing of the practical difficulty of finding a publisher for a first novel of inordinate length, written in an experimental dialogue technique.

Another difficulty was his own attitude towards his subject. He had long since ceased to think of himself as a Catholic,[1] and it would therefore have been most difficult for him to have any real sympathy for his hero, unless he were going to make the struggle between Faith and Reason, the crisis of belief, one of the principal themes of his novel. The temptation of satire would provide another pitfall; and would also tend to remove him from his Tolstoyan model. Tolstoy's influence, however beneficial in the later works, was definitely unfortunate here. He might have observed that even Tolstoy did not commence his literary career with *Anna Karenina* or *War and Peace* (and almost all the other *romans de longue haleine* of this century have been preceded by shorter works, with the exception of those of Thomas Wolfe). Something more modest in scope and scale would have been more suitable; as indeed he was to find with *Devenir*.

[1] cf. Houtin, op. cit., p. 139.

Perhaps the most interesting aspect was the dialogue technique, employed in *Une Vie de Saint*, and, in fact, to a large extent in all his works until *Les Thibault*. He wished to unite the advantages of the novel with the greater immediacy of the drama, in order to increase the illusion of reality and objectivity, to give 'une optique de spectateur'.[1]

On abandoning *Une Vie de Saint*, in January 1908, he felt unable to harness himself to another novel immediately, and spent the remainder of the winter in an attempt to acquire some knowledge of psychology and psychiatry. He visited hospitals and attended the clinical lectures of, among others, Gilbert Ballet, Babinski, Reymond and Georges Dumas.[2] Although this knowledge of psychology must necessarily have been somewhat superficial, he believed that it helped him to 'regarder au fond des êtres',[3] and it certainly furnished him with a good deal of first-hand knowledge of hospitals and medical practice generally, later to be used in *L'Une de nous* and *Les Thibault*. Nevertheless these clinical studies were at best a stop-gap; and Martin du Gard felt seriously demoralized by the failure of *Une Vie de Saint*. He began to doubt his literary vocation, and was seized by a powerful urge to prove himself by bringing out a book, more to convince himself than anyone else. This worry itself provided the solution: he decided to write 'le roman d'un raté'—a novel about the unsuccessful writer which he hoped he was not but feared he might be. *Devenir* was written in a matter of weeks in Spring 1908, at Barbizon, and was published by Ollendorff, at the author's expense, later the same year. The young novelist was finally launched on his career.

---

[1] *Souvenirs*, p. lviii.   [2] Ibid., p. l.   [3] Ibid., p. xlvii.

2

DEVENIR!

MARTIN DU GARD has summarized the theme of *Devenir*, in his Nobel Prize speech:

J'étais encore très jeune, lorsque j'ai rencontré, dans un roman de l'Anglais Thomas Hardy, cette réflexion sur l'un de ses personnages: 'La vraie valeur de la vie lui semblait moins être sa beauté, que son tragique.' Cela répondait en moi à une intuition profonde, étroitement liée à ma vocation littéraire. Dès cette époque, je pensais déjà (ce que je pense encore): que le principal objet du roman c'est d'exprimer le tragique de la vie. J'ajouterai aujourd'hui le tragique d'une vie individuelle, le tragique d'une *destinée en train de s'accomplir*.[1]

'Une destinée en train de s'accomplir . . .' The hero of the novel is André Mazerelles, who believes he has the ability to become a great writer. The novel depicts his various attempts to launch himself in the literary world, all of which end in failure. As a *pis-aller* he marries and settles down on a provincial farm, but even here he has no success: his farm loses money, but is too heavily mortgaged to sell, and the novel ends with his complete disillusionment and despair after his wife's death in childbirth.

The primary theme of the novel is therefore that of failure— the ultimate defeat of ambition. A line from Montaigne is given as epigraph to the last section:

Nous n'allons pas, on nous emporte, comme les choses qui flottent, ores doucement, ores avecques violence, selon que l'eau est ireuse ou bonasse . . . (p. 203).

Devenir treats many of the themes which will occupy Martin du Gard throughout his life, while André Mazerelles is a prototype of the later heroes—Jean Barois and the Thibault brothers, and although *Devenir* was regarded as 'une improvisation de circonstance'[2] the relationship is clear.

[1] *Les Prix Nobel en 1937*, Stockholm, 1938, p. 68.   [2] *Souvenirs*, p. li.

Much of the novel is autobiographical, but he does not identify himself too closely with his hero. By means of the device which Lalou has called the *dédoublement du héros*,[1] André Mazerelles takes on Martin du Gard's own background (and possibly his parents), and has many of his ideas about literature; but the other main character, André's friend Bernard Grosdidier, has the author's actual physical appearance, attends the *Ecole des Chartes*, and holds various other of his literary ideas, notably the belief in planning and hard work. Martin du Gard identifies himself with Bernard, acting as a foil to André, who is throughout viewed critically.

The novel opens at the exact point where his literary career should commence. He and Bernard form part of a group of eight young men beginning their careers after army service; a group based on the author's own friends and his own experiences as a well-to-do student.[2] But all this is subordinated to the principal aim of portraying André's vain struggle towards achievement.

The novel is divided into three sections: *Vouloir!*; *Réaliser?*; and *Vivre*. . . . The punctuation is important; it marks André's progressive disillusionment and disappointments. *Vouloir* shows the group at the threshold of their careers; *Réaliser* shows their progress—in the Diplomatic Service, at *Normale*, in the literary and artistic worlds—contrasted with André's own lack of success. Only one character, Fink, appears to be in a similar position to André, and he extricates himself by marrying and taking up farming. In *Vivre*, André, who is essentially imitative by nature, attempts to follow Fink's example, with tragic results. Martin du Gard himself has described André's basic predicament:

. . . l'impuissance d'un faux artiste à créer une œuvre durable, à vaincre le Temps; c'est la souffrance déchirante et sotte du raté intelligent devant sa vie qu'il gâche consciemment, jour après jour, sans pouvoir autrement.[3]

With no real vocation for literature, he has ideas, but no perseverance, and continually conceives grandiose projects which go

[1] R. Lalou, *Roger Martin du Gard*, Paris, 1937, p. 27.   [2] *Souvenirs*, pp. lviii–lix.
[3] *N.N.R.F.*, 12/58, pp. 1119–20 (letter by Martin du Gard to Pierre Margaritis).

little farther than the title-page. (It is one of the minor ironies of the novel that his father, a dull notary, is probably right when he insists that André should follow him into the legal profession.) André's lack of vocation is closely linked to another weakness: his inability to tolerate solitude. As soon as he is alone with a blank sheet of paper his creative powers escape him. His nearest attempt to actual creation accompanies his brief affair with Ketty at Fontainebleau, yet he is so weak that he breaks with her when he fears that she has fallen in love with him and might be bearing his child.

The theme of solitude will recur in all Martin du Gard's later work: metaphysical solitude, the inability of human beings to make permanent and satisfactory contact with each other. Apparent contact is an illusion, rapidly dispelled. The group of the *huit* breaks up within a year, and André is thrown back on his own resources. Unable to sustain himself, eventually he finds himself leading the same social life he has previously so much despised, making a loveless marriage, and exiling himself to the country in a vain imitation of Fink. Ultimately his solitude only increases.

This sense of solitude and the impossibility of durable, intimate contacts pervade the whole novel. They find expression in André's relationship with his parents, largely one of mutual incomprehension, and even in his friendship with Bernard, who realizes, after only seven months of separation, that a gulf now extends between André and himself (p. 93).

Martin du Gard's comment partly explains his own motives for wishing to write: *vaincre le Temps*. He sees in creative activity the only possibility of survival, the only defence against the destructive effect of time, inevitably culminating in death:

A l'origine de ma vocation d'écrivain, il y a la terreur de la brièveté d'une vie humaine, un désir éperdu de se protéger, de se survivre quelque temps. (. .) La clef secrète de ma vie aurait été l'horreur de l'oubli et de la mort.[1]

The theme of survival, the fight against time, is central to an understanding of André.

---

[1] Quoted by Lalou, in *Revue de Paris*, 10/58, p. 63.

The model for a novel of failure, of unfulfilled promise, is naturally Flaubert's *Education sentimentale*, and this must have been in Martin du Gard's mind, since there are various similarities. There is, however, a much closer parallel—Barrès's *Déracinés*. There can be no doubt that Martin du Gard was influenced by at least two aspects of Barrès's work. Barrès's group of young men arriving in Paris from Lorraine is repeated in the *huit* arriving after their military service; Ketty Varine is clearly based on Astiné Aravian; while one of André's abortive projects is to be a *Déracinés* centred upon his own group (p. 90). The other aspect of Barrès is that of the *culte du moi*. Here the influence is reinforced by that of one of Barrès's own disciples, Jean de Tinan.

Tinan, to whom *Devenir* is dedicated, is almost forgotten today, but he was a leading figure in literary journalism in the nineties, collaborating on the *Mercure de France*, ghosting for Willy, and writing several delicate ethereal works of his own,[1] before dying of consumption in 1898 at the age of 24. The *culte du moi* for Tinan implied a mixture of political and literary ambition, development of the sexual ego, enthusiasm for pseudo-Nietzschean aphorisms. His hero, in *Penses-tu réussir?*, mentioned in *Devenir*, was Raoul de Vallonges, a wealthy young Parisian who effortlessly succeeds in all his enterprises.

It is easy to see the fascination of Tinan, and in some of his descriptive passages Martin du Gard succeeds in recreating the same atmosphere of:

une époque privilégiée où l'amour et l'art étaient les principaux tourments des âmes bien nées. Aux portes de la société ne veillaient pas, casqués, le spectre de la révolution flanqué du fantôme de la guerre . . .[2]

Although he had not completely freed himself from Tinan's influence, he was by no means uncritical. André enjoys the same advantages as Vallonges, but his utter failure contrasts with the latter's success. The more prosaic side of literary creation—perseverance and hard work—finds little mention in Tinan; in *Devenir*, Bernard stresses this to André, who expects life to

---

[1] Cf. A. Billy, *L'Epoque 1900*, Paris, 1951, p. 116.
[2] M. Chaffiol-Debillemont, quoted in Billy, op. cit., p. 117.

follow the Vallonges pattern. Where Martin du Gard has most in common with Tinan is in the scenes in the *demi-monde*, for *Devenir*, like its Flaubertian prototype, is not only a novel of failure but one of sentimental education.

Tinan's influence is also evident in the style. Martin du Gard abandoned his idea of narration in dialogue temporarily and, in view of the speed of composition, we should scarcely expect to find a highly polished style. In fact, he displays far greater spontaneity and exuberance than in any later work. Throughout *Devenir*, the tenses employed for narration of action are the present and perfect; passages of exposition and psychological motivation are largely in the imperfect and pluperfect, and linking passages in the past historic. One result of this is that many of the scenes of direct action or dialogue are written in roughly the same technique as later in *Barois* or *L'Une de nous:*

> L'auto ronfle devant la porte.
> Comme un automate, André descend le perron.
> Contre la voiture, raidi, il reçoit le baiser d'adieu; puis il pousse la portière:
> — Allez . . .
> Machinalement, il dit, à demi-voix:
> — Me voilà seul.
> Il se lèvera, seul; il se mettra à table, seul . . .
> Il reviendra de la ferme: où donc est-elle? . . . Dans le salon, personne; dans sa chambre, personne . . . (p. 203)

This use of crisp, short sentences, frequently unfinished, has many parallels in Tinan.

Other techniques he had hoped to use in *Une Vie de Saint* are absent. Indirect presentation of events is abandoned, and the novel is narrated in the third person in the normal way, with comments, often ironical, about the events and characters. He has not developed an individual style of his own, or shaken off a tendency towards neo-Symbolist preciosity, as Camus has pointed out: 'Le fleuve laiteux du ciel charrie des paillettes d'argent.'[1] Nor has he learnt to take his imagery from life, not from literature:

Un *exerciser* tout neuf pend au mur ripoliné; un jeu d'haltères vernies s'aligne sur la table. On se croirait dans un roman de M. Bourget. (pp. 41-42)

---

[1] A. Camus, Introduction to *Pléiade* edition, p. x; and *Devenir*, p. 26.

André,—qui, pour avoir lu trop passionnément Tinan, affecte de psychologuer dans les lieux dits 'de plaisir' . . . (p. 46)

The exuberance of the style—'François s'élance en courant d'air, brandissant le potage' (p. 32)—occasionally degenerates into juvenile puns:'. . . Phydilé Coczani, (. .) vieille fille efflanquée, qui peint un peu, surtout son visage . . .' (p. 72), and paradox: 'Ce qui frappait dès l'abord, c'est qu'en elle rien n'était frappant' (p. 12). There is also a tendency to exaggerate certain mannerisms, particularly the Flaubertian use of the single short sentence between paragraphs; with a constant tendency towards facile irony and crude generalization, and a somewhat shallow wit. The result of this irony is of course social satire, but the flippant note contrasts badly with the underlying seriousness of the basic themes of solitude and failure. A deeper dramatic irony is sometimes used, to reveal the disparity between dreams and reality. Fink's *cabinet consulat* is an example; originally his pride and joy, it becomes the cause of misery until he furnishes a small room with mementos of his childhood, which better represent his true nature. There is an ironic twist at the heart of André's failure: he attempts to devote himself entirely to creative activity, when he is by nature incapable of it, and would be much happier following parental example in the law. Similarly, as Camus has pointed out,[1] there is a touch of bitter irony in the last lines of the novel:

Il lève les yeux vers sa maison vide . . .

Marie, curieuse, penchée à la fenêtre de Madame suit des yeux l'auto qui descend l'avenue. (p. 203)

The trait is subtle but perfectly clear: André will console himself with the maid, who has already taken the place of *Madame* symbolically.

Devenir is very much a young man's novel. Not only are literary influences imperfectly digested, but the confident enthusiasm with which the novel begins is not maintained. In the opening chapters, Martin du Gard attempts to give thorough psychological portraits of eight young men (one more than

[1]Camus, op. cit., pp. xi–xii.

Barrès), quite apart from subsidiary characters such as André's parents. He also has the tendency, common to inexperienced writers using autobiographical material, to linger too indulgently over his descriptions, such as that of the dinner at the *Café Voltaire* and the visit to Fink's *cabinet consulat*. The result is a certain lack of balance, particularly between the second and third sections, and a jerkiness in the passage of time in the later chapters. There is perhaps also a change in tone about half-way through. Whereas M. Mazerelles is somewhat cruelly satirized in the early scenes, the author's attitude towards him changes roughly at the point where André gives up his attempts to write; and at the same point his attitude towards André hardens. Finally, the *dénouement* is much inferior to the earlier sections; Fink's conversion to the open-air life is highly implausible, and André's imitation of him no less so; the characterization of André's wife Denise is weak, and she is in any case only introduced—and killed off—for the necessities of the plot.

Nevertheless, despite its flaws, *Devenir* is a fair achievement as a first novel. Camus has congratulated Martin du Gard on his characterization,[1] although the young girls, such as Denise or Valentine, are by no means as successful as the male characters. The other women in the book are more successful: Mme Mazerelles may well have been based on Martin du Gard's mother; Ketty owes much to Barrès; and the various *filles* could equally have been taken from the pages of Tinan. The *huit* owe less to literature, and probably had real-life models. In general, Martin du Gard subscribes to a neo-Naturalist conception of character, dependent on the interaction of heredity and environment. It follows from this that a description of milieu is necessary for a complete understanding of personality, and he is careful to fill in the background of his character, following Barrès in the use of group psychology.[2]

Political and religious questions are rarely touched upon. The Dreyfus case, for instance, is never mentioned, although it might

---

[1] Ibid., p. vii.
[2] There is an example of something close to *unanimisme* on p. 74 of *Devenir*, in the passage ending: 'Le conférencier est admis.'

have been expected to be a constant subject of conversation among the *huit*. There is a certain amount of social satire, but the savage note of Barrès's attacks in *Les Déracinés* is absent. Religion receives a little more attention, since André's religious development is outlined (pp. 96–97); but here again an insouciant, irrational 'irreligion' is the keynote of his attitude, rather than partisanship. Amongst the others we find a flourishing agnosticism which will be a point of contact with Antoine Thibault (p. 97).

The character and development of André is the most original aspect of the book. If the *huit* can be traced back to the Barresian concept of energy, and much of the background description and analysis of *sensibilité amoureuse* to the works of Tinan, André exemplifies a completely different attitude to the theme of ambition, so important in the two earlier writers. There seems to be no model for the portrait of the failed writer, except Martin du Gard's fears about himself.[1] André is essentially imitative; his literary ability is critical, not creative—and this lies at the root of his failure. He is fertile in ideas, but can never bridge the gap between conception and execution.

Early in the book André expounds an entire theory of the novel, a 'new art'; and here there can be little doubt that the theory is Martin du Gard's own, since it corresponds closely to that actually carried out in *Barois*:

— Moi, je rêve d'un art neuf... Je voudrais faire un livre qui serait 'de la vie', et rien que ça... Un livre qui ne serait ni 'composé', ni 'écrit', parce que dans la vie les événements ne se lient pas par des coïncidences merveilleuses ...(..)

— Imagine une histoire quelconque, très simple, qui ne prouverait rien, où il ne se passerait presque rien, comme sont celles qui arrivent... Les faits s'y suivraient gauchement, avec des précipitations et des lenteurs inattendues, illogiques ...(..)

— Je commencerais: une description; le récit d'un fait; une analyse de caractère; un autre fait; un dialogue; un fragment de journal; un monologue; un bout de lettre; d'autres faits; d'autres analyses; d'autres dialogues... Des documents, enfin, comprends-tu? Fini, le récit délayé d'où émergent les morceaux qui font le livre! Plus de cette sauce gluante où flottent les aliments solides! Ils en sont arrivés, comme dans les gargotes, à avoir la sauce prête

---

[1] cf. *N.N.R.F.*, 12/58, pp. 1122–5 (letters to Margaritis).

d'avance, et ils nous en versent dans tous les plats, indifféremment . . . Non!
ces aliments-là, moi, je les flanquerai tout secs, tels qu'ils sont, isolés, réduits à
leur forme essentielle . . . (pp. 24-25)

Not the least interesting point in this theory is the attitude to
form and content, expressed in the last few sentences. Martin du
Gard later repeats the image of *aliment* and *sauce* when speaking
about style,[1] distinguishes clearly between the two, and has a
fixed preference for content—*fond*. Style is merely a means to
the end of making content as clear as possible; it should
therefore attempt to become invisible, or at least transparent.
(Technique is not to be equated with style in this connexion;
technique is applied equally to both form and content, since
the master plan at the root of his technique essentially represents content.) Now, when challenged by Bernard about the
unity of the novel he is proposing, André claims that the subject-
matter itself would unify the work:

— L'unité, elle ne sera pas dans la forme, mon vieux, elle sera dans le fond,
et on la sentira tout le long du livre, comme on sent l'échine sous la chair . . .
L'unité ? elle m'est garantie, si je fais la vie ressemblante ; car elle y est, je pense,
dans la vie ? . . . (p. 25)

These are, however, no more than projects, and perhaps the
hardest part of literary creation is the steady work necessary to
execute a project. Maurice Martin du Gard has said that his
cousin found the labour of writing exceedingly difficult,[2] even
after 1918; André finds it impossible, since he does not possess
the resources of method. Throughout the book Bernard is
made to stress the importance of hard work, planning, and
perseverance:

Moi aussi j'ai cru qu'il fallait passer des nuits blanches à attendre l'inspiration.
C'est de la blague, tout ça . . . Le génie, tout le monde en a un peu! ce qu'on
n'a plus, maintenant, parce que, ça, il faut l'acquérir, c'est de la conscience
. . . (. .)
On n'a jamais trop de conscience quand on commence : c'est la seule chance
que les années d'atelier vous profitent un peu . . . (p. 92)

[1] *Souvenirs*, p. cvi (extract from Martin du Gard's *Journal*, 17/3/42). The same image
can be traced back at least as far as Maupassant, where in *Bel-Ami* Mme Forestier says
to Dupuy: 'Je ferai la sauce mais il me faut le plat'. (Manz edition, Vienna, undated, p. 64).
[2] Maurice Martin du Gard, op. cit., p. 470.

There is a constant refrain of similar remarks, and again there is no doubt that Bernard represents Martin du Gard's own belief in method, planning, and steady work. Bernard is probably also expressing Martin du Gard's own preference when he criticizes Jemmequin's poetry (p. 93); dislike of artificiality and preciosity, and approval of what is solid, vigorous, and spontaneous. Despite occasional lapses this remained a permanent feature of Martin du Gard's work.[1] The preoccupation with the technical problems of the novelist shows that he is taking sides against the prevailing Idealist view of aesthetics: that Art is basically Imagination (or conception).

Devenir is an interesting novel, yet it is not a great one. Borgal has suggested that this is because a *raté* will never ordinarily make a hero,[2] but this is an oversimplification: the concept of the 'unheroic hero' is today almost a cliché of criticism. Here it would perhaps be appropriate to judge *Devenir* by Martin du Gard's own criteria as expressed in his Nobel Prize speech:

Le romancier né se reconnaît à cette passion qu'il a de pénétrer toujours plus avant dans la connaissance de l'homme, et de dégager en chacun de ses personnages, ce qui est la vie individuelle, ce par quoi chaque être est un exemplaire qui ne se répètera (sic) pas. Il me semble que, si l'œuvre d'un romancier a quelque chance de survivre, c'est seulement par la quantité et la qualité des vies individuelles qu'il aura su fixer. Mais ce n'est pas tout. Il faut, aussi, que le romancier possède le sens de la vie en général; il faut que son œuvre soit le témoignage d'une vision personnelle de l'univers.[3]

If he fulfils the first of these conditions, creating a memorable character, the 'sens de la vie en général' is lacking. The reader can only view André as an individual case, not as a symbol of mankind with universal relevance; and his fate is more pathetic than tragic. The other weaknesses of the novel—the stylistic mannerisms, the undigested literary influences, the temptation to indulge in satire—merely underline this fundamental deficiency. The significance of the novel never transcends the individual events narrated.

[1] Ibid., p. 470, where he describes some of his cousin's dislikes: Giraudoux—'ce pèse-gouttes'; Valéry's *Monsieur Teste*—'vous supportez cela?'; and even Proust.

[2] C. Borgal, *Roger Martin du Gard*, Paris, 1957, p. 41.

[3] *Les Prix Nobel en 1937*, pp. 68–69.

3

MARISE

WITH the publication of *Devenir*, Martin du Gard felt sufficiently confident to make another Tolstoyan attempt on the grand scale.[1] Once again he chose a biographical theme:

Je projetais encore une fois de composer une longue monographie: l'histoire d'une femme, de sa naissance à sa sa mort. Je rêvais de décrire les premières songeries et les tendres élans d'une adolescence féminine; puis, les aventures, les joies, les déceptions, les souffrances de la jeune femme, de l'épouse, de la mère; puis, l'épanouissement de la maturité et ses derniers feux; enfin, le lent acheminement de l'être qui vieillit; l'abdication progressive, traversée d'ultimes révoltes, jusqu'à l'heure mélancolique de la résignation.[2]

In this conception the theme of death was to be crucial. Death, for Martin du Gard, is the fundamental *donnée* of the human condition; desire for survival and metaphysical solitude are merely subsidiary aspects of this main theme. He proposed to treat the problem of death in its more powerful and direct manifestations—the destructive effect of time and the advent of old age:

Ce thème du 'vieillissement' m'a toujours obsédé; il a tenu une grande place dans la plupart de mes livres. (. .) Je me proposais de consacrer tout un volume aux dernières années de mon héroïne, et de rendre, avec toutes ses nuances, cet apaisement, teinté d'indifférence sinon de sécheresse, qui vient souvent comme une grâce suprême adoucir la fin des destinées tumultueuses; je voulais m'attacher à peindre avec un soin particulier cet âge où tout ce qui passionne les vivants n'éveille plus d'écho dans la sensibilité assoupie; l'âge des 'jamais plus', l'étape finale où, quoiqu'on (sic) veuille, quoiqu'on fasse pour en détourner sa pensée, la mort, même si elle tarde à paraître en scène, même si aucun signe ne l'annonce, compte infiniment plus pour le vieillard que ce sursis de vie dont il jouit encore.[3]

---

[1] *Souvenirs*, pp. li–lii. [2] Ibid., p. lii. [3] Ibid., pp. lii–liii.

(This passage takes on an added significance and pathos when we remember that it was written when Martin du Gard himself was a sick man in his seventies; clearly he had himself in mind as much as Marise.)

Despite all his hopes, *Marise* failed abysmally. He had scarcely gone beyond compiling dossiers of notes, sketches and documentation before he was forced to realize that he could never bring the novel to a successful conclusion. Once more he had chosen a subject too far removed from the range of his own experience, outside the scope of his still insufficiently developed abilities, and found himself overwhelmed by unexpected complications. The character of a woman no doubt presented, if anything, even more problems than that of a priest; already in *Devenir* his weakest characterization had been that of women.

He soon decided that further efforts would be futile, and abandoned *Marise*, destroying almost all his materials. But not quite all: he preserved the section nearest completion, and turned it into a *nouvelle*, *L'Une de nous*, which Bernard Grasset, then establishing himself as a young publisher in Paris, brought out at the author's expense in 1910. The book had no success with the public, and Martin du Gard soon regretted having published it. During the First War he took the opportunity of having all remaining stocks pulped.[1] He excluded it from the collected edition of his works,[2] condemning its 'naturalisme suranné', and its 'sensiblerie et mauvais goût déplorables'.[3] The author's own judgment, though severe, is undoubtedly correct. Nevertheless, *L'Une de nous* repays study, if not for its own sake, for the light it throws on development of technique and on later themes and characters.

The *nouvelle* is divided into three parts. The plot is as follows: Marise, the heroine, as an innocent adolescent, falls in love with her cousin Raymond Lefèvre, a spoilt child become a *noceur invétéré*, who is twelve years older than herself. She keeps her love a secret until a few years later, when Raymond, in one of the intervals in his debauchery, 'tenté par sa fraîcheur', asks

[1] Ibid., pp. liii–liv.   [2] 'J'en ai honte', was his comment to the present writer in 1955.
[3] *Souvenirs*, p. liii.

her to marry him. But the marriage is not successful and Marise, although she tries to turn herself into the sensual creature of her husband's real desires, is unable to hold his fidelity. Then, one morning, he arrives home on a stretcher, after having had a stroke, 'quelque part, dans la nuit'. Gradually she nurses him back to health, despite the fear of a relapse; her mental suffering has been extreme. All this is told in an expositional flashback; the narrative proper, and the book itself, open at this point. After a pilgrimage to Lourdes, Raymond appears much improved, and the Lefèvres have some friends in for the evening, including their doctor, Germain Mussey. While Raymond is out of the room, Marise asks Mussey if her husband is definitely cured. Mussey, in a moral dilemma, is torn between telling the truth, and giving Marise a brief interlude of happiness.

The pages of recapitulation are inserted here; and when the direct narrative is taken up again, Mussey has gone and Raymond is back. In her happiness Marise cradles her head against his shoulder, only to glimpse in his eyes the flash of sexual desire. She attempts to draw back, but it is too late: 'elle reconnaît, à travers les étoffes, le palpement oublié de ses mains. La mémoire physique des caresses, morte depuis un an et ensevelie en elle, ressuscite d'un coup et l'embrase'.[1] The scene which follows is of unequalled sexual intensity, and is clearly what Martin du Gard had in mind when he spoke of 'un mauvais goût déplorable'. At the climax of intercourse, at the very moment of orgasm, Raymond has another stroke. Marise realizes this, but is physically incapable of doing anything until the orgasm is over, when she tears herself away with a terrible cry.

This ends the first section. Part II, consisting of nine fairly short episodes of unequal length, begins some five weeks later: Raymond is still alive, but barely; he is half paralysed and has not the use of his faculties. Their sickly son Jean—congenitally feeble as a result of his father's disease (syphilis is hinted at)—has almost died as well, as a result of shock after being the first on the scene after the stroke. Marise herself has been cruelly shaken and is almost beside herself with grief, but worse is to come.

[1] *L'Une de nous*, Paris, 1910, p. 23.

Slow, agonizing descriptions convey her gradual realization that, as a result of the fateful evening, she is once again pregnant, and is terrified that the child will be even more congenitally stricken than its brother. This is too much for her. She cannot believe that she has deserved it, and as a result she is tempted to reject completely the religion she has previously accepted. The nun sent to nurse Raymond, Sœur Angélina, can offer no real spiritual help. Yet Marise is still in doubt, and a chance remark by Raymond's mother leads her to believe that what is happening is divine punishment for her own weakness—and pleasure—on the night of the second attack. She thinks about an abortion, but when her own amateurish expedients fail, she considers suicide. Even this is impossible; when the full horror of the meaning of death strikes her, she is forced to accept that any kind of life is better than the utter annihilation which death now means to her.

The third section consists of a short epilogue, and is entirely descriptive. Three more months have passed, and Marise is now visibly pregnant. Raymond is a little better, and can even walk about and play children's games with Jean. He has reached the optimum point of his recovery, and may linger on for years in this state of premature senility. Marise is so worn by suffering that she lives in a permanent condition of dull resignation. The book ends on an indeterminate note at this point:

Neuf heures sonnent.
    Machinalement Marise s'est levée, et de sa voix sans timbre:
— Allons, mes enfants, rangez vos joujoux, c'est l'heure du dodo . . .
Nous vous rendons grâce, ô Mon Dieu, pour tous les bienfaits dont votre bonté nous comble chaque jour . . .[1]

There can be no doubt that Martin du Gard's intention was to make his story symbolic. The very title, *L'Une de nous*, clearly indicates that Marise is to be taken as representative of humanity (both *Une Vie de Saint* and *Devenir* had been symbolic titles). Both the closing lines of the book, and the epigraph, from Psalm xxxi—'Jour et nuit, s'est appesantie sur moi ta main'—

---

[1] Ibid., p. 105.

with their unmistakable irony, leave no room for doubt. He was attempting to describe a typical example of the human condition as he saw it. The relationship of *L'Une de nous* to the full-scale novel *Marise* is also fairly clear. Martin du Gard has chosen the crucial episode in Marise's life, the dramatic turning-point in her existence at which the hope of youth gives way to the resignation of advancing age. This, a crisis in itself, is reinforced by the even greater drama of her loss of religious faith, which is motivated by the apparently undeserved suffering which she has to endure, and which is accompanied by a profound realization of the significance of death.

The book's weaknesses are glaring. The *naturalisme suranné* is perhaps a greater fault than the *mauvais goût déplorable*. It is true that the description of Raymond's second stroke, during intercourse, is both daring and designed to shock, but a frank treatment of sexuality is a feature of Martin du Gard's work, and this particular incident is merely one example among several of the 'curieux enlacement des thèmes du désir et de la mort.'[1] The intensity of this scene also recalls that of certain episodes in Zola's novels (although there is no evidence that the neo-Freudian explanation of this aspect of Zola now current has any echo in Martin du Gard). The naturalism finds expression in a strong belief in the transmission of hereditary characteristics.[2]

The greatest weakness of all, however, is that '*L'Une de nous* is a *roman à thèse* in the worst sense of the term. Martin du Gard is attempting to show, first, that Marise's life is typical of humanity generally, and, secondly, that her unfortunate experiences will inevitably lead her to abandon the Catholic faith. Yet Marise is clearly no typical case; loss of religious faith may be psychologically true in this one instance, but it cannot be rigidly demonstrated as inevitable. Martin du Gard has fallen into the same error as other authors of *romans à thèse*, Barrès

---

[1] Camus, op. cit., p. xii.

[2] Jean's infirmity is constantly stressed as hereditary: 'le consanguinage était trop proche, la santé du père trop minée...' (p. 21); 'son infirmité, l'éternelle misère physique; à laquelle il est condamné par sa naissance, n'est que la floraison en ses membres innocents de la tare paternelle...' (p. 37); while Marise fears still worse for the child she is carrying: 'Voici l'enfant d'un père presque sain!... Que sera donc le germe jailli d'un être amoindri, à l'extrême degré de sa déchéance, au seuil de la mort?' (p. 74).

and Bourget (although his thesis is the opposite of theirs); in his illustration of the conflict between reason and faith, he has loaded the dice too heavily in favour of his own view and disregarded all considerations of objectivity. Because of this, *L'Une de nous* loses all claim to universal significance and remains little more than an interesting curiosity, a case-history of human misery.

Nevertheless it is very relevant to the development of Martin du Gard's work as a whole. He was attempting to find a satisfactory vehicle for his basic themes: death, old age, solitude, religion and science, the problem of Evil, and suffering. That the attempt failed merely proved his own immaturity, not the inadequacy of his basic themes, which indeed recur in all his later novels.

One of the most interesting aspects of *L'Une de nous* is his treatment of disease, which is a theme peculiarly suited to his needs. Disease can be rendered into an easily comprehensible form of *Mal*, and the struggle against illness and suffering can take on the symbolic value of the fight between Good and Evil. The doctor can then become a protagonist in this fight; which is what in fact we find in *Les Thibault*. Germain Mussey is undoubtedly Antoine Thibault in embryo.

Disease leads naturally to the theme of death and its implications. In the physical description of Raymond after his second stroke, the ravages of time and illness are portrayed with horrifying realism. At the same time the science/religion conflict can be dramatized. Raymond, like the weakly child Jean Barois, is taken to Lourdes; but whereas the episode in the later novel is treated as irrelevant to Jean's recovery, here it merely serves to raise Marise's unjustified hopes and thereby contributes to the tragedy of the second attack. Medicine, in the person of Mussey, cannot help Raymond, because he is incurable; but religion can offer no lasting solace either. Sœur Angélina, the sturdy young nun, is useful only for her physical assistance; Martin du Gard uses a deliberate savage irony to describe her prayers at the bedside, contrasting the horror of Raymond's physical debility with her confident ignorance.[1]

[1] *L'Une de nous*, pp. 32–33.

But religion is most important in its influence on Marise. Martin du Gard, considering religious faith the product of certain environmental conditions on the individual personality, is attempting to demonstrate that certain other environmental conditions could equally well lead to a complete abandonment of the same faith. He therefore tries to show Marise, at the beginning of his narrative, as a sincere and contented Catholic. The first blow to Marise's faith follows Raymond's relapse, despite the visit to Lourdes. She is forced to realize that all her youthful hopes have already been dashed; and, at the same time, she fully realizes the significance of death. When she discovers that she is pregnant, she cannot understand why God should select her to bear the weight of so much suffering. Her attitude to prayer is shown as essentially egoistic, and her faith is not strong enough to withstand her misfortune. Finally, after the failure of her attempts to procure a miscarriage, she goes to the church, as a last resort, a last attempt to obtain divine consolation. But her devotions are interrupted by a woman passing in front of her with a baby in her arms, and Marise is unable to recapture her previous emotion of semi-ecstasy.[1] Martin du Gard's intention is obvious. He is describing a concrete example of the age-old problem of Evil: if God is both omnipotent and omnibenevolent, what is the source of suffering and evil? Here again, although the episode is one of the weakest in *L'Une de nous*, he is anticipating *Barois*, where he also attempts to motivate loss of faith, with greater felicity.

The consequence, for Marise, of loss of faith, is that she contemplates suicide as the only means of escape from her plight. But she can no longer believe in immortality, and fear of death becomes a more powerful sentiment than the desire to escape. In the face of this, no other course lies open to Marise but the silent resignation with which the book ends: the stoical pessimism which remained Martin du Gard's attitude throughout his life.

Not only the themes, but many of the characters and relationships also anticipate those in the later works. Marise and Raymond recall Mme de Fontanin and Jérôme: the connexion between

---

[1] Ibid., pp. 76-78.

Mussey and Antoine Thibault has been indicated; while Sœur
Angélina has many of same characteristics as Abbé Joziers in
Barois. Mme Lefèvre, Raymond's mother, has something of old
Mme Barois, and even possibly of M. Thibault.

The principal theme —that of failure—also recalls *Devenir*,
and, we may surmise, *Une Vie de Saint*. The protagonist is once
again the young person who sets out in life with the highest
hopes and ideals, only to see them dashed. It is an integral part
of the tragic effect of the book that Marise, like André, is brought
to full realization of the disproportion between her ambitions
and her achievements. In addition, the lack of real contact
between the different characters is constantly brought out; each
lives in an apparently impenetrable cocoon of solitude, and not
one of Marise's friends and acquaintances has any inkling of her
suffering.

The technique Martin du Gard employs in *L'Une de nous* is no
less important, in his general development, than the themes he
treats. *Marise*, no doubt, was intended to be written in dialogue,
but *L'Une de nous* is, in fact, much closer to *Devenir*, stylistically,
than it is to *Barois*, which we may regard as the culmination of
the dialogue technique. This need cause no surprise, since the
book was adapted from what was no more than a preliminary
sketch for *Marise*, and he was probably more interested in laying
down the lines of the action than in polishing details of style.
The present tense is employed in most of the narrative, with
occasional lapses into the perfect to describe events in the
immediate past; and it is reasonable to assume that the whole
of the original sketch was written in this style. In the five-page
flashback, and certain other descriptive passages, Martin du Gard
reverts to the imperfect, past historic and pluperfect; these
passages were probably inserted into the original sketch to act
as exposition. Stylistic difficulties were no doubt one of the
reasons why he abandoned the novel. One of the principal
themes is that of Marise's utter isolation from those around
her, and the intractability of this material to dramatic dialogue
technique is obvious. Insofar as Marise is conscious of her
thoughts and feelings, Martin du Gard can make do with

reported monologue; but when she is not, he can only describe them by means of ordinary third-person narration. And, since the crux of the action takes place within Marise's mind, and goes unperceived by the other characters, he is obliged to dramatize it as best he can, if his psychological observations are not to be limited to a crude behaviourism. The result is that he frequently has to resort to rhetoric or even to melodrama in order to enliven his material or to heighten the tension. Above all there is a fundamental inability to make Marise's suffering clear from her actions and her words, and he resorts to frequent repetitions, which fatally weaken the effect intended, instead of reinforcing it. Martin du Gard's stylistic resources are still at this stage insufficient to take the strain of his material. Nor has he entirely freed himself from the neo-Symbolist preciosity noted in *Devenir*, which indeed gives indications of its primarily Romantic origin, as in the dedication of the book: 'Aux grands arbres de la forêt de Bellême, aux pins écorchés des Sept-Bras, Je dédie ces pages, écrites dans leur ombre tragique.'

Other aspects of style are more successful. If Marise herself is an inadequate vehicle, the other characters, Raymond, Mussey, Sœur Angélina, Mme Lefèvre, are more satisfactory. They are, of course, no more than 'flat' characters, but the careful brevity with which they are sketched is itself a technical advance.

On the whole, the style of *L'Une de nous* shows an improvement over that of *Devenir*, as indeed one would expect. The over-facile satirical irony of the earlier novel has been eliminated, and the deeper irony of situation further developed.

In *Marise*, Martin du Gard's creative inspiration and his technical ability were still not yet ripe. He had already chosen his themes, but had not found a satisfactory vehicle for them, and, lacking this, found himself in difficulties which exposed the weaknesses in his narrative technique. But the effort was not wasted; he was to learn by his mistakes, and translate his themes into a more satisfactory material for his powers. Moreover, had he continued, it might still have been a failure and he would have spent the capital he was to invest so successfully in *Jean Barois*.

4

JEAN BAROIS

AFTER the failure of *L'Une de nous*, Martin du Gard wasted no time before once more launching on a long novel. He decided that Parisian life with its many distractions was incompatible with his methods of work, so withdrew to Berry, to begin his new project: 'une longue monographie masculine, la destinée d'un homme et l'histoire d'une conscience.'[1] *Jean Barois* was begun in April 1910 and completed in May 1913. Again there was difficulty in finding a publisher; although Grasset had agreed to publish *L'Une de nous* at the author's expense, and the next novel at his own, he tried to dissuade Martin du Gard from publishing *Barois* at all, since, in his opinion (and he was after all a publisher of some literary acumen), the book was a failure.[2] Before deciding whether or not to hold Grasset to his word, Martin du Gard happened to meet Gaston Gallimard, a former schoolfellow, and, knowing Gallimard's connexion with the *N.R.F.*, mentioned his difficulties. Gallimard generously offered to read the novel and to submit it to the other members of the *N.R.F.* group. Schlumberger read the manuscript and liked it, while Gide (who about the same time had turned down *Du Côté de Chez Swann*) cabled Gallimard immediately on reading *Barois*: 'A publier sans hésiter.'[3] So Grasset published Proust's novel and Gallimard Martin du Gard's (and no doubt Grasset later had time to regret both his mistake about *Barois* and his decision to sell back to Gallimard his rights in Proust's novel). On its appearance, in late 1913, *Barois* immediately found warm admirers,[4] while it was also an outstanding commercial success, and has been more or less continuously in print

[1] *Souvenirs*, p. liv.   [2] Quoted in *Souvenirs*, p. lv.   [3] *Souvenirs*, p. lvi.
[4] Ibid., p. lvii.

ever since. Success brought Martin du Gard full confidence,
while the contact with the *N.R.F.* took him out of his comparative isolation as a struggling young writer and threw him—on
equal terms—with the most stimulating group of contemporary
literary figures, the *bande à Gide.*

In conception, *Barois* was very similar to *Une Vie de Saint* and
Marise: 'la destinée d'un homme et l'histoire d'une conscience',
an idea close to the German *Bildungsroman.* And, once again,
Martin du Gard wished to give his novel a symbolic, ironical
title—*S'affranchir*—from which he was dissuaded, to his later
regret.[1] The parallel with *Devenir* is evident. Yet there is a distinct change in subject matter: after his failure in attempting the
fictional biography of a priest, then of a woman, he decided to
tackle an easier subject, a scientist and publicist. Throughout
the novel he avoids the problem of having to improvise his
characters' ideas, beliefs and feelings, by closely documenting
them from real life—so much so that practically every episode
in the novel can be tracked down to its source.

The basic theme of the novel is Barois's spiritual development.
As he attains maturity his scientific studies make it more and
more difficult for him to adhere to the Catholic religion, and
finally, after an intermediate stage during which he accepts the
idea that Catholic dogmas are symbolically, if not literally, true,
he breaks away from the Church altogether to become a
crusader for rationalism. His marriage is destroyed in the process. He founds *Le Semeur*, a propagandist review, to further his
ideas, and the review becomes one of the leading advocates of
revision in the Dreyfus Case. When this is eventually achieved,
Barois stands at the height of his career, but, involved in an
accident, has a presentiment of possible weakness in old age,
and dictates a spiritual testament, in which he declares his complete belief in rationalism and disclaims in advance any recanta-
tion which feebleness might later force upon him. The last
chapters in the novel describe the gradual process of weakening

---

[1] *N.N.R.F.* 12/58, p. 1128 (letter to Margaritis, dated 24/8/18). We may also note, in
this connexion, the continued, slightly pretentious, use of epigraphs at the head of each
section of the novel, to stress the underlying meaning.

under the ravages of disease, his reconversion to Catholicism, and his death.

The idea of the spiritual testament gives the clue to the source of the plot—Renan's *Souvenirs d'enfance et de jeunesse*. Towards the end of this book Renan expressed a similar hope: that even in senility he would never be reduced to a state of feeble-mindedness and possibly be led to recant his whole life's work:

> Je serais désolé de traverser une de ces périodes d'affaiblissement où l'homme qui a eu de la force et de la vertu n'est plus que l'ombre et la ruine de lui-même, et souvent, à la grande joie des sots, s'occupe à détruire la vie qu'il avait laborieusement édifiée. Une telle vieillesse est le pire don que les dieux puissent faire à l'homme. Si un tel sort m'était réservé, je proteste d'avance contre les faiblesses qu'un cerveau ramolli pourrait me faire dire ou signer. C'est Renan sain d'esprit et de cœur, comme je le suis aujourd'hui, ce n'est pas Renan à moitié détruit par la mort et n'étant plus lui-même, comme je le serai si je me décompose lentement, que je veux qu'on croie et qu'on écoute. Je renie les blasphèmes que les défaillances de la dernière heure pourraient me faire prononcer . . .[1]

This passage is clearly the origin of the most effective device of the testament (which so impressed Hébert when he read the novel that he made one of his own,[2] and which was borrowed by Mauriac in his *Nœud de Vipères*);[3] and it probably provided the idea for Barois's entire life.

Other sources are also apparent. For the village of Buis-la-Dame, Martin du Gard drew upon his own childhood memories of Clermont-sur-Oise;[4] the *compromis symboliste*, advocated by the abbé Schertz, can be equated with Hébert's position before being forced out of the Church.[5] The *Collège Venceslas* where Barois teaches is based upon the *Collège Stanislas;* Michaelangelo's *Esclave enchaîné*, which stands upon Barois' mantelpiece, as a symbol of his struggle (and was reproduced as a frontispiece to

---

[1] E. Renan, *Souvenirs d'enfance et de jeunesse*, new ed., Paris, 1947, p. 202.

[2] M. Hébert, *Testament spirituel*, Novara, 1914.

[3] Cf. M. Jarrett-Kerr, *François Mauriac*, Cambridge, 1954, p. 13, where Mauriac's use of the device is contrasted unfavourably with that in *Barois*.

[4] The description of the church bells in *Barois* (p. 213) compares closely with a passage in *Souvenirs* (pp. lxxx–lxxxi).

[5] Martin du Gard uses passages from *Dei Filius* already quoted in Hébert's *L'évolution de la foi catholique*, Paris, 1905. Cf. C. Moeller, *Littérature française et Christianisme*, Paris, 1953, vol. ii, p. 184.

the first edition of *Barois*) in fact stood upon Hébert's; Barois's accident and narrow escape, which inspire him to write his testament, recall Pascal's carriage accident on the *Pont de Neuilly* in 1654. Barois's review, *Le Semeur*, although it has no connexion with a Protestant review of the same name which existed in the first half of the nineteenth century, has undoubted affinities with Marc Sangnier's progressive Catholic review, *Le Sillon*, and Péguy's *Cahiers de la Quinzaine*, while the idea of using the review in the novel may derive from Racadot's newspaper in *Les Déracinés*. The attitude of certain members of the *Semeur* group after the *cassation* of the Dreyfus conviction—in particular that of Cresteil—and at the ceremony of transferring Zola's ashes to the *Panthéon*, can only be modelled on Péguy;[1] the discussion between Barois and the two young Nationalists, Tillet and Grenneville, in *L'Age Critique*, illustrates the influence of Barrès and Bergson, as expounded by Henri Massis and Alfred de Tarde.[2] Luce's Socratic death, Martin du Gard himself has admitted, was inspired by a conversation with Hébert in January 1911, in which the latter expressed his hope that he would be granted a serene, lucid, and fearless end.[3]

In addition, Martin du Gard quotes extensively from other writers, or from newspapers, in the text.[4] The historical reconstruction of the Dreyfus case, which takes up a third of the entire novel, and especially the scenes at the Zola trial, are the product of six months of research.[5] This passion for documentation was almost taken to extremes; one cannot fail to recognize the *chartiste* in the following passage, where Martin du Gard admits that *Barois* is largely composed of ideas he had absorbed from ten years of reading—from 1903, in fact, before he even began to write seriously:

---

[1] Cf. C. Péguy, *Notre jeunesse*, Paris, 1910.

[2] Agathon (H. Massis & A. de Tarde), *Les jeunes gens d'aujourd'hui*, Paris, 1913.

[3] *In Memoriam*, p. 575.

[4] E.g. from Brunois (p. 235); Renan (p. 265); the Vatican Council (pp. 266-7, p. 443); Lamennais (p. 319); Bernard-Lazare (p. 357); *L'Aurore* (p. 377); E. Carrière and Daniel Halévy (p. 435); and Björnson (p. 537).

[5] '. . . j'ai travaillé l'affaire Dreyfus six mois pleins, à la campagne, dix heures par jour (j'ai une "bibliothèque" de l'Affaire . . .', *N.N.R.F.*, 12/58, p. 1123 (letter to Margaritis, 23/1/18).

C'est en général un article *qui m'a donné des idées;* et c'est pour retrouver ces idées que je le garde . . . (. .) *Barois* a été littéralement farci d'idées que j'avais notées et mises de côté ainsi. Voilà dix ans que j'amasse. Une grande partie de mes provisions a passé dans *Barois. Barois,* c'est trois ans de travail suivi, mais c'est dix ans de notes quotidiennes, d'articles de journaux découpés *et classés* dans des chemises étiquetées. *Barois* n'a pas été écrit en fumant des cigarettes, mais en bûchant pendant dix ans; en amassant, fragment par fragment, des idées sur tout . . . [1]

As a result of the incorporation of this material, *Barois* is very much a novel of ideas, not so much his own ideas, as ideas generally current in progressive circles during the early years of the century. It is this, the topicality of so much of *Barois*- the struggle between religion and science, and the *crise de conscience* of the Dreyfus case—which no doubt account for the novel's early success. Gustave Lanson, reviewing *Barois* in *Le Matin,* put this point of view succinctly: 'on n'a peut-être rien écrit encore qui exprime avec plus de vérité l'âme des générations de 1880-1890',[2] and there is wide critical agreement on this issue.[3]

At the same time, however, the criticism has been raised that just because of this topicality and of the documentary nature of much of the book, *Barois* cannot really be called a novel, and must therefore be excluded from serious critical consideration. Grasset called the book a *dossier* and others have followed him in the same attitude.[4] Martin du Gard voiced his own opinion on the point, in a letter quoted by Claude Roy:

Tout grand roman est dans son essence un *reportage dépassé,* tout grand reportage (. .) est dans son essence un roman *involontaire.* L'axiome vrai n'est pas: prenez garde à la réalité. C'est: prenez la réalité à bras-le-corps, à bras l'esprit.

[1] Ibid., p. 1126 (letter to Margaritis, 6/2/18).

[2] *Le Matin,* 24/12/13; quoted in Houtin, op. cit., p. 200.

[3] E.g. R. Lalou, *Roger Martin du Gard,* p. 8: '(Il) montrait en pleine lumière les problèmes qui tourmentaient nos esprits et nos sensibilités . . .'; P.-J. Brodin, *Les écrivains français de l'entre-deux-guerres,* Montreal, 1942, p. 187: 'le témoignage d'une génération' D. Mornet, *Introduction à l'étude des écrivains français d'aujourd'hui,* Paris, 1939, p. 91: 'Jean Barois est comme une somme des systèmes philosophiques et sociaux de la génération qui était jeune au moment de la guerre . . .'; J. Prévost, in *Problèmes du roman,* Brussels, 1945, p. 85: '. . . une suite de drames de conscience . . .'.

[4] 'Chronique de premier ordre, roman de troisième ordre', is a remark typical of this attitude (taken in fact from a Cambridge Tripos Paper). Malraux has been defended against a similar attack: W. M. Frohock, *André Malraux and the Tragic Imagination,* Stanford U.P., 1952, p. ix.

Qu'il faille, pour faire un rapport exact, repenser, rerêver, remâcher, oublier, retrouver, truquer, travestir, reformer ce qu'on a vu, ce qui est la matière du rapport—bien sûr. Mais chaque fois qu'on oppose le journalisme (ton dédaigneux) à la littérature (ton noble), le reportage (ton commisérateur) au roman (ton d'admiration vive), on n'oppose pas une esthétique à une autre, un genre à d'autres genres, mais le talent à l'absence du talent, la hâte à la méditation, la facilité à l'effort.[1]

The documentary effect of *Barois* is reinforced by the entire narrative technique: the pseudo-dramatic form, in which lies most of the book's originality. The novel consists of a series of scenes in dialogue, with extensive stage directions, interspersed with letters, extracts from newspapers and pamphlets, and other documents. This is very much in accordance with the idea of the *présentation indirecte des événements*, and of the dialogue novel; it embodies the conception of the novel outlined by André Mazerelles. The individual scenes play the part of the 'série de petites pierres, sèches, dures, bien d'aplomb';[2] but Martin du Gard has taken extra precautions in order to achieve the unity of the whole work. The scenes are collected into groups, so that the novel consists of thirteen groups of scenes, and the groups themselves are divided into three distinct parts, each of which might be said to correspond roughly to an act of a play. In this way the *sauce gluante* of linking narrative is avoided, and also many of the difficulties of dealing satisfactorily with the passage of time. Time, in a novel covering the full span of a man's life, is rarely easy to handle, unless the writer is prepared, like Martin du Gard in *Une Vie de Saint* and *Marise*, to fill several volumes with his narrative. If the flow of time is not kept fairly even, the reader is unable to adjust himself to it sufficiently quickly, and the novel then appears top-heavy, as does *Devenir*. The method in *Barois* is to make time pass between episodes; in each individual episode, just as in a scene of a play, narrative time is equated with real time, with the result that in the entire novel only a few separate hours of Barois's life are directly narrated. What happens in the long periods of time between these separate episodes has to be inferred from the text.

---

[1] Quoted in C. Roy, *Descriptions critiques*, Paris, 1949, p. 66.   [2] *Devenir*, p. 25.

The reader is, in fact, given only the framework of the traditional type of novel, and, by an imaginative effort of his own, has to fill in the gaps—largely the connecting links between episodes—and also to draw his own conclusions from the episodes themselves, just as the theatre audience has to interpret the play. Not unnaturally, much greater demands are made than in the conventional novel, but once the effort is made, powerful dramatic effects can be achieved. Not only are the scenes chosen for direct narration sharply highlighted, but the reader is made to participate in those scenes much more closely than in an ordinary narrative. As Martin du Gard himself has said, 'on se laisse imposer le spectacle direct'.[1]

The unity of the novel is further aided by a deliberate symmetry. Barois's life can be represented by a parabola. The curve begins with his childhood in Part I, until he breaks away from the Catholic faith; then, with Part II, it reaches its zenith with his supreme triumph: success in the Dreyfus Case, after which it once more begins to descend; in Part III, as Barois suffers the ravages of time, is reconverted, and dies, the development of Part I is seen in reverse. The thirteen groups of scenes are all kept deliberately brief—about twenty or thirty pages to each— except for the one dealing with the Dreyfus Case, *La Tourmente* (not actually the central section, since it is eighth in order), which takes up about sixty-five pages. In this way the general symmetry of the plan is followed in its execution; Barois's life and the novel together gradually rise to a climax, hold the climax, for a time, then slowly sink down again to their end. Time between the episodes is made to pass at about the same rate in the first and third parts of the novel, so that the reader is rarely thrown farther forward in real time than he can at once apprehend. It is interesting to compare *Barois* in this respect with Rolland's *Jean-Christophe*. One of the more obvious weaknesses of Rolland's novel is that he devotes, proportionately, too much space to his portrayal of the hero's childhood in the Rhineland. After Christophe's arrival in Paris, Rolland so speeds up the passage of psychological time, besides complicating the narrative with

[1] *N.N.R.F.*, 12/58, pp. 1134-5 (letter to Margaritis, 14/9/18).

the long flashback of *Antoinette* and the static polemics of *La Foire sur la Place*, that by the time Christophe dies in old age the reader is still considering him a young man, or at any rate hardly out of his thirties. It is probable that Martin du Gard—who had done much the same thing in the abortive first draft of *Une Vie de Saint*—was consciously aware of this pitfall, and deliberately pruned down the early chapters of *Barois*. Nevertheless, a certain mystery lingers about the closing chapters. Borgal has quite rightly pointed out that since Barois is over 50 when he dies, and was born in 1866, his death must take place about 1918—or five years after publication of the book.[2] This, however, is perhaps not so important as the fact that Barois is deemed to be an old man, 'rongé par la tuberculose des vieillards' (p. 537), when he is in fact little more than 50. No doubt Martin du Gard was perfectly aware of the anomaly, which is unavoidable if Barois is to be about 20 when he comes under the influence of the Modernist movement, and at his most vigorous during the Dreyfus Case. Although a fault, this is no more than a technical one, which must have seemed preferable to making Barois much older when he died, and putting off his death to the 1920's.

The dramatic method of presentation helps to solve another technical difficulty: the illusion of objectivity. Through his dramatic presentation, Martin du Gard hoped to be able to abolish the omniscient narrator, and to show events themselves happening, so that the illusion of reality would be absolute. Complete transparency is not possible, but he tries to rely upon no more than an unseen 'intelligence', who jots down rapid descriptions of the *external* appearance of characters, their actions and their words. This 'intelligence' is supposed to have no knowledge of the future, and notes down all events as they happen, without space for reflection. The narrative tense is, therefore, the present. (This problem of the point of view of the narrator is, of course, common to many modern novelists: the parallel with James and Proust is evident.) In practice the impersonality of the narrator is not absolute; there are occasional

[2] Borgal, op. cit., p. 113.

lapses where description is really comment, or where the narrator shows knowledge of the past and psychological insight into the present; and even, at times, lapses into the satirical irony of *Devenir*:

Le docteur retire son lorgnon: regard myope, plein de tendresse. Mme Barois se tait. Leurs pensées se reconnaissent et se heurtent: tout un passé entre eux. (p. 210)

(Grenneville) . . . Un visage fin, sans dominante . . . (..) Dans l'ensemble, ce mélange d'assurance et de retenue que le bon élève d'une institution religieuse conserve jusqu'à sa première aventure. (p. 504)

Despite these occasional instances, the illusion of objectivity is for the most part upheld. The documentary content of the novel adds to this. Since the whole book is 'farci d'idées', it is difficult to identify any single character with the author; many of the ideas contradict others, since the aim is to achieve an even balance.

It should be stressed that the dialogue technique is only one of Martin du Gard's stylistic resources. (Nor was it entirely original, for although he was the first to use this device in a full-scale serious novel, something similar had already been attempted years before by Gyp, Henri Lavedan and Abel Hermant.)[1] The so-called stage directions are also significant, as an effort to describe, in a few brief external traits, the total essence of a scene or a character. The author has called this method the *style notatif*, pointing out that it involved considerable effort, since he had to reduce any description to a fraction of its totality, leaving only significant details for the reader to interpret for himself. The contrast which he makes with Balzac is instructive:

La description de la pension Vauquer était indispensable à un lecteur contemporain de Balzac. Un Balzac d'aujourd'hui évoquerait, pour un lecteur d'aujourd'hui, ladite pension avec la même précision, en employant le tiers des mots, en décrivant le tiers des détails, dont beaucoup sont inutiles pour nous, 'vont de soi'. (..)

---

[1] E.g. by Gyp in short stories such as *C'est son père* and *En préparant l'arbre de Noël;* by Lavedan in *Le nouveau jeu,* which is actually subtitled *roman dialogué;* and by Hermant in *La Carrière.* One critic has even attempted to see some influence of Flaubert's *Tentation* (G. Truc, *Revue Bleue,* 3/1/25, p. 17), but this would seem, to say the least, a little tenuous.

... je dirai que les quinze lignes qui présentent la cour d'assises au début du procès de Zola laissent, dans le cerveau d'un lecteur d'aujourd'hui, une image très complète, et que trois pages détaillées, minutieuses, n'y ajouteraient rien. Et je dirai que ce n'est pas une esquisse, ni un croquis. C'est une description très travaillée, très poussée, rentrant dans la catégorie des descriptions 'qui se posent là'. (..) ... la description notative, cinématographique n'est pas un croquis. C'est au contraire une synthèse. Pour la faire, pour la faire bien, il faut commencer par trois pages de description, et puis rayer, biffer, condenser, réduire, mettre en relief l'essentiel.[1]

This is closely linked with the idea of indirect presentation; events which take place between the scenes directly narrated have to be presented indirectly, either through dialogue or the *style notatif*, and this technique is developed to a fine art, which is used again in *Les Thibault*, although the dialogue form is abandoned. Perhaps the best example of this indirect method occurs at the beginning of the section entitled *Le Calme*, where a few brief traits and one side of a telephone conversation serve to outline the progress of Barois's life and *Le Semeur* since the last scene, several years previously in 1900:

Rue de l'Université, plusieurs années après.

L'immeuble entier est occupé par *Le Semeur*. L'entrée est encombrée de rames et de ballots. Le rez-de-chaussée et l'entresol servent de locaux aux machines. Les autres étages sont réservés aux bureaux de la revue et de la maison d'éditions.

Au 3e étage: REDACTION.

Un employé (entrant).—'Monsieur Henry vous demande à l'appareil.'

Le secrétaire.—'Connais pas.'

L'employé.—'C'est pour le *New York Herald*.'

Le secrétaire.—'Ah, Harris? Donnez...'

Il prend le récepteur.

Le secrétaire.—'Allô! Parfaitement... J'en ai parlé à M. Barois, il veut bien: mais pas de phrases, pas d'éloges: les faits, sa vie... A votre disposition; questionnez...

'Depuis l'affaire Dreyfus?' (Riant.) 'Pourquoi pas depuis 70?

'Oui, la besogne actuelle: ça vaudra mieux...

'Si vous voulez... D'abord ses cours du soir, aux mairies de Belleville, de Vaugirard, du Panthéon. Beaucoup d'ouvriers; au Panthéon, une majorité d'étudiants... Oui, insistez: c'est l'idée directrice: tout ce qui peut servir à faire évoluer le cerveau des masses vers la liberté de la pensée.

---

[1] *N.N.R.F.*, 12/58, p. 1133 (letter to Margaritis, 9/9/18).

'Maintenant, il y a son cours aux *Etudes sociales*, deux fois par semaine . . .
'Cette année? Sur *La Crise universelle des religions*. Ça fait un livre par an.
'Enfin, il y a *Le Semeur* . . . C'est le gros morceau . . . deux cents pages tous les quinze jours . . .
'Je ne sais pas, mais certainement une quinzaine d'articles personnels dans l'année. Et puis, dans chaque numéro, une chronique régulière, toutes ses idées du moment . . .' (pp. 438-9)

Thus, in comparatively few lines, the prosperity of *Le Semeur* is indicated, and the nature of Barois's work—a book a year, editing and writing articles in *Le Semeur*, lecturing in a popular university—his modesty, his spreading fame, and so on. Every phrase, every word, even punctuation marks have been chosen to yield maximum effect and fullest information. To quote Martin du Gard himself again, he claims that the *style notatif* necessitated 'une volonté implacable, un émondage perpétuel, un dessèchement' but provided 'des effets précieux, des raccourcis, des touches impressionnistes qui ressuscitent la vie mieux que n'importe quel autre procédé, parce qu'il rend le mouvement, la vitesse des mouvements, la suite mobile et ricochante des sentiments . . .'.[1]

The cinematographic, rather than dramatic, nature of the *style notatif* can be shown by the opening scene of the novel. Here, after the minimum of indications—'En 1878, à Buis-la-Dame (Oise)—Martin du Gard briefly sketches Mme Barois's bedroom:

La chambre de Mme Barois.
Pénombre. Derrière les rideaux, la lune strie de noir et de blanc les persiennes. Sa lueur sur le parquet met en relief un bas de robe, une bottine d'homme qui bat silencieusement la mesure. Deux respirations; deux êtres s'immobilisant dans une même attente.
Par moments, dans la pièce voisine, le grincement d'un lit de fer; une voix d'enfant, sourde, entrecoupant des mots de rêve ou de délire. Dans l'entre-bâillement de la porte, un reflet mouvant de veilleuse. (p. 209)

The 'intelligence' (or invisible observer, or camera) arrives in the room, and can at first see nothing; then, as his eyes grow accustomed to the darkness, he begins to distinguish more than

---

[1] Ibid., p. 1129 (letter to Margaritis, 1/9/18).

merely light and shadow; he detects a woman's dress, a man's boot silently beating time. (A striking comparison can be made with the opening lines of Sartre's *Les Jeux sont faits*, an actual film scenario:

Une chambre dans laquelle les persiennes mi-closes ne laissent pénétrer qu'un rai de lumière.

Un rayon découvre une main de femme dont les doigts crispés grattent une couverture de fourrure. La lumière fait briller l'or d'une alliance, puis glissent le long du bras, découvre le visage d'Eve Charlier . . . Les yeux clos, les narines pincées, elle semble souffrir, s'agite et gémit.

Une porte s'ouvre et, dans l'entre-bâillement, un homme s'immobilise . . .[1]

The resemblance may be a coincidence, but the camera technique is unmistakable.)

One of the consequences of this method of composition is that careless, slipshod passages are almost impossible; every scene is deliberately and consciously selected for its significance as a part of the whole work; in each scene, every line, every phrase is again selected for its significance. In this way, the final narrative contains nothing which is not essential, and is throughout closely packed with meaning and ideas. This is perhaps one of the marks of the great novelist: the significant detail transforming the ordinary into the memorable (one thinks of many instances in Flaubert, or in Tolstoy of Karenina's protruding ears, which somehow symbolize his whole nature). In *Barois*, Martin du Gard shows great ability in careful preparation, in order to hint at the arm of fate behind events and actions, thus achieving a deeper level of meaning. An example is the situation of the Barois house in Buis, built right up against the church:

Le vieux logis des Barois est au sommet de la ville.

Le bâtiment du fond, adossé au clocher, étaye l'église; les deux ailes, basses, couvertes en tuiles, avancent vers la rue; un mur de prison les relie, que ferme un large portail.

L'espace ainsi clos est mi-cour, mi-jardin. Plusieurs fois par jour, le son des cloches s'engouffre dans ce puits sonore et l'emplit jusqu'à ébranler les murailles. (p. 213)

[1] J.-P. Sartre, *Les Jeux sont faits*, Paris, 1947, p. 7. The comparison may also be made with the opening scene of Malraux's *Condition humaine*.

When these church bells are made to clash with Dr. Barois's
exhortation to his son to struggle against his illness, to have
the will to live, it is as though science and religion are trying
to drown each other's voice, and alone influence the young
Jean.

Nevertheless, dramatic effect is not achieved without some
sacrifices. The greatest disadvantage is found in characterization.
Since Martin du Gard is largely refraining from all but external
description, he voluntarily deprives himself of most of the
possibilities of analysing characters, either through introspection
or by means of the third-person narrator. Like Zola, he fully
accepts the artistic convention that man's external appearance
and his inward personality coincide, that 'le portrait explique
l'homme' (one of those conventions, such as that of plausibility
or of the exclusion of sentimentality, which are more strictly
enforced in the novel than in real life). His characters, at their
first appearance, are presented in a brief sketch, after which
almost all other description is dispensed with, and the reader
himself has to interpret words, gestures and actions. These
sketches are carefully prepared, and the characters appear to be
sharply delineated:

Breil-Zoeger: la trentaine.

Né à Nancy, de parents lorrains. Mais, dans la coupe de visage, quelque
chose de japonais, qu'accentue sa maladie de foie: un teint jaune, un masque
élargi aux pommettes, des sourcils bridés, une moustache maigre et tombante,
un menton pointu.

L'arcade sourcilière est très saillante: au fond des orbites, les prunelles,
toujours dilatées, d'un noir luisant et dur, ont une expression fiévreuse, aiguë,
aride, qui contraste avec la douceur générale des traits.

La voix est monotone, sans timbre, agréable au premier abord—mais d'une
implacable sécheresse. (p. 303)

Harbaroux: un gnome malingre.

La figure, sans âge, est d'une laideur, mais d'une intelligence satanique. Un
visage étroit, s'élargissant aux tempes, puis s'effilant en lame jusqu'a la pointe
d'une barbiche roussâtre. Des oreilles dressées de faune. La fente des paupières,
la bouche, sont comme des trous brutalement creusés avec une spatule dans
de la cire à modeler. Regard aigu, tenace, sans douceur.

Bibliothécaire à l'Arsenal. Travailleur acharné. S'est d'abord spécialisé dans
le droit au moyen âge. Puis s'est consacré à l'histoire de la Révolution. (p. 317)

One consequence of this technique is that great importance is attached to the characters' expressions and, especially, eyes. The *regard* of most of the characters is enough to indicate clearly their nature; we read of Luce's 'yeux clairs . . . (. .) d'un gris fin, caressants et limpides' (p. 336), of the abbé Miriel's 'regard pâle, d'une lucidité avertie et sans indulgence' (p. 288), of Marie's 'yeux clairs et sans douceur'; and the trait is repeated in every case. The method permits some most striking effects, as when Dr. Barois, dying, gazes at his son:

Les yeux du mourant, qui vaguaient, effleurent Cécile, puis Mme Pasquelin, et soudain se fixent sur Jean avec une hostilité catégorique, une lueur aiguë de rancune . . . puis une supplication déchirante, aussitôt dissipée.
    Jean a compris cet éclair:—'Tu vis, toi! . . .' (p. 258)

and again when Barois's relationship with Julia is both begun and symbolized by one glance:

Le regard qu'il lui jette est brutal et pénétrant comme un viol: et elle le reçoit, comme une femelle consentante. (p. 379)

The sketches are incisive enough as far as the minor characters are concerned, but many of them are little more than embodiments of abstract ideas, with most human qualities except physical appearance left out of consideration. The three abbés, for example, represent little more than three different aspects of Catholicism; and he merely has to devise an adequate physical vehicle for these ideas, and a name for the completed characters. (Martin du Gard also accepted the convention that the names of characters should not be purely arbitrary, but should reflect the personality of their bearer. Schlumberger has remarked that he actually had lists of suitable names for different types of characters,[1] and the connotations of, say, a name like Luce (*lucide*, *lumière*, etc.) are at once apparent.) But because of this very technique of brief sketches, the characters, with the exception of Barois himself, and possibly Luce, never become more than 'flat'; little or no development of their personality can take place, and the Tolstoyan portrait in depth becomes impossible. One can in fact go further and claim that none of these characters,

---

[1] *N.N.R.F.*, 12/58, p. 1071.

Luce included, really exists independently; all are only significant in so far as they cast light on Barois himself.

This is not to say that Martin du Gard has not shown considerable skill in characterization. The priests, Joziers, Schertz and Lévys, are both plausible and interesting: Joziers with his unflinching missionary optimism; Schertz with his Modernist ideas—and perhaps a hint of Protestantism; Lévys with his pragmatic faith in the beauty and efficacy of Catholicism.

The *Semeur* group are most clearly seen as functions of the central character Barois. As in *Devenir*, Martin du Gard evidently wishes to show the interplay of ideas and personality within a small group of men, an aim eminently suitable for his dramatic method of presentation, carried out very successfully in the scene of the first *Semeur* conference (pp. 316–35). But Barois's six colleagues, vigorous and convincing in this episode, swept away by their common ideal, are less imposing as individuals. Roll, Portal and Harbaroux have little part to play in the action, nor do they represent any distinct ideas; they are scarcely more than a means of making the actions of Barois and Luce appear those of a collectivity, a closely-knit group. Cresteil is more original: a renegade officer, aristocrat, royalist and Catholic, with Péguy's thirst for purity and disgust at the political outcome of the Dreyfus Case. His bitterness and disillusionment are not only political; Art, as well as Justice and Truth, is now a meaningless word for him, and his pessimism is absolute.

Si j'avais mon existence à recommencer, j'anéantirais en moi toute ambition, je me *payerais ma tête*, jusqu'à ce que j'aie bien renoncé à croire en quoi que ce soit! je m'appliquerais à n'aimer la vie que sous les formes minimes,—les seules qui ne contiennent pas trop d'amertumes à avaler en une fois... Ramasser le bonheur par miettes... C'est la seule chance que l'homme ait d'en récolter un peu... avant de mourir... puisqu'il faut toujours en arriver là... au trou...' (p. 469)

Shortly afterwards, he commits suicide, after having tried to conceal all evidence of his identity. 'Il devait logiquement en arriver là', comments Breil-Zoeger, brutally yet accurately (p. 496). Thus Cresteil achieves greater stature; but his rôle is still closely linked to that of Barois by what might be called the 'echo' technique. Just as Fink, in *Devenir*, to some extent echoes André's development, at least until the final stages, Cresteil's progress foreshadows that of Barois himself. The basic theme in both cases is the same: the inability of the young man's ideals and enthusiasms to resist the disillusionments of life and the ravages of time. Fear of death and metaphysical solitude finally overcome them both.

This same 'echo' technique finds even more powerful expression in Jean's father, Dr. Barois. His life follows almost identically the same course as his son's, and the resemblance cannot be coincidental. He is brought up as a Catholic, but his medical studies draw him away from the Church. The struggle between Jean and his wife which breaks up their marriage is foreshadowed in the disagreement between Dr. Barois and both his wife and his mother. At this point Dr. Barois is the representative of science and truth in the battle against ignorance and prejudice (and has, as Ikor has pointed out, some of the qualities of Antoine Thibault and Dr. Philip).[1] Later in life, a sick man himself, he returns to the fold under the fear of death. Thus the whole course of Barois's development is prefigured, although this is not stressed too heavily at the time, so that Barois's own declining years are unexpected, but on reflection are seen as perfectly natural.

There is something of the same technique in the character of Woldsmuth, who is Jewish, and, even in the *Semeur* group, feels isolated. His first contribution to *Le Semeur* is not an article but simply a copy of a letter from Russia, describing a recent pogrom, while it is he who introduces Bernard Lazare's-pamphlet to the group, and thus brings about their connexion with the pro-Dreyfus movement. Above all he 'echoes' Luce's gentleness of nature, and stands with Luce on one side of Barois, in deliberate contrast with the implacable sectarian approach of Breil-Zoeger, whose attitude is itself reflected in Dalier towards the end of the book. It is Woldsmuth who recounts, in a letter to Barois, Luce's Socratic death, which reinforces his own faith in progress through scientific discovery. The postscript to the letter illustrates his own attitude of hope; he has devoted his

[1] R. Ikor, *Europe*, 6/46, p. 30.

whole life to a vain attempt to create living matter, yet he does not despair at his failure.

Breil-Zoeger is more simply a foil for Barois, whose attitude can be measured against Zoeger on the one side, and Luce on the other. He is a fanatical anti-clerical, lacking almost all human qualities, particularly sympathy and understanding. There is a powerful streak of jealousy in his nature: he takes Julia from Barois, and *Le Semeur* after his illness; and after the conversion no feelings of loyalty or pity prevent him from making a savage attack on his former colleague.

Luce is a more complex character, clearly intended to stand out from the other members of the *Semeur* group. It has been suggested that Luce was based upon Gabriel Séailles, Marcellin Berthelot or Scheurer-Kestner,[1] but although he may have elements in common with these public figures, Martin du Gard is again using the technique of *dédoublement*. Just as he split his own personality into Bernard Grosdidier and André Mazerelles, in *Devenir*, using Bernard as a foil to point the weaknesses in Andre's character, he is now doing something similar with Barois and Luce. But Luce is more than a foil for Barois; he is very much an ideal figure who shows up and corrects Barois's weak points. His public position, also, belongs more to wish-fulfilment than to real life: a Professor at the *Collège de France*, and a Senator, he is 'revendiqué à tour de rôle, par tous ceux qui veulent assurer le triomphe de quelque noble pensée' (p. 336). He is a paragon of virtue on all sides; and notably succeeds where Barois fails, in creating satisfactory human relationships and building up a happy family life. Luce is always able to dominate his emotions, to accept setbacks without bitterness, and above all to face death without fear. Barois's own death, preceded by re-conversion, has been attacked as being *truqué*, but it nevertheless remains perfectly plausible; Luce's Socratic death is as improbable as his life. Its existence in the novel is too patently for the purposes of contrast with Barois's death shortly afterwards.

With Barois himself one has at times the same impression—that

---

[1] R. Jardillier, *Arts et Livres*, No. 7, 1946, p. 87. C. Delhorbe also suggests Scheurer-Kestner in *L'Affaire Dreyfus et les écrivains français*, Paris, 1932, p. 314.

he exists less in his own right than as a vehicle for the themes treated. Since the themes of *L'Une de nous*—religion and science, belief and unbelief, ignorance and knowledge, old age, the ravages of time and death, metaphysical solitude—all find expression in the novel, they must have preceded the conception of Barois as a character. He must therefore have been constructed round them. Barois is made to come into contact, during his career, with elements of all these themes, together with one or two more treated in *Devenir*—vocation, and ambition—while his life is closely linked with the political issue which had split the country and which symbolized the two opposing streams of thought in France in the Third Republic: the Dreyfus Case. It is to this that the novel owes its great topical interest and much of its success: Barois's life illustrates almost all the political and philosophical problems which occupied the intelligent man in the street (more than the mature intellectual: we look in vain for the ideas of the really influential philosophers of the age—of Bergson, Sorel, or Nietzsche. Martin du Gard is only dealing with ideas in popular circulation). As a result of this Barois tends to be a passive character, since ideas can only be shown in their effect upon him. Because of this passivity he lacks a dominating personality. The section of the book entitled *L'Age critique* illustrates this aspect; put into contact first with Dalier, an uncompromising young atheist, Barois first reacts towards scepticism about the value and effect of the *Semeur's* rationalist crusade; then, facing Tillet and Grenneville, the pragmatic Catholics and Nationalists, he reacts away from them back towards what he had been criticizing in Dalier. By this time he is a sick man and his powers are weakening, it is true, but throughout his life a similar tendency is apparent, particularly when he is placed in contact with Luce.

Another serious deficiency in his character lies in his inability to create any lasting human relationships with women. His emotional life is unusually barren—a brief student affair with Huguette, his short-lived marriage with Cécile (only resumed in the weakness of his closing years), and an equally brief affair with Julia. It may be remarked here that in none of Martin du

Gard's works is there any love affair or marriage which is both happy and lasting. Without going as far as Borgal, who finds an autobiographical basis in the break-up of Barois's marriage,[1] it is clear that this inability to achieve sexual happiness is an integral part of Martin du Gard's fictional world, a symbol of ultimate pessimism. Here again Barois's own experience is anticipated by his father, who comments, somewhat bitterly, 'Les femmes, on cherche à les comprendre, et c'est impossible . . . (. .) elles sont *autres*' (p. 256); and Luce's nine children and happy family life are too artificial to dispel the general impression of emotional failure in the novel. Certainly unbelief, for Barois as for Luce, has nothing to do with desire for sexual indulgence; indeed, the opposite is the case, since Barois deprives himself of female companionship almost ascetically.

This illuminates another important aspect of his character. He has essentially a religious outlook, in the wider sense (like Renan again). At the time of his first doubts, he confides to Schertz: 'Il existe peut-être des gens qui peuvent se passer de religion? Moi pas. J'en ai besoin, besoin, comme de manger ou de dormir.' (p. 237), and when he does make the break from Catholicism, it is only to replace the Christian religion by the religion of free thought. Leading the crusade for this free thought is in no way necessitated by the break, but is a deliberate resolve, and Barois becomes, one might say, a missionary of atheism. Until a corrective is applied, he plunges into this new religion almost fanatically; Luce shows him that the true humanist ideal must always be one of tolerance, that free thought depends on the spiritual freedom of the thinker. The break from religion is a break from servitude to the dogmas of a collectivity, and it is worthless if another set of dogmas immediately replace those abjured. This is partly a question of vocation; only in one's true vocation can one truly develop one's individuality and achieve a really valuable life. In Luce's words:

. . . ne jetez pas votre personnalité dans le creuset commun. Conservez-vous à vous-même, obstinément; ne cultivez en vous que ce que vous est propre. Nous

---

[1] Borgal, op. cit., p. 16.

avons tous une faculté particulière—un don, si vous voulez,—par lequel nous resterons toujours absolument distincts des autres êtres. C'est ce don-là qu'il faut arriver à trouver en soi et à exalter, à l'exclusion du reste. (p. 341)

This is a further development of the idea of energy, deriving from Barrès, which we saw in *Devenir;* choosing one's true vocation implies canalizing that energy properly, which was exactly what André Mazerelles was unable to do. Dr. Barois earlier says that life is a continuous battle—'L'existence tout entière est un combat; la vie, c'est de la victoire qui dure . . .' (p. 216)—but it is more than that, and his own moral energy is only usefully employed because he has found a vocation: medicine. Barois is impressed by this aspect of his father, but he himself is more attracted to teaching, despite its greater risks, than the career already mapped out for him in medicine. Later, editing *Le Semeur,* he remains a teacher, more than an original thinker, and, until his intellectual powers fail, is strikingly successful, because he has chosen his correct vocation. This theme of vocation is echoed in other characters, in Woldsmuth, and even in Barois's daughter Marie, in her determination to become a nun. Whatever the truth about religion or science, there can be no doubt about the genuineness of Marie's vocation, and therefore about its value. Here Barois's confidence in the crusade for free thought is badly weakened by the realization that so many of mankind, perhaps even the majority, certainly his own family, are immune to the logical arguments so compelling to himself.

Barois is never able to escape his environment and heredity, and thus his return to the Church he had fought is, paradoxically enough, itself an illustration of determinism. In his characterization Martin du Gard accepts entirely the ideas of Félix Le Dantec, who was also one of the primary sources of his material. Le Dantec, who lived from 1869 to 1917, was one of the last representatives of militant nineteenth-century materialism, and a vigorous popularizer, writing no less than thirty-nine works between 1891 and his death. For him life was no more than a chemical process, and mind an epiphenomenon. Responsibility, liberty, religion, and the whole of metaphysics were all arbitrary ideas which could only remain alive in a favourable environment: 'peut-être quelques générations rationalistes suffiraient-elles à faire disparaître de l'hérédité des hommes le besoin métaphysique'.[1] He reduced Taine's *race, milieu, moment* to two concepts, heredity and environment (*éducation*), which between them were adequate to explain human personality—the famous A × B:

L'homme est le produit de l'hérédité et de l'éducation; j'entends par hérédité l'ensemble des propriétés de l'œuf dont l'homme provient, et par éducation, l'ensemble des inconstances qu'a traversées l'œuf depuis sa formation; l'homme est le produit de ces deux facteurs, et de ces deux facteurs seulement.[2]

Early in his life, Barois is exposed to forces—*éducation*—which determine his development away from the Church, since they are powerful enough to outweigh the other environmental influences which would normally keep him within it; but the change is only temporary, since the greatest influence of all— fear of death—is only checked by the enthusiasm and optimism of youth, which is by definition temporary. Thus his entire development is inevitable, determined from birth.

In one respect Martin du Gard implicitly criticizes Le Dantec's attitude. This is in his treatment of the theme of death. Barois, in 1900 writes, about death in *Le Semeur:*

Pourquoi craindre la mort? Est-elle si différente de la vie? Notre existence n'est qu'un passage incessant d'un état à un autre: la mort n'est qu'une transformation de plus . . . (. .)
Pour moi, depuis que j'ai compris le néant qui m'attend, le problème de la mort n'existe plus. J'ai même plaisir à penser que ma personnalité n'est pas durable . . . Et la certitude que ma vie est limitée augmente singulièrement le goût que j'y prends . . . (pp. 496–7)

These ideas are almost identical with those of Le Dantec:

La mort est le triomphe de l'athée . . . (. .)
. . . l'athée ne redoute pas la mort, puisqu'il est convaincu que la différence

---

[1] Quoted in D. Parodi, *La philosophie contemporaine en France*, Paris, 1919, p. 56.
[2] F. Le Dantec, *Les influences ancestrales*, Paris, 1905, p. 207. Quoted in Parodi, op. cit., p. 55. Le Dantec's ideas are chiefly seen in the earlier Barois, in Breil-Zoeger, and in Dalier.

n'est pas essentielle entre la vie et la mort; il croit au néant qui suit la vie, et l'on ne saurait redouter le néant; l'athée ne craint pas de devenir *rien* parce qu'il est convaincu qu'il n'est *rien* qu'un mouvement momentané de matériaux ayant subi par hérédité un certain arrangement . . . (. .)

. . . l'athée n'a aucune peur de la mort; il est sans cesse prêt à mourir . . .[1]

But Barois, a few years after he wrote these lines, is appalled by his own temerity, and they are only quoted to show how untenable his optimism was : 'Il est écrasé par ce qu'il a osé écrire, jadis, *sans savoir* . . .' (p. 497). Free thinking and atheism are no help in the face of death, and a sense of proportion is restored to the issue of rationalism when it is thus overshadowed by the more important theme. This aspect of the novel might almost be said to be Promethean: Barois has attempted to wrest immortality from the gods, by denying the existence of death. In his closing years he is cruelly punished for his pride, with true irony of fate.

Weakness in characterization are to a large extent concealed by the introduction of the Dreyfus Case into the novel. There was nothing original about the use of a near-contemporary political event in the novel; indeed, the Dreyfus Case itself had already been the subject of several novels. The grafting of fictional characters on to political events had been Barrès's method in *L'Appel au soldat* and *Leurs Figures*, dealing with the Boulanger episode and the Panama scandal; and in view of the connexion between Barrès and Martin du Gard already noted, we might be justified in assuming some influence. The attraction of political matter in the novel lies mostly in its topical interest, and it is therefore a two-edged weapon: the two Barrès novels have both suffered from a decline of interest in—even perhaps knowledge of—the political events they are concerned with. This risk seems to be tacitly acknowledged in the *Pléiade* edition of *Barois*, since a seventeen-page *résumé* of the whole *Affaire* is included,[2] for the reader who finds the account in the novel itself inadequate. Topical interest must have played some part in the decision to introduce the episode, but more important, Martin du Gard needed a symbol for the crusade of *Le Semeur*,

---

[1] F. Le Dantec, *L'Athéisme*, Paris, 1907, pp, 102–4.   [2] *Pléiade* ed., vol. i, pp. cli–clxvii.

a concrete issue to crystallize dramatic interest. The struggle between science and religion—in which science is identified with absolute truth—is at best somewhat abstract and arid. Now, by equating the scientific case with the *Dreyfusistes*, with their ideal of absolute justice, he is able to add to the intellectual implications of his story and to dramatize it in doing so. (Any trial is in itself dramatic, and the Dreyfus Case, packed with events and surprises, eminently so.) So the Case itself provides an object for Barois's energy, a symbol of his success, and a natural focus of dramatic interest; while the aftermath, with its disillusionment and anticlimax, is aptly fitted to accompany his spiritual decline.

Success in treatment of the Case is beyond dispute: *Barois* is one of the most popular general histories of the whole *Affaire*— 'ce livre, qui a résumé pour bien des années ce que le grand public a su de l'Affaire . . .'[1] The method of inserting this historical material is skilful. The actual participants in events remain in the background; being seen and described only at second hand, or, like Zola, appearing only briefly. Some of the generals are seen for longer periods at the Zola trial, but since Martin du Gard is relying entirely upon newspaper reports of this, there can be no danger of any discrepancies between his account and contemporary views, as these were based upon the same reports. The *Semeur* group remains in the foreground, and the chief technical problem was to graft their actions on to historical events and to create the illusion that they were actually influencing them, without falsifying the events themselves. In this Martin du Gard succeeds, partly by suppressing most mention of the other *Dreyfusistes*, and making it appear as if the Semeur group were the real leaders in the fight for revision. He does, however, distort events on one occasion, when he makes Colonel Henry's arrest, confession and suicide all take place on the same day, whereas in fact the suicide came a day later. The reason is artistic; he wished to show the dramatic effect on the *Semeur* group of all these events happening in quick succession, in one scene alone. The end of this scene is

[1] Delhorbe, op. cit., p. 312.

one of the most revealing in the whole novel: the reaction of
these idealists, humanitarians and rationalists to the news of a
man's suicide—whatever his crimes—is an hysterical outburst of
savage emotion, exactly what they are trying to abolish from
the world. Only Luce—the ideal figure once more—does not
share this reaction:

> Le journal lui tombe des doigts. Ils se l'arrachent; il passe de main en main:
> tous veulent avoir *vu*.
>
>   Un cri sauvage de triomphe, un long hurlement, un véritable délire . . .
>
>   Luce (la gorge serrée).—'Henry mort, c'est fini: il y a des choses de l'affaire
> que personne ne saura jamais . . .'
>
>   Ses paroles se perdent dans l'ivresse générale. (p. 409)

Passages such as this, showing a profound understanding of the
darker passions of man, normally suppressed, are among the
most convincing, powerfully expressed without recourse to
melodrama. This may be contrasted with Zola's interest in
passion and violence; Zola frequently exaggerates and Martin du
Gard is the more convincing for not doing so.

The use of the Dreyfus Case and religio-scientific material
marks a significant trend in the modern novel. The focus of
interest moves from the purely psychological to cover material
which might previously have been treated in works of biography,
history, philosophy, sociology and so on. The result is that the
writer can make contact with his reader on several levels, not
merely on the purely psychological one. The intelligent reader,
whatever his views and beliefs, could not help feeling the
relevance of *Barois* to his own intellectual life. As Thibaudet put
it, 'Quand on verra l'Affaire Dreyfus avec quelque recul, peut-
être estimera-t-on qu'un démiurge subtil la disposa spécialement
pour placer la France en état de clarté dramatique',[1] and Martin
du Gard was able to draw on the stock of emotional and intellectual reactions which already existed in his public when the
novel appeared. All that was needed to achieve balance was to
present all beliefs and attitudes as accurately as possible, without
distortion. Most critics, even the Catholics whom one might

---

[1] A. Thibaudet, *Les idées de M. Maurras*, Paris, 1920, p. 86.

expect to be hostile, admit that he succeeded.[1] But at the same time this means that the novel can scarcely be judged by the normal criteria; in fact, this type of novel is more often spoken of in terms of significance than in terms of beauty, and it is impossible to separate the aesthetic from the non-aesthetic in appreciation of *Barois*. Its appeal is well characterized by its recommendation as a popular text-book,[2] and by Philippe van Tieghem's statement that in his student days *Barois* acted as an infallible litmus paper to separate the Right and Left politically, and at the same time the non-believer from the believer, merely by the reader's reaction to it.[3] It follows from all this that the popularity of the novel depends very much on the general climate of opinion. In France, the problems treated in *Barois*, its content as a sociological document, have for the most part remained alive, perhaps only as a result of political and cultural developments. In Britain and the United States, on the other hand, the religious issue in *Barois* is no longer a crucial one; while the Dreyfus Case itself is hardly a *crise de conscience* rooted in the heart of the country's political life.

Martin du Gard was well aware of this, and as early as 1918 sharply criticized his book for the 'fatras idéologique, érudit, documentaire, qui alourdit *Barois*, et qui menaçait d'étouffer des dons naturels certains...'[4] He feared that the heavy content of documentary and philosophical matter might have sacrificed the novel's value, 'for all time', merely for brief notoriety, 'of an age', and claimed that:

Ce qu'il y a de meilleur dans *Barois*, sans conteste, c'est ce qui est 'touchant'.

---

[1] E.g. in Moeller, op. cit., p. 198: 'J'ai donné raison, pour l'essentiel, au tableau historique que brosse Martin du Gard.' Moeller's chapter on Martin du Gard is by far the most intelligent appreciation of him from the Catholic side, although he admits that he is chiefly concerned about the effect of *Barois* on Catholic students: 'J'ai choisi ce livre parce qu'on le lit encore énormément, surtout dans les milieux d'étudiants catholiques...' (p. 32). Moeller's view is to be contrasted with Claudel's: in 1931 the latter refused to allow a play of his own to be put on at the *Comédie des Champs-Elysées* immediately after *Un Taciturne*, presumably for fear of contagion. According to Gide (*Journal*, 6/12/31, p. 1096) *Barois* was the real cause of Claudel's attitude.

[2] J. A. Gunn, *Modern French Philosophy*, London, 1922, p. 179: 'Those who desire to study the religious psychology of France during our period cannot find a better revelation than that given in the wonderful novel by Roger Martin du Gard, entitled *Jean Barois*. Cf. also Delhorbe, op. cit., p. 343: '*Jean Barois* pourrait porter comme titre: *Histoire résumée des Idées de mon temps*.'   [3] *N.N.R.F.*, 12/58, p. 1067.

[4] Ibid., 12/58, p. 1130 (letter to Margaritis, 1/9/18

C'est le vieillissement de l'intelligence, l'évolution sénile dans le domaine des idées, (..)—le vieillissement tragique de l'homme, dans son corps et dans son cœur, sa déchéance physique, cette angoisse mortelle devant la maladie, l'inespérance de l'âge et de la mort . . .[1]

There can be little doubt that he was wrong. If *Barois* is stripped of all its ideas, hardly the substance of a full-scale novel remains. (We may perhaps note here that Malègue's novel *Augustin*, which deals with the same theme of loss and recovery of religious belief, from a Catholic viewpoint, possibly as a reply to *Barois*, never transcends lifelessness despite numerous 'scènes de sentiment pur'.) The ideas are an integral part of the novel and of any appreciation of it. Just as the characters in the novel cannot escape their environment, both physical and historical, the novel itself is bound to the intellectual environment of its time. The scenes which seemed, in 1918, to be valuable to Martin du Gard—and in 1955 he still affirmed this opinion[2]—are meaningless taken in isolation, away from the context of Barois's life, which is dominated by ideas. The theme of death is not enough —and can lend itself to excessive sentimentality.

Nevertheless *Barois* is a considerable work, and alone would mark Martin du Gard as a major novelist. In it he succeeded in carrying out the programme outlined in *Devenir*, of the novel composed exclusively of dialogue and documents, without the *sauce gluante* of connecting narrative. He proved he had outgrown the weaknesses of being too much tied to autobiographical material, by objectivizing his vision and experience of life into a non-personal framework. The plot of *Barois* provided him with a much more adequate vehicle than *Marise* for his themes, and allowed him to show a much deeper understanding of them: the contrast in *Marise*, largely in terms of ignorance and knowledge, is recalled only in the first section of *Barois*, in the relationship between Dr. and Mme Barois, while the remainder of the novel is on a more subtle plane. The originality in technique is undeniable, and Martin du Gard shows mastery in it, although perhaps, like many technical innovators, he tended

---

[1] Ibid., 12/58, p. 1119 (letter to Margaritis, 18/1/18).
[2] In a conversation with the present author in June 1955.

to see an end in what was no more than a means, not realizing
that *Barois* was a *tour de force* which would not easily allow of
repetition, and not recognizing its disadvantages—above all,
that dramatic tension remains constant, at too high a level,
broken only by the insertion of documents, and that variation
of focus becomes difficult. (Since *Barois* the dialogue technique
has suffered the fate of all innovations, and has become merely
one tool among many available to the novelist.) The symmetry
of Barois's life is excellently brought out, echoed as it is in the
lives of his father and of Cresteil: symmetry of form, of the
passing of psychological time, and symmetry of scene: the novel,
and Barois's life, begin in the narrow family circle at Buis, and
although he breaks away and spends most of his life in Paris, it
is to Buis that he returns to be reconverted and to die. Martin
du Gard's belief in determinism, which might have fatally
flawed his vision, is brilliantly transformed into the wheel of
Fate, from which Barois cannot escape, as he himself is finally
forced to realize:

Pendant longtemps, on croit que la vie est une ligne droite, dont les deux
bouts s'enfoncent à perte de vue aux deux extrémités de l'horizon: et puis,
peu à peu, on découvre que la ligne est coupée, et qu'elle se courbe, et que
les bouts se rapprochent, se rejoignent . . . L'anneau va se boucler . . . (p. 464)

Throughout his life his spiritual development is exactly paralleled
by his physical state; the reader accepts his fate as both inevitable
and fitting. Furthermore, the actual end of the novel is finely
contrived, with the sudden flash of recognition of the testament
and the irony of Cécile's destruction of it. Yet here too a balance
is achieved; whatever the reader's own views, there is no need
for him temporarily to 'suspend his disbelief', and whatever his
own scale of values, the novel has meaning for him. Unity,
objectivity, and balance are all achieved.

At this point Martin du Gard's own measured judgment of
Barois may usefully be recalled. He admits *Barois's* faults, yet
comes to a judicious conclusion about its true value:

C'est un livre lourd et long, sans génie, sans cette aisance des œuvres de génie.
Mais c'est tout de même une espèce de 'chef d'œuvre' (dans l'ancien sens,

bien entendu); une maîtresse pièce, de l'ouvrage bien fait et qui peut être retournée (sic) en tous sens. Solide et rationnelle. De la bonne besogne. C'est un livre qui n'a rien pour plaire, pour attirer l'émotion; qui n'aura jamais la gloire joyeuse des livres qui subjuguent une foule et qui vivent dans toutes les mémoires. Mais c'est un livre bien d'aplomb, plein de choses, bien foutu, ordonné, *et qui bravera le temps*, comme tout ce qui est composé et convenablement réalisé.[1]

This judgment could be repeated today with scarcely a word changed. By setting his sights lower than the hoped for Tolstoyan epic, Martin du Gard achieved success.

[1] *N.N.R.F.*, 12/58, pp. 1127–8 (letter to Margaritis, 24/1/18).

5

LES THIBAULT

OVER eight years separated *Barois* from the next novel: *Le Cahier gris*, the first volume of the *Thibault* series. Certain critics have seen in this long interval evidence that Martin du Gard almost abandoned the novel for the theatre,[1] but this is an exaggeration. It is true that *Barois* was immediately followed by the peasant farce, *Le Testament du Père Leleu*, which was put on at the *Vieux-Colombier* in February 1914. But from the outbreak of war in August that year until February 1919, he was serving in an army transport column, with scarcely enough time to carry on correspondence, let alone set about another novel. Nor did the experience of war produce any prompt aesthetic response; in fact we have to wait for *Vieille France*, in 1933, for the first reference to it—itself an indication of its traumatic effect. Martin du Gard's sole production during the war years was his obituary article on Hébert.[2]

Given his way of writing, the planning, documentation, and his need for solitude, it is not surprising that he went no further than projects for the future. One of these was the *Comédie des Tréteaux*, an idea deriving from conversations with Copeau before the war. Another was a vast Tolstoyan epic, to be entitled *Le Bien et le Mal*. We have extensive documentary evidence about this in the letters to Pierre Margaritis, published in the obituary number of the *N.N.R.F.*[3] These letters, dated from January to September 1918, are of great importance in Martin du Gard's development; in them he discusses at length his vocation; whether he was primarily a thinker—'un manieur d'idées'—or a psychological novelist—'un manieur d'émotions'.[4]

---

[1] e.g. Borgal, op. cit., p. 61.   [2] *In Memoriam*, Pléiade ed., pp. 561–76.
[3] *N.N.R.F.*, 12/58, pp. 1118–34.   [4] Ibid., p. 1119 (letter of 18/1/18).

Despite the success of *Barois*, he had fears, which gradually hardened into conviction, that his desire to 'farcir (son) œuvre littéraire (. .) de spéculation idéologique' was really just his own form of *bovarysme*.[1] Finally he resolved to give up taking endless notes on social and political problems, and to devote himself instead to purely psychological observation. Only in this way could he return to the Tolstoyan ideal: 'Il faut *étouffer le chartiste et ressusciter le poète* de mes quinze ans.'[2]

This also meant, he believed, a complete change in his methods of work: 'mon *Anna Karénine* doit se faire en *promenade;* tandis que mon *Barois* a dû se faire *au bureau*'.[3] The only danger was that his careful planning provided a deliberate discipline, and he was a little afraid that without it his natural laziness might get the better of him: 'J'ai le travail lent, l'effort lent. Je dois me donner tout entier à ce que je veux faire',[4] (and in fact *Les Thibault* was eventually written very much *au bureau*, if, at least in the early volumes, without the 'spéculation idéologique'). As yet he had no clear idea of the plot of his next novel; hitherto he had considered another novel of ideas, and a reference to an entire 'rayon de bibliothèque' on Alsace-Lorraine[5] hints at politics or the events leading up to the war as a likely subject. But *Le Bien et le Mal* is only vaguely described:

. . . je le vois comme un pur roman, un conte volumineux et rebondissant, un grouillement d'êtres vivants, attachant comme le spectacle même de la vie.[6]

This tells us little more than the intention of writing another *War and Peace*, more an ideal than a plan. Finally his attention turned to the style of *Barois*, the *style notatif*. He considered changing to a more normal style: '. . . me laisser aller, écrire en un style coulant, narratif, coloré . . .',[7] and, after the Armistice, when he began to write his *souvenirs* to while away the time in Germany, he experimented with this manner. But for the time being he came down in favour of a freer version of the *style notatif*:

[1] Ibid., p. 1118 (letter of 18/1/18).   [2] Ibid., p. 1127 (second letter of 6/2/18).
[3] Ibid., p. 1124 (letter of 23/1/18).   [4] Ibid., p. 1123 (letter of 23/1/18).
[5] Ibid., p. 1123 (letter of 23/1/18).   [6] Ibid., p. 1132 (letter of 1/9/18).
[7] Ibid., p. 1129 (letter of 1/9/18).

... ne pas renoncer à ce style notatif, irremplaçable. Mais en user avec beaucoup plus d'aisance, ne pas en être obsédé, gêné. Laisser courir la plume par endroits, chaque fois qu'au lieu d'avoir à présenter un lieu précis, un jeu de scène, une suite rapide de sentiments, j'aurai à créer une atmosphère floue, à mettre de l'air coloré autour des scènes, à résumer une évolution de sentiments ou de pensées.[1]

On demobilization, however, Martin du Gard did not set to work directly on a new novel, but instead helped Copeau to re-establish the *Vieux-Colombier*. Not until early in 1920 did he eventually begin work on *Les Thibault*:

Dès janvier, pendant le répit que je m'étais accordé après la réouverture du Vieux-Colombier, j'avais été brusquement séduit par l'idée d'écrire l'histoire de deux frères: deux êtres de tempéraments aussi différents, aussi divergents, que possible, mais foncièrement marqués par les obscures similitudes que crée, entre deux consanguins, un très puissant atavisme commun. Un tel sujet m'offrait l'occasion d'un fructueux dédoublement: j'y voyais la possibilité d'exprimer simultanément deux tendances contradictoires de ma nature: l'instinct d'indépendance, d'évasion, de révolte, le refus de tous les conformismes; et, cet instinct d'ordre, de mesure, ce refus des extrêmes, que je dois à mon hérédité.[2]

There may be more to this than he claims. Unless *Le Bien et le Mal* was intended to have an entirely different subject, he could scarcely have been 'brusquement séduit' by the idea two years after he had written at length to Margaritis about it. The idea, in any case, was not new: *Devenir*, *Barois*, (and *Jean-Christophe*) are built round a similar *dédoublement*. What actually happened in 1919 must, for the present, remain doubtful. Maurice Martin du Gard has stated that his cousin was greatly depressed in 1918 and 1919, quoting from Roger's *Journal* in support.[3] The release of tension at the end of the war and Margaritis's death may have had some connexion with this (Margaritis, who died on October 30th 1918, was an intimate friend, and was apparently the model for Jacques Thibault).[4]

However, planning and documentation for *Les Thibault* continued steadily from January 1920. Martin du Gard was warmly encouraged by Gide,[5] and in May retired to Berry in

[1] Ibid., p. 1130 (letter of 1/9/18). [2] *Souvenirs*, p. lxxviii.
[3] Maurice Martin du Gard, op. cit., p. 469. [4] *N.N.R.F.*, 12/58, p. 1117.
[5] *Souvenirs*, p. lxxix.

order to establish a detailed plan. His dossiers completed, he began to write, and by 1920 was able to discuss the first draft of *Le Cahier gris* and half of *Le Pénitencier* with Gide, and the two volumes were published in April and May 1922 respectively. The original edition was accompanied by a note regretting the impossibility of bringing out the novel-series as a whole, and announcing that later volumes would appear 'à quelques mois d'intervalle'.[1] These 'few months', however, soon stretched to years, and the final volume only came out in 1940. Consequently a certain degree of unity is essential in each individual volume, as well as development of the general action. This unity is achieved by the technique which Mme Magny has well named the *nœud d'événements:*

Martin du Gard a évité le risque de dispersion en entrelaçant ses diverses intrigues pour en former des *nœuds d'événements*, où se trouvent superposées et concentrées en un point unique de la durée plusieurs occurrences importantes quasi simultanées; ou bien qui annoncent et préfigurent à travers le fait présent (relativement insignifiant) un événement capital encore à venir, soudant ainsi dans l'espace ou dans le temps des destinées independantes.[2]

In this way only limited periods of psychological time need be narrated directly: in fact the range extends from *La Belle Saison*, spanning several months, to the fourteen hours of *La Consultation*. The entire novel thus falls into a number of short episodes, with long stretches of time between volumes. It is, in fact, the structure of *Barois* on a larger scale, and the construction in dramatic *tableaux* is unmistakable.

The first two volumes deal principally with the adolescence of Jacques Thibault and his friend Daniel de Fontanin. *Le Cahier gris* is taken up with the *fugue* of the two boys, who run away from home to the South of France, in an unsuccessful attempt to reach North Africa. Caught near Toulon, they are brought back to Paris by the police, and the volume ends with the contrast in their treatment, Daniel being welcomed back, but Jacques severely punished. This punishment takes the form of incarceration in the reformatory from which the second volume,

[1] *Le Cahier gris*, Paris, 1922, p. 9.
[2] C.-E. Magny, *Le roman français depuis 1918*, vol. i, Paris, 1950, p. 310.

Le Pénitencier, takes its name. Nine months have passed, when Antoine Thibault is seized with doubts about his brother's welfare, and visits the reformatory, where his suspicions are amply confirmed. He forces his father, the domineering M. Thibault, to allow him to bring Jacques back to Paris under his own wing. Jacques is thus gradually brought back into normal life, and the volume ends with his final surmounting of the sexual crisis of adolescence.

With the third volume, *La Belle Saison* (October 1923), Martin du Gard made a strong attempt to broaden the scope of his novel by introducing several sub-plots. Five years have passed, and Jacques, as the volume opens, is successful in the *Concours* of the *Ecole Normale Supérieure*. The events cover the summer months which follow: Jacques's awakening love for Daniel's sister Jenny; Antoine's love affair with the exotic and sensual Rachel, Daniel's life as a promising young artist; and the relationship between his parents, Mme de Fontanin and her husband Jérôme. The action which completes the novel is Rachel's decision to leave Antoine and return to her former lover Hirsch in Africa.

A gap of several years followed before the appearance of the succeeding volumes—*La Consultation* in April 1928, *La Sorellina* in May of the same year, and *La Mort du Père* in March 1929. The interval was, however, the result of external causes: first, the composition of *La Gonfle*, a second peasant farce, as creative relaxation; then the death of Martin du Gard's parents in 1924 and 1925, and problems connected with the inheritance. *La Consultation*, the shortest volume in the series, is a technical *tour de force;* simply a description of one day of Antoine's life as a doctor. Indirectly, from the description, the threads of the general narrative can be perceived: three more years have passed, and we discover that Jacques had disappeared shortly after the events of *La Belle Saison*, that M. Thibault is now fatally ill, and that Antoine's career is flourishing. Little real action takes place; intervening events are merely inferred from the descriptive *tableaux*. With *La Sorellina* the narrative returns to its previous form. The time interval is a mere six weeks, which allows M. Thibault's illness to have reached a critical stage. A letter addressed to Jacques has finally put Antoine on his track, and he searches him out in Lausanne, where, under an assumed name, he is living as a revolutionary journalist, and persuades him to return to Paris before his father dies. The volume ends with the brothers on the train back; and *La Mort du Père* follows directly on this, at about the same tempo. The first half of the book deals with the events leading up to M. Thibault's agonizing death, and the second one with the aftermath, when the release of tension allows sub-plots to be taken up again, and preparations to be made for later volumes.

From this it can be seen that the primary interest thus far in the novel is psychological. The initial two volumes deal almost entirely with the problems of adolescence, in particular the crisis of puberty, while later the focus is on the themes of vocation, love, solitude, and death. Political, philosophical, and religious preoccupations fade into the background, to re-emerge only in isolated sections of *La Consultation* and *La Mort du Père*. The basic problem of composition was to combine treatment of these themes, in adequate depth, with a comparatively limited number of basic characters. (There is no attempt to cover the entire range of *milieux* in France; Martin du Gard is content to portray only that section of the Parisian *bourgeoisie* which he belonged to and thus knew at first hand.) The themes were therefore dealt with primarily in terms of the different characters: adolescence in Jacques and Daniel, love in Antoine, and, to a lesser extent, in Daniel, Jacques, and Jérôme, death in M. Thibault; while the characters are brought together by means of the *nœud d'événements*. Thus, in *Le Cahier gris*, the *fugue* to Marseilles is made to happen contemporaneously with several subsidiary episodes: Jenny's illness and apparently miraculous cure, Daniel's sexual initiation, the dray accident on the Toulon road, the Thibault *conseil de famille*, and Mme de Fontanin's search for Jérôme. The technique remains similar throughout.

Besides the *nœud d'événements*, we have other evidence of Martin du Gard's methods of composition. There is, first, the passage in the *Souvenirs*—justly described by Borgal as 'une véritable page d'anthologie'[1]—where we see the author, 'seul avec mes liasses de notes', surrounded by a dozen tables representing the different chronological periods of the novel, covering a total of about forty years. By sorting his *fiches* into the appropriate piles, the main lines of the novel, its characters and episodes could take distinct form. In addition to this proof of documentation, in a letter quoted by Roy, Martin du Gard describes his composition, 'avec la collaboration du temps'.[2] He would visualize a scene—such as Antoine's visit to the *pénitencier*, or Jacques's interview with Jalicourt—and would then jot down everything he could imagine about the scene, without the slighest attention to style. And so on with the next scene. It might be months or years before the rough draft was looked at again—but the scene was now 'fixed' in his memory and had taken on 'la consistence d'un souvenir réel.' It could not be changed any more than a real memory—he instances his arrival at his army barracks to begin military service. All that remained was to rewrite the scene and work it into the general narrative. In this way he was able to separate conception from execution and put his taste for method to best use.

Fundamentally, then, the composition of *Les Thibault* is a simple development of that of *Barois*. The only distinct change is the abandonment of the dialogue form. What finally convinced Martin du Gard was an experiment—another example of painstaking thoroughness—in which he wrote an entire episode both in dialogue and in traditional narrative.[3] The dialogue version was undoubtedly more dramatic, with more *relief*—but it was three or four times as long. This would have drawn out the length of the series so much that he was obliged to opt for concision. There was also the final consideration that the dialogue form, forcing the use of the present tense alone, deprived him of the valuable stylistic resource of variation in tense. He made his choice and never regretted it.

Another interesting document is a page from Martin du Gard's diary which shows Gide comparing their methods of work.

[1] *Souvenirs*, p. lxxix; Borgal, op. cit., p. 73.   [2] Roy, op. cit., pp. 66–67.
[3] *Souvenirs*, pp. lix–lx.

For Gide, Martin du Gard's method consisted of a simple chronological narrative, and he illustrated the point by shining a torch along a straight line drawn on a piece of paper. His own method, in *Les Faux-Monnayeurs*, he claimed, was circular, and he revolved the torch from a fixed point on the paper. Martin 'du Gard's lighting was steady and continuous, unlike his own:

Chez vous, rien n'est jamais présenté de biais, de façon imprévue, anachronique. Tout baigne dans la même clarté, directe, sans surprise. Vous vous privez de ressources précieuses . . . Pensez à Rembrandt, à ses touches de lumière, puis à la profondeur secrète de ses ombres. Il y a une science subtile des éclairages; les varier à l'infini, c'est tout un art.'
—'Un art? Ou un artifice?'[1]

And despite Martin du Gard's rejoinder, it is clear that in *Les Thibault* he is using the *science des éclairages*, especially since he is no longer tied to the present tense. Gide's description is in any case inaccurate, since even in *Barois* the *éclairage* is by no means completely regular: Luce's death is narrated indirectly, the story of Barois' mother is told entirely in snatches of conversation between Dr. Barois and the grandmother, and, above all, the use of documents provides a certain range of emphasis and variation of focus. Still, in *Barois* this *présentation indirecte des événements* was both limited and rigid; in *Les Thibault* it is transformed into a subtle skill approaching virtuosity.

The dramatic nature of the *nœud d'événements* technique is further illustrated by the method of exposition. Throughout Martin du Gard prefers presentation to statement, and almost every volume begins with a plunge *in medias res*. Until the general lines of the narrative have been fixed the emphasis is on swift-moving action, with little static description. The pattern is constant:

Au coin de la rue de Vaugirard, comme ils longeaient déjà les bâtiments de l'Ecole, M. Thibault, qui pendant le trajet n'avait pas adressé la parole à son fils, s'arrêta brusquement . . .
Les deux frères longeaient la grille du Luxembourg. La demie de cinq heures venait de sonner à l'horloge du Sénat . . .[2]

---

[1] *Notes sur André Gide*, p. 1372 (entry dated 12/20).
[2] Pp. 581 and 814 respectively. The similarity here is increased by use of the same milieu and vocabulary.

The single exception is *La Mort du Père*, which can be explained since there is no time interval, the narrative overlapping that of the previous volume. The gain in direct interest—and plausibility —of this dramatic presentation is immense; incident and character are thus made into a much more effective vehicle for the essential themes of the novel.

Dramatic presentation implies a different, and more subtle, method of characterization. The stylized short sketch of *Barois* has given way to the device of inserting a series of brief traits into the action, gradually building up the required impression, from page to page, chapter to chapter. Thus with M. Thibault we are at first given only the briefest descriptive traits expressing character through physical behaviour: '(il) s'arrêta brusquement . . .', 'frappa du pied . . .', 'les dents serrées' (p. 581). Slightly longer indications follow: '(il) secoua les épaules, et tourna vers l'abbé son visage bouffi dont les lourdes paupières ne se soulevaient presque jamais . . .', '(il) prit une chaise et s'assit; son esprit agile suivait diverses pistes; mais le visage, paralysé par la graisse, n'exprimait rien . . .' (p. 582). Longer passages follow and the full picture slowly forms. The narrator is omniscient, as in the traditional novel, with no inhibitions about internal psychological description. The total intention is to produce the illusion of psychological development as well as to present them dramatically: since the characters have been fully planned beforehand, the only way to simulate development is to suppress the complete picture, revealing it only gradually in the course of the novel. This process remains broadly true, except in *La Consultation* and the Packmell episode in *La Belle Saison*, where the need to present numbers of minor figures quickly forces a return to the *Barois* technique in the case, say, of Favery, Ernst, or Rumelles.

Conception of character shows an equally mature development. Martin du Gard, like Proust, James, and Gide, has adopted the view that personality is not an absolute, as in the traditional nineteenth-century novel, but is a complex pattern of different, even contradictory, elements. Characters are, therefore, not only portrayed indirectly, from different standpoints, but largely in relation to each other. The total impression is only created in the reader's mind at the conclusion of the final volume, but it is one of correspondingly greater depth. The relationships themselves may change, as with Daniel and Jacques, and the psychological variations and possibilities are almost infinite; the only drawback is that only a limited number of figures can be treated in this way, or the complexities will tend to get out of hand.

Indirect presentation is also used in characterization. Jérôme is first shown, in Le Cahier gris, through his wife's attempts to find his mistress's address; this search, itself dramatic, provides a clear indication of his character, and to a lesser degree of his wife's. Jacques and Daniel are shown entirely at second hand for the first half of the same volume, through the reactions of their parents, while the nature of their relationship is most clearly seen from their correspondence in the grey notebook. Thus suspense can be maintained, since the reader has as little idea of their whereabouts as the parents; while nothing could so well illustrate the artificial, hothouse nature of their friendship as the adolescent letters written to each other in class, with their mixture of undigested literary influences and puerile enthusiasms.

Of Martin du Gard's gallery of characters, M. Thibault is the most dominating in the early volumes, possibly because he is seen entirely from outside. He is at the height of his power and worldly success in Le Cahier gris, easily overshadowing Antoine; and the relationship between the two constantly changes from then on. At first Antoine's reaction to his father's domineering attitude is no more than one of sceptical amusement—on the subject of uncensored reading, for instance (pp. 584–5). In Le Pénitencier he challenges his father directly, and his own stature increases as his father's diminishes. By La Belle Saison no more than lip-service is paid to the old man's wishes (and the final break with Jacques is seen only at second hand). In the next three volumes, his part is entirely passive, the active rôle having passed on to his sons, and the reader sees the dying man very much in terms of contrast with the authoritarian of Le Cahier gris.

The bullying father is indeed almost a stock figure in the bourgeois novel, and makes an easy target for satire. This temptation is avoided here. Martin du Gard rarely makes personal comments about his characters, going little farther than expressing his disapproval indirectly in the shape of Antoine's thoughts. The contrast between his methods of upbringing and Mme de Fontanin's is clear enough; and, as a result, a figure who might have been no more than a caricature is given depth and consistency, while there is no risk of damage to the comparative objectivity of the style. Martin du Gard's determinism adds to this effect. M. Thibault's chief characteristic is his egoism, expressed in ambition and will-power; and this binds him to his sons instead of separating him from them, for it is fundamental in their own personalities. 'Broyer sa volonté,' is M. Thibault's cry when he sends Jacques to the reformatory; and despite his anger when Antoine tries to bring Jacques back, he is somehow proud of these 'actes d'indépendance' as well (p. 729). And since he is no more and no less the product of his particular heredity and environment than any other character, irony is tempered with sympathy: 'Comme tout créateur authentique, Martin du Gard pardonne à tous ses personnages. Le véritable artiste, bien que sa vie soit d'abord lutte et combat, n'a pas d'ennemi'.[1]

The other main element in M. Thibault's personality is his *amour-propre*, the self-satisfaction deriving from realized ambition. This again is treated sympathetically, more with kindly irony than with cruel satire:

Son prénom était Jules; mais M. Thibault, par considération pour lui-même, appelait son secrétaire 'Monsieur Chasle'. (p. 720)

A later instance is his change of the family name to Oscar-Thibault (a trait probably taken from Martin du Gard's father-in-law, whose name was, or became, Albert-Foucault. This may not have been the only resemblance). It is not only an expression of vanity, as Antoine mockingly supposes, but represents the old man's desire for survival, an aspect of the theme of death developed further in *Epilogue*. On this occasion Jacques intuitively understands his father's motives, because of his own preoccupation with death.

[1] Camus, op. cit., p. xxviii.

The counterpart of egoism is of course isolation, from which M. Thibault suffers increasingly as the novel moves on. Isolated in his pride, physically symbolized by his growing deafness, he is no longer wanted by his family; and he becomes merely a nuisance, almost contemptuously deceived by Antoine and Thérivier about the gravity of his illness. This is later balanced by M. Thibault's own pretence of dying; the total effect is to deprive him of his dignity as a human being, bringing him down to the common level of humanity, and this too is reinforced by the ignominious way of his death. But at the same time this redeems him, since it makes him a pathetic figure, worthy of sympathy. Although his reaction to the knowledge that he is dying is wild panic, in which he screams obscenities and abjures his God and everything he has stood for, he is brought round by Abbé Vécard from childish entreaty to acceptance of his fate. Admittedly his self-condemnation, his confession of his 'jeunesse dévorée d'ambition', is somewhat implausible, since hitherto he has been incapable of self-analysis (it is stylistically weak too, since it is stated, not presented); but the complete episode is still effective.

It is only after M. Thibault's death that the portrait of him is fully rounded. There is, of course, a good deal of irony in the old man's attempts to project his *amour-propre* beyond his own lifetime; the funeral service at Crouy is a set-piece of satire, with the assembled dignitaries thinking of the eulogies which will sometime be made in their own honour, so that their orations are the more generously sprinkled with praise, for it is indirectly praise of themselves. But Antoine's reactions to these speeches, if sometimes comic, are also profound; he is proud of his father, who was, after all, no ordinary man, and realizes the truth: 'On n'arrive à comprendre un homme qu'après sa mort' (p. 1357). A whole chapter is devoted to M. Thibault's posthumous papers, in order to lift the veil from the lesser known aspects of his life. The technique is simple: extracts are given from diaries and documents, and Martin du Gard can invent at will to illuminate the psychological facets required. Some lend themselves to ironic treatment, such as the long, precise, and pompous instructions about the funeral; others show M. Thibault's generosity, like the careful list of bequests in the will. His letters to his wife show a new side of him: '. . . personne jamais ne s'est aimé comme nous . . .' (p. 1330). For Martin du Gard the sexual side of man is crucial in an understanding of him, and this had previously been omitted, necessarily. Now there are hints at love affairs after his wife's death, the possibility of remarriage, and talk of 'mon péché'; the technique is that of the oblique remark, the sous-entendu, maintaining an air of mystery, continued by the mysterious woman, with the Parma violets, whom Jacques sees on the train to Crouy. Thus the rock-like obstinacy of the old man in the earlier volumes is belied: reading the papers, Antoine sees much of Jacques in his father: '. . . Mêmes sensibilités contractées, même violence secrète des instincts, mêmes rudesses . . .' (p. 1338). There is also the revelation that, in his later years, he had been growing less serene, despite his outward appearance, and had been torn by inner conflicts. The egoistic attempt to replace human affection by the admiration of others has only resulted in pathetic loneliness.

The total picture is, then, much more complex than the traditional crude satirical figure of the self-satisfied bien-pensant bourgeois.

The character of Jacques is essentially built round the same quality of egoism as his father's. The difference is that the latter —and Antoine—direct their efforts towards material worldly success, while Jacques is the natural rebel, psychologically incapable of making any concessions to society, which he sees personified in his family. The portrait is highly successful, so much so that later in life Martin du Gard grew tired of adulatory letters from misunderstood adolescents who identified themselves with Jacques.[1]

As in Barois, psychological qualities are expressed in physical appearance—'la forte mâchoire des Thibault' (p. 591), and Jacques is constantly described with this in mind:

. . . ses cheveux roux, durs et broussailleux . . . (..) . . . cette figure plutôt ingrate, enlaidie par un semis de taches de son, les yeux, d'un bleu dur, petits, encaissés, volontaires . . . (p. 630)

[1] N.N.R.F., 12/58, p. 1145.

This technique of physical description, verging in some cases into a *leitmotiv*, is not gratuitous; since five years separate *Le Pénitencier* from *La Belle Saison*, and three *La Belle Saison* from Jacques's reappearance in *La Sorellina*, stress on the physical aspect helps to create the impression of psychological continuity.

Jacques's character in *Le Cahier gris* is shown almost entirely through his friendship with Daniel. Both boys are passing through the crisis of puberty, and it is this which inspires their artificially passionate letters, misinterpreted by Binot and M. Thibault in terms of homosexuality. In fact the friendship is completely innocent: in the hotel at Marseilles the two boys are ashamed to undress with the light on. The theme of adolescence had, of course, become more and more popular from the beginning of the century onward;[1] and *Les Faux-Monnayeurs* is equally constructed round a *fugue* (there may have been some friendly rivalry here), but for Martin du Gard adolescence is treated as essential in the development of the adult—the child explains the man—rather than purely for its own sake. 'Dis-moi ce qu'a été ta puberté, et je connaîtrai ta nature, et je saurai tes secrets', we read in the *Journal de Maumort*.[2] Of the two boys, it is Jacques who dominates; Daniel would have scarcely dared to run away alone. But his sexual initiation in Marseilles permanently changes the nature of the relationship, since the crisis of puberty is then surmounted, and his intimacy with Jacques is weakened by concealing his experience. Fundamental divergencies of character are also brought to light by the severe trial of the *fugue*, and from this point the friendship fades, so that the link between the two families gradually becomes Jacques's love for Jenny—itself partly an attempt by Jacques to recapture the lost purity of his friendship with Daniel.

Jacques's incarceration at Crouy is a natural result of the escapade; it also enables Martin du Gard to introduce a social theme, that of penal life. The picture of the reformatory is realistically drawn, not overtly critical, but with an ironic contrast between first impressions and the underlying reality.

[1] Cf. J. O'Brien, *The Novel of Adolescence in France*, New York, 1937.
[2] Quoted in *Souvenirs*, p. cxxxiv.

(The adverse effect on the reader is carefully balanced in later volumes by letters from former detainees expressing their gratitude.) The theme has dated rather: the present-day reader is usually better informed about, and therefore less interested in, penal reform.[1] But the reformatory is more necessary for its effect on Jacques, who, with true dramatic irony, has been corrupted, not by his crime, but by his punishment. After nine months of imprisonment, he is in a psychological state more familiar today than in 1922 (destruction of personality after solitary confinement or 'brain-washing'). Only after his return to Paris can he recover from this traumatic experience.

This reintegration into ordinary life is treated primarily in sexual terms. Even Antoine's desire to have Jacques under his own wing is assimilated to his unfulfilled need for love and affection (p. 700). Martin du Gard's technique for treating this theme remains the same throughout the novel: in order to avoid all suggestion of salaciousness or obscenity, he avoids direct statement and comment as far as possible, preferring the more delicate method of oblique hints and suggestions. Thus it is clear that Jacques has been indulging in excessive masturbation in the reformatory, and that he has been homosexually corrupted (p. 719), but this has to be inferred from the narrative. Back in Paris, the concierge's niece, Lisbeth Fruhling, is introduced as the instrument of Jacques's sexual maturity. She comes briefly from Strasbourg twice, and the necessarily short period of her stay forces her relationship with Jacques to be only temporary, ending with a clean break. Although Lisbeth is only a minor character, little more than a technical necessity for the plot, several pages are spent on a careful portrayal of her and her life in Strasbourg. This type of plump, good-natured, complaisant German girl is perhaps more common in literature than life, which may account for the extensive background material.

---

[1] Martin du Gard also collected similar documentation about prison life to be used in a later volume when Jean-Paul was to be sentenced to a term of imprisonment (cf. *Souvenirs*, p. xcv). Even in 1955, he regretted, in a conversation with the present writer, that he had never been able to make use of all this painstakingly assembled material, and confessed that he had often thought of writing a *nouvelle* on the subject, in order not to waste it.

The entire episode is subtly treated: Lisbeth sleeps with Antoine —as a matter of course—and is at the same time encouraged by him to seduce Jacques, to put his sexual instincts back on the right track. By breaking her stay into two parts, it is also possible to interpose another scene at the Fontanins': motivated by Jacques's intense loneliness after Lisbeth's departure (sexual motivation again). In the final chapter she returns and succeeds in seducing him; this act is clearly shown as the final surmounting of the crisis of puberty:

La glace lui offrit sa svelte image, et pour la première fois depuis bien long-temps, il contempla, sans trouble aucun, les particularités de son corps. Au souvenir de ses égarements, il eut même un haussement des épaules, suivi d'un sourire indulgent. 'Des bêtises de gosse', songea-t-il; ce chapitre-là lui semblait définitivement clos, comme si des forces longtemps méconnues, longtemps déviées, eussent enfin trouvé leur véritable carrière. Sans réfléchir précisément à ce qui s'était passé cette nuit, sans même penser à Lisbeth, il se sentait le cœur joyeux, l'âme et la chair purifiées . . . (p. 812)

Treatment of Jacques in *La Belle Saison* is largely in terms of vocation. After years of sustained work, he succeeds brilliantly in the *concours* for the *Ecole Normale Supérieure;* but even before the results are posted, he doubts whether he really wants to spend three years in the cloistered, hothouse atmosphere of the *Rue d'Ulm.* He is obviously not yet mature, and has a mythomaniac streak: but this also indicates his intense inner life and lack of balance. The Packmell episode serves to repel him from the unbridled sensuality so attractive to Daniel; and the feeling of flatness which is the aftermath of his *Normale* success leaves him merely with confused feelings of revolt and a need to escape. None of his literary projects attract him, now he has leisure for them; but he cannot bring himself to put his subconscious wishes into effect and spend the summer travelling. A vague resentment and bitterness paralyse all power for decision and action, and at times we are reminded of André Mazerelles; the total picture is one of an undeniable intellectual and spiritual egoism:

Mes professeurs! Mes camarades! Leurs engouements, leurs livres de pré-dilection! Les auteurs contemporains! Ah, si seulement quelqu'un au monde pouvait soupçonner ce que je suis, moi,—ce que je veux faire! Non, personne n'en a l'idée, pas même Daniel. (..) 'Oublier tout ce qui a déjà été écrit', songeait-il. 'Sortir des rails! Regarder en soi, et dire tout! Personne encore n'a eu l'audace de dire tout. Quelqu'un, enfin: moi!' (p. 819)

With this thirst for absolute individuality, the stage is now set for Jacques to fall in love with Jenny; but the two have to be placed in close contact. The needs of the plot provide the prime reason why Jacques must be kept at Maisons despite his need for escape, and to do this Martin du Gard has to use a rather crude device: the feeling of destiny—'. . . il sentait qu'une mystérieuse destinée l'enchaînait ici, cette année, et que, partout ailleurs, il traînerait une détresse pire' (p. 908).

In all this, the need for a true vocation is paramount. This is an extension of the problems of adolescence treated in the first two volumes, but whereas earlier he was a passive figure, the onus of decision resting on his father, now he is responsible for his own life and fate. The problem is also transposed into sexual terms. His resentment of Daniel and Antoine for their aggressive and confident sexuality, which offends his own sense of purity, makes him feel a powerful need for sympathy and affection, tending to fix itself upon Gise; yet at the same time he feels the spiritual attraction towards Jenny which had begun in *Le Pénitencier*. Later, his inability to resolve the confusion and the ambiguous emotions caused by this play a large part in his flight to Africa.

Jacques's relationship with Jenny is described in spiritual, not physical, terms; it thus provides an antithesis to Antoine's affair with Rachel. It is never fully analysed, but left as intuitive sympathy between incestuous natures: in Jenny, though she is more passive, Jacques recognizes the mirror image of his own character. But they are held apart by their pride and immature awkwardness, which makes them conceal their emotions; only gradually does the feeling ripen. Both are described in the same language; both feel misunderstood in a hostile world, and are repelled by Daniel's promiscuity. At this point in the novel, of course, both are in a transitional stage; Martin du Gard is laying down the foundations of psychological verisimilitude for future volumes, when Jacques's rebellious attitude and inability to identify himself with any part of society will have developed into political revolt. Here again egoism is the fundamental cause, an egoism fully equal to his father's thirst for status or Antoine's single-minded ambition. But whereas they at least recognize their aim and so find it easier to realize, Jacques is confused and unbalanced, unable to solve his problems.

Jacques does not reappear until *La Sorellina*, and even then is seen at second hand in most of the volume—a technique analogous to the *fugue* in *Le Cahier gris*. We see, first, Jacques in retrospect, in relation to Jalicourt; this episode is evidently regarded as important, since we see it from two widely different points of view. The mainspring of both Jacques and Jalicourt is once again egoism: Jalicourt is not really interested in Jacques, but only in himself and in his influence over the young, which forces him to make strenuous efforts to understand what is 'modern'. Nor is Jacques interested in Jalicourt, except in that he believes, mistakenly, that the Professor personifies one of his own ideals. The meeting is a disappointment: instead of receiving moral support to bolster his own indecision, he has to listen to an outpouring of the conventional ideas he so much detests. There is in fact little common ground between them. Yet Jalicourt has the merit of realizing this utter lack of contact, and it is this which provokes his outburst of sincerity (which his pride had prevented him from revealing to Antoine in their interview.)

The whole episode provides another aspect of the theme of vocation; Jalicourt, despite his worldly success, is at bottom profoundly dissatisfied, because he, as a young man, had not followed the advice of the *maître* of the time, Zola: to go into journalism. He enjoins Jacques in a powerful speech to do so, to give himself over to the 'plongeon dans la fosse commune':

Démenez-vous du matin au soir, ne manquez pas un accident, pas un suicide, pas un procès, pas un drame mondain, pas un crime de lupanar! Ouvrez les yeux, regardez tout ce qu'une civilisation charrie derrière elle, le bon, le mauvais, l'insoupçonné, l'ininventable! Et peut-être qu'après ça vous pourrez vous permettre de dire quelque chose sur les hommes, sur la société—sur vous! (p. 1237)

In the next three years Jacques follows this advice to the letter.

(This episode may have been inspired by Martin du Gard's own career: in particular his resolve, in 1918, to give up solitary study and seek inspiration in life itself. The desire to present this theme dramatically explains the use of Zola—with characteristic reticence his name is never specified, but the reference is clear.)

The scenes in Lausanne in the closing chapters, and in Paris in *La Mort du Père* show Jacques once more in his relationship with Antoine. Even the *nouvelle*, *La Sorellina*, is intended not only to give Antoine the clue to his brother's whereabouts, but also to show up certain psychological refinements, such as Antoine's feeling for Gise. As Antoine understands the *nouvelle*, Jacques's relationship with Gise had gone as far as intercourse, almost incestuous in nature; and this realization hurts Antoine's pride so much that his reconciliation with Jacques is clouded until he discovers the innocent truth.

The Lausanne meeting is a key episode: although Jacques at first meets Antoine with crude hostility and resistance, he is vulnerable to affection. Soon he is forced to realize that he has not been able to free himself from his heredity and former environment after all:

. . . il venait d'apercevoir combien vite il se rattachait malgré lui à son frère, à tout le passé! Hier encore, un fossé infranchissable . . . Et la moitié d'un jour avait suffi . . . (pp. 1249-50)

And even previously he had not been able to divorce himself completely from his real identity: all his aliases—Jack Baulthy, Jacques le Fataliste, J. Mühlenberg—prove that he did not want to lose even his name without trace. His individualism is by now tempered by experience: he is not so different from the rest of humanity as he had thought.

In *La Mort du Père*, Jacques's rôle is more passive. It is one of the ironies of the novel that after Antoine's efforts to bring him back, he arrives too late, not to see his father die, but for any possible reconciliation to take place. His reaction is more emotional than rational, and is thus contrasted with Antoine's. He realizes that it is his own past that has disappeared with the physical presence of M. Thibault, and the hours he spends beside the corpse form an 'émouvante confrontation avec sa jeunesse' (p. 1306). As a sign of his fundamental immaturity, a literary memory continually surges before his eyes, despite his zeal for 'la fosse commune': the final scene from Chekhov's *Uncle Vanya*, and the refrain: 'Nous nous reposerons'. This is linked in his mind with the idea of suicide, and both the refrain and the idea seize him again during his visit to Crouy. Martin du Gard is preparing for his ultimate fate: suicide is the logical conclusion of his constant desire to escape the present, to flee his own past and environment. At Crouy again, he feels a sudden impulse to set the reformatory alight, as if this could somehow purge the memory of his months there; his first emotion on returning to Paris is to want to flee to Switzerland again, to escape the bitter memories evoked by Gise's room. His state of *dépaysement* is made explicit:

L'évocation du passé soulevait en lui des sursauts de rancune. Rien, dans l'existence qu'il avait vécue, ne trouvait grâce. A aucune époque de sa vie, nulle part, il ne s'était senti d'aplomb, à sa place, sur son vrai sol enfin,— comme Antoine. Dépaysé partout. (..) Et non seulement dépaysé, mais traqué. Traqué par les siens; traqué par la société, par les conditions de la vie . . . Traqué par il ne savait quoi, qui semblait venir aussi de lui-même. (p. 1319)

This key passage goes far to explain Jacques's conduct throughout the novel; only one element in his make-up is stronger, one which he normally can suppress completely: his fear of death.

In this volume Jacques and Gise are once more brought together, and their relationship is finally resolved. This is done in two stages, in Chapters IX and XI. At first nothing is settled; Jacques is once again seized with tenderness, but realizes that love is impossible; in the second, he is filled with blind fury, his usual reaction to mental obstacles, followed by remorse, but Gise has an intuition that all is over. The scene is treated again as an exercise in egoism: Jacques knows that he is damaging her life, but cannot sacrifice his personality to her (while he is still subconsciously in love with Jenny); Gise's desire to marry him shows no understanding of his real nature and is basically no less egoistic. Jacques appears to make the active decision to part which she passively accepts, but this difference is illusory: both really act because of the demands of their personality, which in turn is the product of their heredity and environment. The incompatibility between them is fundamental, springing from factors beyond their own control, and thus outside the scope of ethical judgments.

By the end of *La Mort du Père*, Jacques has been fully reintegrated into the general narrative. At the same time his potentialities have been reduced. He has had to come to terms with his family, or rather with Antoine; he has finally broken with Gise; and his friendship with Daniel, though little more than a hollow shell, has been resumed. Only his relationship with Jenny remains to be resolved, and the transition from rebel to revolutionary to be analysed. This is done in *Été 1914*.

Antoine, though his life is not so dramatic as his brother's, can be regarded as the most important character in the novel. Indeed, in many ways, *Les Thibault* is more a *Bildungsroman* centred upon Antoine than a family chronicle: the fulfilment of his medical ambitions is accompanied by increasing social awareness and involvement. His special status in the author's eyes can be inferred from the use of interior monologue in certain episodes, notably in *Le Pénitencier* and *La Consultation*. Only in his case are we given such a wealth of reported thought; and the technique is doubly revealing of his character, since it can be used indirectly to betray his ambition and self-satisfaction, with an ironical effect.

In *Le Cahier gris* Antoine is very much under his father's domination, despite a difference in attitude to Jacques's escapade. We only see him as a personality in his own right during his interview with Mme de Fontanin. Camus has written of Antoine's relationship with her, which from the start is implicitly on a sexual level, without ever going beyond an intuitive sympathy.[1] (This is an excellent example of what the same writer has called Martin du Gard's *trouvailles*, the psychological insights of the great novelist. Clearly no technique alone could enable such

---

[1] Camus, op. cit., p. xxi.

insights to be improvised, but only creative inspiration; yet this subtlety of portrayal, the 'poursuite têtue d'une vérité psychologique' [1] remains a hallmark of the entire novel.)

At the end of the volume we see a further facet of Antoine's character, as he tries to gain Jacques's confidence; this is the first confrontation and acceptance of responsibility round which Antoine's entire development is constructed. *Le Pénitencier* marks a vital stage in this development, no less than in Jacques's. The visit to Crouy and the resulting quarrel symbolically represent a final break from M. Thibault's influence, also shown on the physical plane by Antoine's removal to the ground-floor apartment. Although Antoine's vanity is one of his motives— 'un beau rôle à jouer' (p. 679),—this only makes his actions more human; with typical complexity, the whole episode falls into place as a natural step in the realization of his ambitions. Thus Antoine too is dominated by his egoism and *volonté*, though better balanced and socially integrated than his brother. He now stands at the crossroads: he can follow his father in the pursuit of purely wordly success, and feels strongly tempted to do so; or he can seek happiness through human relationships, which would involve some sacrifice of his personality to others. This problem is left until *La Belle Saison*.

So far we have learned little about Antoine's emotional life. His attitude to sex is obviously casual, and in practice almost cynical, in the matter-of-fact way he sleeps with Lisbeth and at the same time persuades her to seduce Jacques. His affair with Rachel fills in the gap, and indicates another vital stage in his development.

The scene of the operation provides a most effective introduction to the relationship. Besides illustrating Antoine's ability as a surgeon, it is a set-piece of description, naturally dramatic in its own right, as a race against time; and the accuracy of the clinical details has attracted professional praise.[2] At the same time a keen impression of atmosphere is created, with unmis-

---

[1] Ibid., p. xi.

[2] E.g. in G. Alméras, *La médecine dans Les Thibault*, Paris, 1946; P. Mauriac, *La médecine et l'intelligence*, Bordeaux, 1949; M. Laparade, *Réflexions sur quatre médecins de roman*, Bordeaux, 1948.

takable sexual overtones. The first person Antoine sees in the flat is not the injured child, but Rachel, 'la femme en peignoir rose' (p. 868), and there are repeated sensual references to her, so that when she suddenly kisses him it is a perfectly natural consequence of what has already happened.

The affair forms a complete and lengthy episode in itself; though Antoine is unaware of it at the time, it will be the only love of his life, the only affair in which he is not entirely egoistic. Rachel is a curious character, carefully drawn to show the sexually emancipated woman who could treat Antoine on equal terms. The origin of the conception is not hard to find: Ketty Varine in *Devenir*, and through Ketty to Astiné Aravian in *Les Déracinés*. The comparison with Barrès is particularly striking in that both writers firmly identify the erotic with the exotic: Astiné's tales of Asia and the Caucasus are matched by Rachel's memories of Africa with the mysterious Hirsch. (In the choice of Africa, there is an echo of Gide: Africa is the home of *immoralisme, par excellence*, and it is towards North Africa that both Jacques's *fugues* are directed.) Rachel represents almost pure sensuality, and the exotic elements are stressed in the picture of her: she is half-Jewish, an Opera dancer, then almost a circus-rider, her mother is insane, her brother a probable suicide. Above all Martin du Gard uses the personality of Hirsch to explain Rachel. He is the strangest character in the whole novel, and, perhaps because he might appear implausible if seen in the flesh, is shown only at second-hand, through Rachel's descriptions. He stands for the immoralist attitude taken to its logical extreme, no sensual experience or crime, even incest and murder, is too much for his appetite. Since the total portrait can only be reconstructed from Rachel's disjointed, almost incoherent, stories, the reader is not tempted to analyse his character too closely.

Antoine's affair with Rachel parallels Daniel's discovery of the *Nourritures terrestres*, but while Daniel is only confirmed in desires he already feels, Antoine becomes aware of a wide range of emotional experience previously unknown in his life based on the concept of energy and ambition. He is now seized with the desire to escape from an ordered existence, to 'courir des risques, utiliser, pour des actes libres et gratuits, cette force qu'il avait été si fier d'asservir à des fins laborieuses' (p. 1029). The Gidean vocabulary is significant. The happiness caused by the affair brings about a complete transformation in him, physically symbolized by shaving off his beard. But the episode does not end on this plane of happiness; the affair ends in Rachel's departure and Antoine's misery and solitude, another aspect of the destructive effect of time. This, a difficult theme to present dramatically, is brilliantly treated in the chapters dealing with the visit to Rachel's daughter's grave, and the final separation in Le Havre, which contain several *trouvailles*. The moment when Antoine clears the grass from the gravestone, partly uncovering the inscription, so that Rachel's name appears, is followed by the train journey back to Paris, where 'des arbres, des maisons, touchés par la lueur des lanternes, se dressaient un instant comme des spectres' (p. 1036). Again, at Le Havre Antoine goes to the end of the mole to catch a last glimpse of Rachel, but is prevented by the mist; then goes back to the hotel and restaurant both had visited the previous day, only to find them impersonal and hostile. This portrayal of human unhappiness, a difficult feat, is highly successful.

In *La Consultation*, Antoine becomes the central character; other leading characters—Jacques, Daniel, Jérôme—have dropped out from the narrative temporarily. This volume is essentially transitional, taking up certain threads of the previous narrative and preparing for later volumes. There is very little completed action, but the medical material is important for its effect on Antoine, since it provokes the introspective analysis with which the volume closes. This analysis is centred on the moral problems facing the doctor, which are stressed as Antoine interviews his patients: should he tell the truth to Ernst, whose child is suffering from congenital syphilis, or to M. Thibault; should Héquet's baby be put out of its agony? Reflecting on these problems, the same evening, Antoine is suddenly overwhelmed by the pointlessness of life, the omnipresence of suffering and death; and, for the first time, he realizes that his philosophy of action is not adequate to face these problems. He is obliged to search for the ethical imperative which, as a complete materialist, he thought he no longer needed. This long monologue was evidently considered important, we deduce from an entry in Gide's *Journal*:

Longue conversation avec RMG—tapi dans son matérialisme comme un sanglier dans sa bauge. Le Dantec, Taine sont ses évangiles; à tout ce que je lui objecte, il tient à voir une manifestation de mon hérédité chrétienne. Il apparaît (..) qu'un de ses Thibault l'habite, de sorte que c'est moins Roger qui parle, qu'Antoine, ce qui me rassure un peu, mais bien peu, car il ne me paraît pas que l'auteur, ici, domine en rien son personnage, ni qu'il s'en puisse beaucoup échapper. Il veut écrire un monologue d'Antoine dont 'Au nom ce quoi . . . ?' scrait le leit-motiv, ou le refrain. Il n'admet pas que rien puisse arrêter l'homme sur la pente de ses instincts, sinon la crainte d'un Dieu-gendarme; auquel il ne croit pas . . .[1]

In fact, Antoine can get no further than a general principle: 'Liberté complète, à la condition de voir clair', an idea intimately connected with the theme of vocation, the full development of his powers which lies behind his ambition: 'Se prendre exactement pour ce qu'on est. Comme corollaire: s'accepter tel qu'on est . . .' (p. 1124). Finally he has to admit the possibility that personality is not an unchanging entity, but may be made up of different, even contradictory instincts, some of which escape the grasp of consciousness and reason.

This section is possibly disingenuous on Martin du Gard's part, and Gide's criticism that 'il ne domine en rien son personnage' is justified. The material is really philosophical, and might have been more appropriate in *Barois* than here; while Antoine's claim that no philosophy had ever fully satisfied him, ignores the fact that the concept of man as a bundle of instincts, towards which he is edging, was widely current long before 1913, the date of the action. In fact, Antoine's problems had received so frequent formulation as to be commonplace.

The closing episode in the volume is more successful: Antoine's depression is abruptly dispelled by a sexual encounter in the restaurant, in which his natural ebullience reasserts itself, physically represented by his zest for food. The power of the human body to ignore the suffering of others—a fundamental

[1] Gide, *Journal 1889–1939*, pp. 831–2 (entry of 1/3/27).

egoism—has been re-established, and Antoine's daydreams can now accept, even include, the prospect of his father's death.

In *La Sorellina*, Martin du Gard is more concerned with bringing Jacques back into the narrative than with further development of Antoine's personality, which is left for *La Mort du Père*. There is an interesting scene between Antoine and Jacques's mistress, Sophia Cammerzinn, which is imbued with sexual overtones, and at the same time is a triple exercise in egoism. Antoine suspects that Sophia is making sexual advances, and, despite all the circumstances, would have yielded if she had locked the door; Sophia is afraid that her lover will abandon her; Jacques has in fact already done so mentally.

In *La Mort du Père*, the moral problem of the continued deception of M. Thibault is not treated; instead, Antoine feels professional pride in his skill at convincing his father that he is recovering. This further aspect of egoism persists: the mercy killing of the old man is more for the sons' sake than for his, and their relief at his death is expressed in their spontaneous appetite at supper afterwards—the same symbol as in *La Belle Saison*, where after Noémie's funeral, Jérôme 'mordait dans un pain au jambon' (p. 948). Later, Antoine is made to consider the full implications of his act; he realizes that selfishness was mixed with pity in his motives, but has no regrets. Indeed, he feels a greater man: the act has contributed to his psychological development—'une de ces expériences essentielles qui ont sur l'évolution d'un homme un retentissement profond' (p. 1309). Later, the problem will be turned round on himself, with cruel irony.

With the relief of tension after M. Thibault's death, Antoine's development is taken further. It is Jacques who feels the loss of his father more profoundly: Antoine is little more than conventionally moved, and betrays his true feelings in a flash of impatience with Anne de Battaincourt: '—"Rassurez-vous, Madame: je n'aimais pas mon père"' (p. 1314). But the perusal of M. Thibault's papers gives him more insight and sympathy, causing him to reflect on metaphysical solitude and death. The volume can thus end with the long dialogue between Antoine and Vécard on the train back from Crouy—another episode which Martin du Gard discussed with Gide.[1] This conversation continues the theme of the point of life, and is, in fact, a confrontation of the two basic attitudes, Catholic and agnostic, almost taking up the theme of religion where it had been left in *Barois*. Both sides are now more sophisticated—although Gide's retouches may have some bearing on this.[2] Needless to say, neither is convinced by the other's arguments: Vécard stresses the pragmatic side of religion, its beauty, dignity, and powers of consolation; while Antoine counters that beauty and utility have no logical connexion with truth. He admits that many men have a vague religious sense, though he himself has not; but in any case he sees a gulf between this vague religious sense and the formal Catholic dogma. Science may not be able to disprove Christianity, but it does not prove it either; it is agnostic, positivistic, like himself: 'L'univers nous est incompréhensible. J'accepte cela comme un fait' (p. 1390). Yet Antoine still has doubts, a metaphysical, if not religious 'inquiétude', based on the same question as before—'au nom de quoi?'. (This will, of course, later becomes one of the basic existentialist problems: what, in the absence of God, is the point of life?) In contrast, Vécard returns to the essence of the matter: the inevitability of death, which might change Antoine's ideas, and Antoine has to admit the solace of faith *in extremis*. By the end of the discussion there is still no real common ground, and *Cloisons étanches* was the title of the episode when it was published separately in the *Revue de Paris*. With it, a stage in Antoine's career is completed; he is now head of the family, poised for further development in later volumes.

The other characters are all of lesser stature. Although the Fontanin family seem to balance the Thibaults in the opening volume, their part in the action becomes more and more circumscribed. But the conception of the second family, whose lives are partly interwoven with those of the first, is, though it owes much to Tolstoy, one of the most brilliant in the novel. Above all it facilitates the creation of *nœuds d'événements*, and

---

[1] Ibid., p. 879 (entry of 17/4/28). [2] Ibid., p. 879.

presentation of character by means of relationships: in addition to the general contrast between the two families, there are the individual relationships between Jacques and Daniel, Jacques and Jenny, and Daniel and Antoine. It could perhaps be said that if the Thibaults are fundamentally conceived in terms of will, the Fontanins' dominating trait is sensuality. Jenny is the exception, since she is made to reflect Jacques's personality: but the relationship between Mme de Fontanin and Jérôme is inexplicable except for her sensual weakness for him, despite his incorrigible vices. Meanwhile Daniel is, possibly unconsciously, following in his father's footsteps. Sexual success comes easily, too easily, to him, from his first experience in Marseilles onwards, and after the *fugue* we see very little of his life except its sexual aspects. Although his adolescent development follows a more normal course than Jacques's, its consequences are clearly shown in *La Belle Saison*, where Martin du Gard gives full treatment to what Ikor has described as *gidisme*.[1] Taking what was at the time Gide's most influential work, *Les Nourritures terrestres*, he shows its enormous effect on Daniel, for whom it becomes, with Whitman's *Leaves of Grass*, almost a bible. The ground is of course well prepared for the most convincing episode where Daniel first comes into contact with Gide's book—'une de ces idées qui font soudain battre le cœur et qui éclairent toute une vie', as Sartre has put it.[2] Daniel builds his philosophy of life on this book, and the events of *La Belle Saison* provide a searching moral judgment on the entire doctrine.

Whereas Jacques was more affected by the note of rebellion and escape he found in the *Nourritures*, for Daniel it is a justification for his sensual desires, overcoming any lingering moral scruples. By now Daniel has become a creative artist, his talent recognized, although he is self-taught. He is very much the artist of inspiration, not of steady effort; in fact, the dilettante ideal of the artist (and the resemblance to Gide himself is obvious).

---

[1] Ikor, op. cit., p. 36.   [2] J.-P. Sartre, *Situations II*, Paris, 1948, p. 44. Cf. also E. Jaloux in *Les Nouvelles littéraires*, 26/1/24 (quoted in O'Brien, op. cit., p. 79); and the description of the effect of the book given by Rivière and Alain-Fournier in their *Correspondance*, especially the latter's reactions, which are in many ways similar to Jacques's (J. Rivière—Alain-Fournier, *Correspondance 1905–1914*, vol. ii, Paris, 1930, p. 229).

His artistic development has flourished because of his lack of moral restraint, and he is certain of his glittering future (rather like one of Tinan's heroes who had so impressed Martin du Gard years before). It may be commented here that the portrait of Daniel as an artist is much less effective than that of Antoine as a doctor, since it is stated, rather than presented dramatically, and his ability can thus never be demonstrated convincingly.[1]

The Rinette episode is skilfully chosen to make the parallel between Daniel and Jérôme, and is an exercise in dramatic irony. At Packmell's Daniel elbows Jacques aside, ignoring the friend whose success is being celebrated, in his eagerness to conquer Rinette, and later risks his job to snatch her from Ludwigson— the danger merely making the adventure more piquant. (The search for *recherché* sexual sensations implies that the ordinary casual affair has lost its savour through excessive repetition.) He little realizes that her attraction to him is due to his resemblance to Jérôme, her original seducer; and what is for her evidently a profound experience, since she wants to bear his child, is merely a 'souvenir royal' for him, when Jacques later asks about her and Daniel has no idea what has become of her (p. 951). He had been entirely egoistic, not even wishing to reveal his name— 'Il n'aimait pas à se livrer, si peu que ce fût' (p. 857), and he never considers that as Ludwigson's mistress she would ultimately be much better off, or that her fate will now be to sink into a brothel. The implied moral criticism of him is as evident as the implied moral criticism of the reformatory in *Le Pénitencier*. The same theme of the sordid reality behind the bright façade of sexual enjoyment is echoed in the Packmell scene, where Paule has a slight heart attack but begs Jacques to say nothing: mercenary sexual relations are not innocent, for they are bought at the cost of the health and even lives of the girls. This same egoistic attitude is repeated in Jérôme's utter inability to resist the slightest temptation. He originally destroyed Rinette: Daniel drags her farther down. If anything, Jérôme gains from the comparison,

[1] The difficulty of successful characterization of a creative artist has rarely been overcome, tempting though the subject is to the novelist, who can easily identify with his character. Martin du Gard may again have had *Jean-Christophe* in mind here.

since he at least searches for her and gives her enough money to escape prostitution, although even this action betrays him as the plaything of his impulses. Rinette herself is portrayed as a good-hearted girl: Martin du Gard takes the view that prostitutes are nonetheless human beings (and it is a prostitute who looks after Jacques on his return, utterly distraught, from Crouy in *La Mort de Père*). For Jérôme, Rinette was only a casual affair, and at first he can scarcely remember who she was; but she thinks of him without resentment. A later passage stresses the further flaw in the philosophy of sensuality: not only does it damage others, it is itself peculiarly vulnerable to the ravages of time, and renders old age doubly repugnant. Jérôme, after watching his children play tennis at Maisons, is contrasted with Daniel, a cruel picture of advancing age alongside youth (p. 985).

The episode of Noémie's death in Amsterdam links the themes of death and of time, besides providing an instance of merciless physical description (anticipating that in *La Mort du Père*), and an analysis of conflicting egoisms. It is typical of Martin du Gard's technique that he makes it quite clear to the careful reader that Noémie is dying from the effects of an abortion, without ever going further than oblique hints. Jérôme's responsibility for her death must therefore be very great; but he feels no remorse:

Là gisaient maintenant six années de vie commune, de ruptures, de jalousies et de reprises, six années de souvenirs et de secrets, jusqu'au dernier de tous, le plus tragique, et qui aboutissait là.

'Après tout,' songea-t-il, 'cela pouvait se terminer plus mal encore . . . Je souffre peu . . .' (p. 946)

But he is not alone in his egoism: his wife, who had come from Paris, bringing with her a large sum of money she cannot afford, 'dut convenir qu'elle ne réussissait pas à penser que la mort de Noémie fût un grand mal. Pour personne. Elle aussi, comme Jérôme, s'habituait à cette disparition' (p. 944). And when Nicole arrives, her reaction is no less egoistic: her mother's death has removed the 'seul point noir' (p. 948) threatening her marriage with Héquet.

The Fontanin family play little part in the next three volumes of the series, possibly to reduce complications in the plot: Jenny and her mother are in Provence, Daniel is on military service at Lunéville, and Jérôme is still the same, with 'des histoires à n'en plus finir', in Austria. Undoubtedly the Fontanins were to be treated further, but their part in the novel was truncated by the change of plan in 1931.

Jenny is a special case, and is perhaps less successful. Like Jacques, she is intensely introspective, but since this is not accompanied by revolt, as in Jacques's case, it can never be presented dramatically, merely stated in rather vague terms: 'elle paraissait née pour une vie différente des autres' (p. 794); 'il n'aurait pas su exprimer ce qu'il voyait de sa nature' (p. 799). Most of her colouring has to be taken from her relationship with Jacques, although she is shown through Daniel's eyes in *La Belle Saison* as a 'petite âme mal poussée, mal partie, sans équilibre . . . (. .) . . . trop mûrie par la réflexion, la solitude, les lectures . . . Et tellement ignorante de la vie!' (p. 983). With his greater experience, Daniel can realize that she is in love with Jacques, and add a dimension to the portrait of her; nevertheless, since she has not yet reached maturity, her personality is latent rather than actual, and the effect on the reader is weakened accordingly.

Parallel to Jenny is Gise, another character who never reaches full maturity; the ultimate development of both Gise and Jenny was originally dependent on a long *explication* between the two, at Hyères, in the destroyed volume *L'Appareillage*.[1] Gise is in fact something of a stock character, the passive Creole, and is described in language approaching a *leitmotiv*: 'avec ses beaux yeux de chien' (p. 670); 'ses bons yeux de chien . . . (. .) son petit corps potelé de sauvageonne' (p. 749); 'la sensualité d'un animal jeune' (p. 761). After Jacques's disappearance, her refusal to believe that he is dead leads Martin du Gard to some slight implausibilities, when he has to make the nervous Mlle de Waize and the authoritarian M. Thibault allow her, despite her strict upbringing, to live abroad. Nicole Noémie-Dutreuil is similarly not fully satisfactory: she impresses more by her

[1] *Souvenirs*, p. xciv.

situation and by her actions than by her personality, serving as a foil to Daniel and other characters.

The minor characters are on the whole well drawn. However, as Jacques de Lacretelle has pointed out, Martin du Gard is at his best when dealing with characters he knows at first hand; with others he is less skilful: 'En deux lignes il peindra un vieux paysan de la Beauce ou un gosse de Paris et les rendra vivants. Tandis qu'il lui faudra une demi-page pour un Anglais ou un Russe; et ce sera souvent moins bon'.[1] This criticism is peculiarly apt if applied to Gregory, the Christian Science pastor, who is especially implausible, not only as a whole but also in the strange anglicized French he speaks. Gregory is not essential for the plot: Jenny's apparently miraculous cure from meningitis is not intended to be caused by his prayers and intercession;[2] while Mme de Fontanin's reconciliation with Jérôme in Le Pénitencier could easily be otherwise motivated. Although he does perhaps provide a certain amount of relief from tension, he cannot be considered a truly comic character, in contrast to M. Chasle who, with his squeaky shoes and absurd mannerisms, is throughout comic in intention. Possibly Gregory was intended partly to balance the Catholic–Protestant relationship: if Mme de Fontanin's charitable Protestantism is treated more kindly than M. Thibault's rigorous Catholicism, Gregory comes out badly from the contrast with Vécard. Vécard is throughout presented sympathetically, as able, intelligent, tolerant and humane—a man of integrity, if subtle; at M. Thibault's deathbed his sincerity is undoubtedly more dignified than Antoine's comforting equivocations. (This is another example of Martin du Gard's ability to show sympathy for characters whose beliefs he does not share.)

Other minor characters are adequate, and sometimes memorable. We may instance Faîsme, the cheerful and apparently harmless reformatory director, completely different from the traditional prison bully; Favery, the *normalien*, in the Packmell episode; almost all the characters introduced in *La Consultation* —Ernst, the pathetic German teacher; Anne de Battaincourt,

---

[1] J. de Lacretelle, *L'heure qui change*, Geneva, 1941, p. 36.
[2] This was verbally confirmed by Martin du Gard to the present writer in 1955.

wealthy and sensual; Rumelles, the suave politician, power-hungry and ambitious, but, behind his façade, insecure—'Sans la moustache, ce fauve aurait eu le profil d'un mouton' (p. 1081); Jalicourt, the pompous but pathetic *Normale* professor. Some of these characters were undoubtedly intended to be developed further in later volumes; some, such as Anne and Rumelles, are, in the revised plan: but even if this were not so, their single appearance, if brief, is nonetheless effective. The character of Philip, Antoine's *patron*, deserves more attention. By *La Consultation*, the focus of the novel has considerably narrowed, nearly down to the single character of Antoine, who becomes almost too obviously the centre of Martin du Gard's own interest, and even a mouthpiece. In earlier volumes the figure of M. Thibault had dominated the novel, acting as a means of giving perspective; now, sick and passive, he can no longer fulfil this rôle, and Philip may well have been intended as a counterweight, replacing him in this function, rather than merely to introduce the theme of admiration, as Camus suggests.[1] His relationship with Antoine has something in common with Luce's to Barois, although on a more subtle plane; he can act as a curb for Antoine's excesses, like Luce, but Antoine also reacts away from Philip's scepticism as well as being directly influenced by his humanistic approach. Character as a function of relationships is explicitly stated here:

Dès qu'Antoine se trouvait auprès de Philip, insensiblement, sa personnalité se modifiait, subissait comme une diminution de volume: l'être indépendant et complet qu'il était l'instant d'avant retombait automatiquement en tutelle. (p. 1063)

But, again, conception of character depends as much on creative ability as on technique; and Martin du Gard is successful on both counts.

It can be seen, then, that the early volumes of *Les Thibault* are primarily psychological in interest, and that Martin du Gard's themes can be integrated into psychological narrative. In his conception of character, egoism is fundamental, and this egoism

---

[1] Camus, op. cit., p. xxiii.

can best be presented by placing individual characters in relationship with each other. This technique is used constantly, as we have seen, and provides some brilliant effects, as in Jacques's interview with Jalicourt, Antoine's meeting with Sophia Cammerzinn, or the powerful scene between Gise and Mlle de Waize after M. Thibault's death, where Gise has been finally abandoned by Jacques, and wishes to return to her convent in England, while the old lady also cannot face her own future, at 78. Their misery is equal, but separate; and the very lack of contact between them makes it worse. This egoism is fundamentally an aspect of the theme of metaphysical solitude, which is treated in terms of incompatible wishes. On the one hand, the various characters attempt to conquer their solitude by human contacts: Jérôme through sex, Antoine through his affair with Rachel, Jacques through his adhesion to political comradeship; on the other, none of these human contacts is adequate to resist the destructive effects of time, while sometimes even the contact is impossible to establish in the first place, as with Jalicourt and Jacques. This dilemma is in the nature of it insoluble, but dominates Martin du Gard's conception of character.

It is also closely connected with the theme of death, which runs through every volume before it receives exhaustive treatment in *La Mort du Père*. In *Le Cahier gris*, there is the episode of the dray accident, in which a horse is killed; this is deliberately made to follow close after the two boys' first view of the Mediterranean, their first experience of real beauty (as opposed to their artificial literary experiences), and the significance of the juxtaposition is clear: death is central to even the finest experiences in life. In the next volume, this scene is deliberately linked in Jacques's memory with the sight of the corpse of Mme Fruhling, and again the episode has overtones, since it is this death which brings Lisbeth back to Paris and motivates Jacques' sexual initiation. Again, in *La Belle Saison*, the themes of sex and death are linked: when a dog is killed in a road accident, this acts as a catalyst in the relationship between Jacques and Jenny, starting their first really intimate conversation together. By this time, Jacques is obsessed by death: 'la plupart de mes pensées me ramènent à cette idée de la mort' (p. 956); and the theme is taken up once more in the episode at Amsterdam relating Noémie's death. Then, in *La Consultation*, the theme is brought to the foreground, when Antoine reflects on the patients he has seen: 'Un sinistre cortège défila devant lui: tous ceux de ses malades qu'il jugeait condamnés . . .' (p. 1119). Chief among these is his father, and in *La Sorellina* and *La Mort du Père* Martin du Gard has given one of the most powerful descriptions of death in literature. It is here that Martin du Gard approaches closest to Tolstoy. Although there is the general intention to paint a vast fresco of life on Tolstoyan lines, there are few detailed points of comparison; but between *La Mort du Père* and Tolstoy's *nouvelle*, *The Death of Ivan Ilyitch*, the parallel is very close.[1] A long, agonizing, harrowing death is common to both, almost more unbearable to the witnesses than to the dying man himself. It is preceded in both cases by a long illness; the day-to-day deterioration is so slight that self-deception is possible, and those around the sick man become forced into deceit, airily prophesying recovery. The same odour of decay and decomposition hangs over the sickbed; finally both men realize they have been cruelly deceived, and physical pain is accompanied by mental torture, with the only escape an illusory retreat into childhood memories. In friends and relatives pity is soon extinguished by egoism, and the basic attitude when death finally takes place is one of profound relief. These parallels may be fortuitous, and both writers may have had other literary models in mind, notably the death of Emma Bovary, but the resemblance is striking. There are of course considerable differences. Above all the ethical problem of euthanasia is absent from *Ivan Ilyitch*. But the intensive psychological analysis of the idea of death, from the point of view of the dying man as well as of outsiders, is common to both.

The theme allows some fine effects, as when M. Thibault simulates approaching death, making a solemn speech in front of his assembled household, warning them he is dying, while at the same time he alone does not believe it. The dramatic irony is evident. There is then the shattering realization later,

[1] Cf. H. Peyre, *The Contemporary French Novel*, New York, 1955, p. 40.

after overhearing Mlle de Waize, that he is doomed: this is shown as an emotion so devastating that the human mind is paralysed by it:

La lucidité même lui échappe: il ne parvient plus à réfléchir. L'intelligence humaine est si essentiellement nourrie de futur que, à l'instant où toute possibilité d'avenir se trouve abolie, lorsque chaque élan de l'esprit vient indistinctement buter contre la mort, il n'y a plus de pensée possible. (p. 1253)

Whereas death has previously been an abstract concept, applicable only to others, never to himself, its sudden immediacy and inevitability are intolerable. Now, more than ever, he is isolated from his fellow men. In this section Martin du Gard must have also had in mind his own feelings about death; his words to Gide, already seriously ill, in May 1949, are recalled: 'C'est à des moments comme ceux que vous traversez (..) qu'il serait merveilleusement consolant de se croire une âme immortelle.'[1] We may well believe that in the description of M. Thibault's death he was keenly concerned to give an account of the comfort afforded by firm religious belief, and which the old man feels once his initial panic has been overcome. Yet he himself cannot bring himself to believe, which probably explains the note of irony which creeps in: 'L'Esprit-Saint planait' (p. 1265). And Antoine's professional pride, earlier, at his ability to deceive his father with elaborate talk about drugs, is matched by Vécard's 'satisfaction d'avocat qui a gagné le procès' (p. 1265), notwithstanding his sincerity. There is a further personal note here; after Vécard's ministrations, M. Thibault is scarcely of this world:

Tout lui était égal; définitivement, totalement égal. (..) L'univers formait un tout, étranger, hermétique, où lui, mourant, n'avait plus de place. Il était seul. Seul avec le mystère. (p. 1267)

This total estrangement, not only from others, but also from one's own past life, *l'optique de la mort*, is again treated in the deeply moving letter written by Martin du Gard to his old friend Marcel de Coppet, a few months before his own death. He tells of an idea he has had for a long time, to write a Chekhovian short story, called *La Salle d'Attente*. In this story,

---

[1] *Notes sur André Gide*, p. 1423.

an engineer who has lived in a town for years, being largely responsible for its services and amenities, is waiting one night in the railway waiting-room. Before dawn his train will arrive, but exactly when he does not know. While he is waiting the townspeople come to beg him not to leave, since they will not know what to do without him. Yet all his achievements, indeed the whole of his past, now mean nothing more to him. This is exactly the sentiment felt by M. Thibault, and in the letter Martin du Gard describes how it has turned into reality for himself. All he feels is a 'vide total', an utter detachment: 'Plus je vais, plus j'avance en âge, moins j'ai le sentiment de vivre parmi des *semblables*'.[1]

M Thibault's death is described in physiological as well as psychological terms. Martin du Gard deliberately chooses a complicated and harrowing form of cancer, which is carefully and realistically documented:[2] he wishes to show death in its full horror, as in *Ivan Ilyitch*, with no distortion or omission of unpleasant details, at the same time motivating the euthanasia by which the old man's death is finally brought about. The horror is achieved by simple factual description, and a total refusal to yield to any demands of *bienséance*. The tone is set by the picture of the sickroom, which is treated in terms of smell, not of sight, with the mingled odours of ether, iodine, and, above all, 'les relents de ce corps déchu' (p. 1251). The descriptions of the dying man are merciless, down to the soiled sheets, and the scene of the bath is deliberately selected to illustrate this aspect. There is something indecent about the old man's body exposed in front of his sons; while Martin du Gard connects it with a memory of Jacques's time in Tunis, where he had seen the similarly swollen and naked body of an old Italian who had committed suicide. The universal sweep of death eventually reduces all men to the same level of decaying flesh and naked indignity—another Tolstoyan trait.[3] The ironic contrast

[1] *N.N.R.F.*, 12/58, p. 1164.   [2] Cf. Alméras, op. cit., p. 50.
[3] Cf. F. W. J. Hemmings, *The Russian Novel in France, 1884–1914*, Oxford, 1950, p. 43: 'The lowest common denominator, for humanity, is the physical, the animal being, and in Tolstoy the highest of the high are brought down to the level of the lowest by the attention the author gives to the corporal detail.'

between the pompous style of M. Thibault's life and the ignominious manner of his death is accentuated when Mlle de Waize
fulfils her promise to recite the *Litanies de la bonne mort* at the
dying man's bedside.

Metaphysical solitude and death are universal themes, and
when the characters are placed in this context, they merge their
individual significance into a wider meaning, becoming universal
symbols of Man. But various other themes are integrated into
the narrative. The theme of vocation, and of ambition, is worked
out in detail in the lives of Jacques, Antoine and Daniel, while
the ultimate implications of two basic attitudes to life—pursuit
of sensual pleasure and of wordly status—are shown in Jérôme
and M. Thibault. The psychological theme of vocation runs
parallel to the social one of education, and Jacques's strict
Catholic upbringing is contrasted with the affectionate treatment
of Daniel, to the obvious advantage of the Protestant side. In
Le Pénitencier, the visit to the reformatory is not only a fine set
piece of description, but treats a social theme. The same is true
of the theme of euthanasia, which produced outbursts of righteous
indignation in some critics at the time.[1] The theme, however, is
not only used for its intrinsic psychological interest, but for
reasons of dramatic irony, since the euthanasia concerns Antoine's
own father (and ultimately will concern himself).

Martin du Gard's style in *Les Thibault* has been well characterized by Gide: 'Je ne connais pas d'écriture plus neutre, et qui
se laisse plus complètement oublier. Il ne s'agit même plus ici de
transparence; le lecteur entre directement en contact avec les
personnages que présente l'auteur.'[2] As in *Barois*, he attempts to
reduce aesthetic distance to a minimum; style is the lens through
which characters and events are seen, but which is itself invisible.
To achieve this, all techniques may be valid on occasion, as long
as they do not obtrude and destroy the general illusion of
objectivity. Not that Martin du Gard believed in the possibility
of attaining complete objectivity; it is not diametrically opposed
to subjectivity, but is merely a matter of greater skill, or tact, on

---

[1] E.g. P. Souday, *Les Livres de Temps* (3e série), Paris, 1930, p. 265 (à *propos* of the
Héquet case in *La Consultation*).   [2] A. Gide, *Divers*, Paris, 1931, p. 199.

the part of the writer. Any stylized form of writing would tend to interpose itself between the narrated events and the reader, and Martin du Gard's only temptation on this score is the occasional striking image:

—'Quoi? La huguenote?' balbutia M. Chasle en se reculant, comme s'il venait de poser le pied dans une flaque de la Saint-Barthélemy. (p. 601)

The primary narrative tense is the past historic, since the change from the dialogue technique had freed him from his servitude to the present tense, and it is indeed astonishing that this point had not struck him before, especially since Flaubert's *Correspondance* had been favourite reading of his since the turn of the century. There are however many incursions into the imperfect for affective reasons, particularly *style indirect libre*, and into the pluperfect for variation in time. The following passage shows the flexibility aimed at:

Ce fut seulement vers onze heures, repassant pour la centième fois devant le café où, la veille, ils s'étaient fait indiquer le bureau des messageries,—ah! il était là!

Jacques se précipita à travers tables et chaises. Daniel, plus maître de lui, s'était levé:

—'Chut . . .'

On les remarquait; ils se tendirent la main. Daniel paya; ils sortirent, et tournèrent dans la première rue qui s'offrit. Alors Jacques saisit le bras de son ami, s'accrochant à lui, l'étreignant; et, tout à coup, il se mit à sangloter, le front contre son épaule. Daniel ne pleurait pas: il continuait à avancer, très pâle, le regard dur fixé au loin en avant, serrant contre son côté la petite main de Jacques, et sa lèvre, relevée de biais sur les dents, tremblait.

Jacques raconta:

—'J'ai dormi comme un voleur sur le quai, sous une bâche! Et toi?'

Daniel se troubla. Il respectait trop son ami et leur amitié: pour la première fois, il lui fallait cacher quelque chose à Jacques, et quelque chose d'essentiel. L'énormité de ce secret, entre eux, l'étouffa. Il fut sur le point de s'abandonner, de tout dire; mais non, il ne le pouvait pas. Il demeurait silencieux, hébété, sans pouvoir écarter l'obsession de tout ce qui avait eu lieu. (pp. 643-4)

Altogether Martin du Gard has forged a supple instrument, equally well fitted for vigorous narrative and psychological analysis, and none the less effective because it necessarily goes unnoticed by the ordinary, perhaps careless, reader. At times the apparent facility of the narrative style conceals the technical difficulties inherent in the material, as in Mme de Fontanin's meeting with Jérôme, when the sexual undertones are made evident by the presence of Daniel, made more perceptive by his experience in Marseilles:

Daniel, ne sachant trop que répondre, s'était tourné vers sa mère: et il surprit alors sur le pur visage maternel, il n'eût pas su dire quoi, quelque chose de si particulier, de si intime, qu'il détourna la tête avec un sentiment de pudeur. Il avait perdu à Marseille jusqu'à l'innocence du regard. (p. 656)

It can easily be seen that Martin du Gard is no longer insistent on removing the *sauce gluante* of linking narrative. This is most noticeable in his use of documents, which are practically always worked into the continuous narrative, instead of standing alone, and this implies an advance in smoothness of style. Documents are again used principally to impart information indirectly and succinctly, as in the letters in the grey notebook, the *Tout-Paris* entry which summarizes M. Thibault's worldly achievements, or the many extracts from his papers after his death. At times, of course, the use of documents leads to considerable technical problems: although it is fairly easy to devise a telegram or to simulate a directory entry, the composition of a series of letters requires more skill. This is most evident in the *nouvelle*, *La Sorellina*.

The idea of a story within a story was not original: to mention only one example, Balzac's *Albert Savarus* provides a parallel; but it obviously tempted Martin du Gard as an excellent opportunity to demonstrate technical virtuosity. The story provides the best instance of indirect narration in the whole series, giving, fictionally, Jacques's account of the events leading to his disappearance; it also plays an integral part in the plot, since it gives Antoine an opportunity to trace his brother's whereabouts and bring him back to Paris. Martin du Gard's chief problem was to invent a style which would be easily enough distinguishable from his own to be plausible, and yet impulsive and passionate enough to appear to spring naturally from Jacques's personality. With typical thoroughness he devised a feverish, brusque, highly impressionistic style, and, although only brief extracts from the supposed *nouvelle* are actually quoted—those which especially strike Antoine during his reading—he went to enormous trouble to write the story out in full, a task which occupied several months.[1] *Maisons* in the *belle saison* of 1910 is transposed into the Bay of Naples; M. Thibault becomes 'le conseiller Seregno', the Fontanins are renamed the Powells, an English family, and all events are so barely disguised that Antoine can follow the story perfectly. After a final quarrel with his father about Jenny, Jacques had left home; with a neat touch the same words Antoine had heard in his father's delirium are repeated in the story: 'Va-t'en, mauvais fils!' The style of the *nouvelle* is well illustrated by its last lines:

Pas l'une sans l'autre, eh bien, ni l'une ni l'autre. Renoncer, oublier, mourir. Non, pas mourir, être mort. Disparaître. Ici l'envoûtement, l'infranchissable obstacle, l'interdit.
Ici, la vie, l'amour sont impossibles.
Adieu.
Attrait de l'inconnu, attrait d'un lendemain tout neuf, ivresse. Oublier, recommencer tout.
Demi-tour. Filer jusqu'à la gare. Le premier train pour Rome. Rome, le premier train pour Gênes. Gênes, le premier paquebot. Pour l'Amérique. Ou pour l'Australie.
Et tout à coup, il rit.
Amour ? Hé non, c'est la vie que j'aime.
En avant. (p. 1192)

The main features are short, often verbless sentences, short, often one-sentence paragraphs, giving the effect of brief traits noted down without further polishing. No logical connexion is maintained between different ideas, or even between different speakers: this is left for the reader to elucidate. There is no constant narrator: third-person narrative gives way to reported thought or speech without any visible change of style:

Son père. Les sentiments de Giuseppe pour ce père. Inaccessible coin de son âme, buisson d'épines, brûlure. Des années d'idolâtrie inconsciente, enragée, rétive. Tous les élans naturels rebutés. Vingt ans, avant de s'être résigné à la haine. Vingt ans, avant d'avoir compris qu'il fallait bien haïr. De plein cœur, haïr. (p. 1173)

The predominant narrative tense is the present, to give greater dramatic immediacy, combined with the perfect for anterior

---

[1] *Souvenirs*, p. xciii.

events; but there is also use of the imperfect for past description. Jacques's inexperience as a writer shows in the excessive stylization and in the confusion about the position of the narrator; and, as in all highly stylized techniques, there is something of the *tour de force* about the story (as well as Martin du Gard's use of it). It rapidly tires the reader: Jacques has mistaken a means for an end, a technique for an infallible method. Dramatic immediacy is gained only at the cost of losing all differentiation, all variation in *éclairage*. In fact at times the technique approaches the *style notatif* of *Barois*, especially in the description of Conseiller Seregno (p. 1176).

Nevertheless, on the whole, the *nouvelle* is successful in fulfilling its function, and one may doubt the justification of Gide's criticism: 'Ne faites pas de prestidigitation . . . (..) on voit vos mains, tout le temps!'[1] At the same time, several months seem a disproportionate period of time to spend on one single episode, and Martin du Gard was undoubtedly carried away by the desire for technical achievement.

Another stylistic device frequently used, to bring to an effective end particular episodes, is that of ironic juxtaposition. This is seen at its best at the end of *La Belle Saison*, where Antoine's grief at Rachel's departure is suddenly interrupted:

La phrase de Rachel lui vint à la mémoire: 'J'ai pensé me tuer . . .' Oui; en finir! Le suicide, seule issue à de telles angoisses . . . Un suicide sans préméditation, presque sans consentement, simplement pour échapper, n'importe comment, avant qu'elle ait atteint son paroxysme, à cette souffrance dont l'étau se resserre!

Tout à coup, il sursauta, et, d'un bond, fut debout: un homme, qu'il n'avait pas vu venir, lui touchait le bras. Il faillit, d'un geste réflexe, le repousser, l'abattre d'un coup de poing.

— 'Ben quoi?' fit l'homme.

C'était un vieux, qui poinçonnait les billets.

—'Le . . . le train de Paris?' bégaya Antoine.

— 'Troisième quai.'

Antoine fixa sur l'homme deux yeux de somnambule et s'élança d'un pas mou vers le hall.

— 'Vous avez le temps, l'est pas formé!' cria l'autre. Puis, comme Antoine,

[1] Ibid., p. xciii.

avant de disparaître, s'était, en flageolant, heurté au battant de la porte, le vieux haussa les épaules:
— 'Et ça veut faire le costaud!' grommela-t-il. (p. 1050)

This device is often used in the short story, especially in Maupassant, and in addition to providing a 'dramatic cut-off', it is a powerful means of creating aesthetic perspective, by contrasting the intensity of Antoine's emotions with the total unconcern of the rest of the world.

A somewhat similar use of dramatic irony terminates *Le Pénitencier*, when Jacques, brimming over with self-satisfaction after his night with Lisbeth, misinterprets her wave to him, completely unaware that she is leaving and that this is her last farewell. The underlying pathos becomes immediately evident:

A quatre heures, on sonna, il courut ouvrir: son professeur de latin! Il avait oublié qu'il avait répétition ce jour-là.
Il suivait distraitement l'explication d'Horace, lorsqu'on sonna de nouveau. Cette fois, c'était elle. Elle aperçut, dès le seuil, la porte de la chambre ouverte, et le dos du professeur courbé sur la table. Quelques secondes, l'un devant l'autre, ils s'interrogèrent des yeux. Jacques ne soupçonnait guère qu'elle venait lui faire ses adieux, qu'elle repartait par le train de six heures. Elle n'osa rien dire, mais elle eut un léger frisson; ses paupières battirent, elle leva son doigt malade jusqu'à sa bouche, puis, de tout près, comme si déjà le train l'emportait pour toujours, elle lui jeta un baiser bref, et s'enfuit.
Le répétiteur reprit la phrase interrompue:
— *Purpurarum usus* équivaut à *purpura quâ utuntur*. Sentez-vous la nuance?'
Jacques sourit, comme s'il eût senti la nuance. Il songeait que Lisbeth allait lui revenir tout à l'heure; il revoyait, dans l'ombre de vestibule, son visage sous le voile levé, et ce baiser qu'elle avait comme arraché de ses lèvres pour lui, avec son doigt enveloppé de linge.
— 'Continuez', dit le professeur. (p. 813)

Irony is in fact one of Martin du Gard's favourite techniques, another important development since *Barois*. It pervades the novel-series at all levels, acting both as a defence against sentimentality, and as a method of preserving detachment. Temptation to satire is less evident, but occasional indulgence in it can be noted:

Du premier coup d'œil (M. Thibault) aperçoit Jacques et ne peut se défendre d'être ému. Il s'arrête cependant et referme les paupières; il semble attendre que le fils coupable se précipite à ses genoux, comme dans le Greuze, dont la gravure est au salon. (p. 668)

(The use of the dramatic present tense stresses the significance of the scene.) Again, Antoine's immediate—and only—reaction, when Rachel describes how she had slept, on impulse, with a negro: 'Diable . . . un nègre . . . sans examen préalable . . .' (p. 1002).

Irony of language is overshadowed by irony of situation, from which many vigorous effects are drawn. Perhaps the best example can be seen in the treatment of M. Thibault's illness in *La Sorellina*, which is tragi-comical throughout: the old man's pretence that he is dying, in order to provoke comforting expressions of grief in his household; M. Chasle's incoherent tale of his visit to the police-station; Mlle de Waize's pathetic preoccupations with lost baskets of vegetables; Antoine's demonstration of the power of suggestion, with his imaginary injections, N 17 and D 92. By these means the effect of the scenes is greatly heightened; avoiding more obvious ways of producing an atmosphere of horror, and stressing the comic aspects of the situation, a level of macabre drama can be attained, once the true significance penetrates, which would otherwise have been impossible, and which itself will act as a contrast with the actual deathbed scenes in *La Mort du Père*, where the physical horror is unconcealed.

The meeting of Jérôme and Rinette in the *Rue de Stockholm* brothel is another set-piece of irony. At first Jérôme can hardly recognize her:

Il cherchait désespérément les traits enfantins de Cricri sur le visage maquillé de cette jolie fille, un peu bouffie, aux cheveux coupés courts; il ne retrouvait même pas la voix fraîche et paysanne d'autrefois. (p. 1012)

Here the irony is double, for Rinette's appearance is also deliberately contrasted with her *début* at Packmell's, only a few months earlier:

Elle était charmante, en effet: des yeux clairs, des joues pures de fard . . . (. .)
Près d'elle, aussitôt, même les plus jeunes semblèrent défraîchies . . . (p. 839)

There is a further twist in the irony when Jérôme gives her the money to return to Brittany, taking on the accents of a missionary as he urges her to leave her 'working' clothes behind:

... avec une ferveur qui faisait trembler les finales de ses phrases, il lui prêcha l'abandon de ses toilettes de prostituée, le renoncement, le retour total à la simplicité, à la pureté de jadis. (pp. 1018-19)

But he has no sooner finished congratulating himself on his good deed—'je vaux tout de même mieux qu'on ne croit'— than he sees Rinette in her peasant clothes once more, the same girl who had attracted him six years before, and he is seized by sexual desire again. The significance of the sexual act is here underlined by its identification with completely different sentiments (and the rhetorical questions, a rare device in Martin du Gard, emphasize this):

N'était-ce pas le seul témoignage de reconnaissance qu'elle pût offrir? Et n'était-ce pas, pour Jérôme, le seul geste capable en cette seconde d'exaltation mystique, d'exprimer jusqu'à l'épuisement cette pitié religieuse dont son âme était surchargée? (p. 1020)

And, as a final irony—the note on which the episode ends— Jérôme decides to leave to his wife the details of the allowance which he will send Rinette—'elle a tant d'ordre, elle n'y manquera jamais' (p. 1021).

Antoine's consultation with Rumelles in *La Consultation* is also treated in a distinctly ironical, almost comical, manner. The contrast between the pretensions of the man and the humiliating nature of his disease—gonorrhoea—makes him an easy target: while he is sitting, naked, in pain from his ignoble injections, Antoine visualizes him accompanying the Queen of Serbia to an exhibition immediately afterwards. But the irony is also at a deeper level: Rumelles's ambition has completely isolated him from other men—'depuis dix ans, la politique l'avait condamné à vivre isolé derrière un barrage de camaraderie hypocrite et méfiante' (p. 1085), and his sickness has separated him from the single person in whom he could still confide—his wife. The irony provides a further illustration of the theme of solitude.

Irony is not the only means of achieving detachment. A high degree of objectivity is frequently attained—especially in scenes of a sexual nature—by simple, matter-of-fact description and refraining from all comment or judgment. As a result even the most daring scenes can be shown as happening quite naturally, as concrete facts, rather than as a basis for moralizing. This technique is again found in *Confidence africaine;* and it is reinforced by the use of indirect suggestion and oblique hints rather than direct statement in some rather *risqué* episodes as Jacques's indulgence in masturbation, Noémie's abortion, or Rachel's relations with Hirsch. In these cases not only is there no comment on the action, but the unobservant reader may very well fail to realize exactly what is being referred to. The same device can be used to create an atmosphere of mystery and suspense, thus maintaining dramatic interest at a high level, as in the restaurant scene at Lausanne, where casual, almost incomprehensible remarks are strung together to give a sense of dangerous but fascinating adventure:

— 'Leur manège ne peut pas réussir', prononça Jacques, après avoir réfléchi. 'De deux choses l'une . . .'
— 'Oui, voilà ce qu'on peut dire!' s'écria l'autre, sans attendre, avec une sorte de reconnaissance et de chaleur imprévues. 'Mais il ne faudrait pas que la presse politique nous fasse sauter avant.'
— 'Sabakine disparaîtra, dès qu'il flairera quelque chose', souffla Jacques, en baissant la voix. 'Et Bisson aussi, vous verrez.'
— 'Bisson? Peut-être.'
— 'Mais, ces revolvers?'
— 'Non, ça, c'est facile à prouver. Son ancien amant les avait achetés à Bâle, à la vente d'une armurerie, après décès.'
— 'Ecoutez, Rayer,' dit Jacques: 'ne comptez pas sur moi, ces jours-ci, je ne peux rien écrire d'ici quelque temps. Mais allez trouver Richardley. Qu'il vous remette les papiers. Vous lui direz que c'est pour moi. Et, s'il a besoin d'une signature, qu'il téléphone à Mac Laher. N'est-ce pas?' (p. 1218)

This technique of briefly mentioning names, revolvers, signatures, and so on, without explaining them, is in fact extremely easy but none the less effective.

The very length of the novel-series has one undeniable advantage: it permits a wide choice of stylistic devices, and we notably find many set-pieces of description. At the same time this is rarely gratuitous but skilfully dovetailed into more dramatic narrative. Antoine's visit to Crouy, for example, lends itself to lengthy description of the reformatory as a static background to the dramatic confrontation of the two brothers; while an identical technique is seen in his journey to Lausanne, or in Mme de Fontanin's visit to Noémie's deathbed in Amsterdam. By now Martin du Gard possesses the extensive vocabulary and delicate feeling for language of the experienced writer, and almost any theme or scene which interests him can be judiciously worked into the fabric of the novel without much disturbing its general balance. Often, indeed, it can be made directly to serve the purposes of the action, as in the Packmell episode, which is not only a fine example of social description, and preparation for future action, but above all permits the threads of the first two volumes to be caught up, and the five-year time-gap to be successfully overcome, so that the difference in age—from 15 to 20—in Jacques and Daniel is not obtrusive.

Occasionally the descriptions are poetic, even lyrical, but without the tendency to neo-Symbolist mannerism which had marred similar passages in *Devenir*. Antoine's night in Le Havre after Rachel's departure provides the best example:

La ville était morte et ruisselait sous le brouillard. De tragiques nuées la couvraient encore; d'autres nuages s'amoncelaient à l'horizon; et, entre ces deux restes d'orage qui cherchaient à se joindre, une pâle tranche de ciel semblait fondre. (p. 1046)

At times even the pathetic fallacy is employed:

Il était seul dans les rumeurs mêlées du vent, et du large. Juste en face de lui, une lueur crémeuse indiquait l'est, où sans doute, pour d'autres, se levait un soleil d'hiver. A ses pieds, un escalier, taillé dans le granit, s'enfonçait vers l'abîme invisible de l'eau: même en se penchant, il ne pouvait apercevoir les vagues qui battaient le môle; mais il entendait, au-dessous de lui et tout près, leur respiration régulière, faite d'un long soupir et d'un sanglot mou. (p. 1047)

These passages might have been taken directly from a Romantic writer—Chateaubriand, even Hugo—but they are not inserted gratuitously or in imitation. In each case the intention is to deepen the psychological effect at a moment of great intensity.

Another interesting example of technical range occurs in the use of affective memory, when Mme de Fontanin enters Jérôme's room in search of his address, only to be assailed by the involuntary memory of having seen him, from a tram, two years previously, with a girl in tears (pp. 602-3). No imitation of

Proust need be implied by this, which merely exemplifies Martin du Gard's eclecticism: his total style is an amalgam of all technical methods which may suit his purpose. Thus we find frequent use of interior monologue, both to emphasize Antoine's privileged position in the author's eyes, and to enliven passages dealing primarily with ideas or thought; incursions into the dramatic present tense to heighten dramatic effect, as when Antoine reads the *nouvelle*, *La Sorellina*, in a café; and several techniques deriving from Naturalism. The most important of these is perhaps the attempt to reproduce dialogue realistically. This attempt takes the form, not so much of phonetic representation (although we find Gregory's broken French or the ticket-collector with his 'ben quoi . . . (. .) L'est pas formé'), as of an attempt to show how people speak, with unfinished sentences, non-sequiturs, rhetorical questions. The reader has to infer from the dialogue just as much as he is informed directly by it. Rachel's monologue while she and Antoine are looking at her collection of photographs—her defence against time—is a *tour de force* of conversational naturalism, with Antoine's replies and gestures indicated entirely through her own words.[1] The counterpart of this scene occurs in Chapter VIII of *La Consultation*, where Anne's governess —and Lesbian partner?—Miss Mary, returns to try to obtain morphine from Antoine. This is another *tour de force*, since the entire significance of the episode and its psychological nuances are made clear without a single word being spoken on either side.

The narrative tempo of *La Consultation* deserves special note. Since the whole volume covers only fourteen hours, Martin du Gard can afford to spread himself on individual scenes, thus approaching the *Sekundentechnik* of German Naturalist drama. There is also a partial return to the dramatic technique of *style notatif* of *Barois*, except that the past tense is generally maintained and that reported thought is included. The volume opens very much in the same way as an episode in *Barois*:

Midi et demi, rue de l'Université.
Antoine sauta de taxi et s'engouffra dans la voûte.
'Lundi: mon jour de consultation,' songea-t-il . . . (p. 1051)

---

[1] This is, incidentally, the narrative technique adopted by Camus in *La Chute*.

Full use is made of brief, impressionistic traits, and verbs are omitted to increase the tempo as Antoine rushes round his flat:

Aussitôt les enfants partis:
— 'Vous pouvez servir, Léon!'
Puis, au téléphone:
— 'Allô . . . Elysées 01-32 . . .' (p. 1055)

A final naturalistic trait is the use of technical detail, principally in the medical scenes, and although some of the cases described are highly complicated (M. Thibault, the Héquet's baby, Huguette), they are depicted both accurately and dramatically, without appeal to sentiment or melodrama.[1] This material had to be documented carefully and amounts to an application of local colour: to the lay reader the terminology is impressively professional: 'Lésions curables . . . (. .) Tout l'appareil ganglionnaire était tuméfié . . .' (p. 1077); 'Nous avons trouvé toutes les complications possibles: mastoïdite, naturellement; infection du sinus latéral, etc . . .' (p. 1067).

The keynote of Martin du Gard's style can thus be seen as virtuosity taken to almost Flaubertian lengths, and the contrast with the contempt shown for *sauce gluante* in *Devenir* is striking. Martin du Gard is indeed occupied primarily with the *fond*, but problems of presentation of that *fond* are increasingly important. The aim is, fundamentally, an impersonal style, almost unnoticeable, rather than a highly personal one, as in Gide or Proust, where technical virtuosity is equally the aim, but the result is none the less effective. At the same time, technical ability alone cannot make a good novel unless it is accompanied by creative power, and it is possibly in the visualizing of significant incident and detail that the essence of Martin du Gard's art lies—in the *trouvaille*. One need only instance a few scenes—where Nicole, fleeing from her mother and Jérôme, takes shelter with Mme de Fontanin; later, she recognizes in Daniel's livid face the sensual expression of his father (p. 803); the pathos of Jacques's sudden discovery, in his dying father's ravaged features, of 'la figure en larmes d'un gamin qu'il n'avait pas connu' (p. 1295); or the double level of Antoine's conversation of Anne de Battain-

---

[1] Cf. Alméras, op. cit., pp. 45–46, 50–51.

court, after M. Thibault's death, where the underlying sexual manoeuvring is more important than the actual words spoken.

No final judgment is necessary on the volumes of *Les Thibault* as far as *La Mort du Père:* since these were originally to form no more than about a third of the series, they must have been intended, to a large extent, as being no more than introductory. We may in fact surmise that the experience of war was to play a central rôle in the development of the novel, even before the 1931 change of plan. The first two volumes deal with the crisis of adolescence, after which the tension drops. In *La Belle Saison,* Martin du Gard presents the highest point of optimism in the novel: his characters are, for the most part, at the stage of life where they seem to have control over their destiny, but in the course of a single summer, the tragic aspect of life reasserts itself. and the destructive effects of time pursue their course. From *La Belle Saison* onwards, there is a constant rise in tension, symbolized by the increasing gravity of M. Thibault's illness, although caused no less by the disappearance and rediscovery of Jacques. This tension reaches a climax with M. Thibault's death, and then is allowed to dissolve. The way is now open for the next important development in the action. It is arguable that *La Consultation,* an entire volume given over to detailed description of the life of only one of the principal characters, damages the general balance; and it is probably true that Martin du Gard made his subsequent task more difficult because of this desire to exhibit technical skill, especially since the new characters of the volume were not, in the event, further utilized. Otherwise, the level of dramatic interest remains high and fairly evenly balanced, because of the constant creation of suspense by not fully explaining incidents until after their narration. The unity of the different volumes is also reinforced by the deliberate recall of earlier scenes, especially in *La Sorellina.*[1]

----

[1] E.g. When Jacques thinks of Lisbeth Fruhling (p. 1208); when Antoine, visiting Jalicourt, remembers accompanying Jacques to see the *Normale* results posted up (p. 1163); and, above all, when Antoine recalls Rachel's departure (p. 1166), an episode which now gains added significance because it exactly coincided with Jacques's disappearance, the news of which was withheld from the reader at the time.

Yet it must be said that despite the general success of the first six volumes, and the individual brilliance of several episodes, notably the death of M. Thibault, their ultimate value can only depend on what follows in later volumes. The key themes have been introduced, but not exhausted; the protagonists have been brought to the threshold of maturity, but it is their further development which will be crucial: only now are Antoine and Jacques no longer overshadowed by the figure of their father, whose disappearance indeed leaves something of a vacuum in the narrative. It is appropriate at this point to consider the time-scale of the series. Not until *La Consultation* is the date of the action definitely stated: Antoine's diary entries for October 13th 1913, are reproduced in the first chapter. In *La Sorellina* it becomes possible to establish the complete time-scale of the series by working backwards: *La Belle Saison* must have taken place in 1910, *Le Pénitencier* in 1905, and *Le Cahier gris* in 1904.[1] The reasons for delaying all exact dating until *La Consultation* remain doubtful, although one may suspect that Martin du Gard wished to leave himself the maximum freedom in the earlier volumes, rather than risk involving himself in unnecessary complications forced by the time-scale. But there are considerable disadvantages: after *Barois*, a work of undeniable originality, central to an intellectual understanding of pre-1914 France, the early volumes of *Les Thibault*, with their return to psychological themes, must have seemed at first sight something of an anticlimax.[2] The point made by Crémieux and repeated by Borgal is valid[3]: the reading public, which had recently undergone the inescapably traumatic experience of a war of previously unimagined dimensions, naturally expected that war to be a central theme in any significant novel. The first six volumes of *Les Thibault* have only taken the reader to 1913, the threshold of the war; and the ultimate value of the total novel-series will largely depend on the treatment of it.

---

[1] In *La Mort du Père*, Martin du Gard himself makes a slip in chronology: he makes Antoine think that 1906 was the year of Jacques's incarceration at Crouy, whereas in fact this must have taken place during the winter of 1904–5.

[2] Cf. the comments by Duhamel and Coppet quoted in *Souvenirs*, p. lxxxiv and pp. lxxxii–lxxxiii respectively.

[3] B. Crémieux, in *N.R.F.*, 1922, quoted by Borgal, op. cit., p. 114.

6

CONFIDENCE AFRICAINE
AND VIEILLE FRANCE

AT THIS point it is convenient to consider the two shorter works separating *La Mort du Père* from the next volume in the series, *Eté 1914*. The first of these, a *nouvelle, Confidence africaine*, was written in 1930 and published in the spring of 1931; the second, *Vieille France*, was completed in 1932, appearing in 1933.

Confidence africaine appeared with a prefatory note to the editor of the *Nouvelle Revue Française*, Jean Paulhan, explaining why, despite his claim that 'tout ce que j'ai à dire passe automatiquement dans mes *Thibault*' (p. 1107), Martin du Gard had decided to write a *nouvelle*. In actual fact, this was by no means the first time that he had interrupted his novel-series to write some shorter work. There had been his second peasant farce, *La Gonfle*, completed in 1924 and published in 1928, while the short story, *Noizemont-les-Vierges*, had also appeared during the latter year. This would appear to belie the claim that all he had to say went into *Les Thibault*. We may indeed surmise that the constant concentration on a single work tended to tire him, and that the lesser works were written partly at least as relaxation. There may, too, have been the challenge of a new genre: the desire to demonstrate technical virtuosity which had become more insistent in the years since the war. It would moreover have been difficult to integrate into *Les Thibault* every theme which interested Martin du Gard, at least with adequate treatment. This is especially true of the theme of incest, central to *Confidence africaine*. This theme had already been skirted in *Les Thibault*: in the relationships between Jacques and Gise, and between the mysterious Hirsch and his daughter. But the difficulty of fitting a fairly lengthy treatment of this theme into the series, without changing the entire plot, would evidently be insurmountable.

Martin du Gard's interest in the theme is clearly related to his interest in sexual psychology in general; it is the aesthetic interest, common to so many realist and naturalist writers, in the extraordinary—the 'pathological case'—and the treatment is deliberately amoral and neutral. He goes out of his way to make clear his attitude to the events, putting his point of view into the mouth of Barbazano, the male protagonist:

Et voilà.

Ces choses-là, vous voyez comme ça peut arriver tout naturellement. C'est même tout simple, n'est-ce pas, quand on y pense, quand on retrouve à peu près l'enchaînement des détails. (p. 1121)

This completely amoral attitude is further justified by the corollary: that life is composed, not of normal, but of exactly such extraordinary cases: 'Est-ce que la vie n'est pas faite presque uniquement de détails exceptionnels?' (p. 1114); and because he claims to be merely describing facts he knows to be true, Martin du Gard takes no responsibility for these facts, although admitting in his letter to Paulhan that they might be 'de nature à scandaliser certaines gens' (p. 1107).

The basic plot is simple, almost excessively simple. He merely intends to show how easily a relationship of this kind could arise. Leandro Barbazano and his sister Amalia, four years older than himself, grow up in close intimacy in one of the large towns in French North Africa, called 'Y' in the story and not further described. Their domineering father, of Italian stock, rules their lives in a strict patriarchal manner; their mother dies while they are still small children and the whole family then live in one room behind the father's bookshop. After some five years, the father takes a serving woman as his mistress, and a large room, with a partition between two beds, is rented for the two children on a higher floor in the building. Both continue to live there for over ten years, when the boy is 17 and has already been involved in various amorous escapades with local girls, culminating in an episode when he brings into the room the daughter of a neighbouring tenant. A fierce quarrel breaks out between Amalia and himself as a result, ending in a nocturnal fight on his bed, which turns into a scene of love. The incestuous relationship continues for four years, until it is ended by Leandro's military service and Amalia's forced marriage to her father's partner, a man already in his fifties. Although Barbazano returns to the household after his period of service, the relationship with his sister is not resumed; by now she has given birth not only to a child of his, conceived shortly before her marriage to Luzzati, the partner, but also to another, legitimate, child.

Such is the basic plot of the story. Martin du Gard, once again, is very much preoccupied with technique. Primarily, he wishes to create an absolute illusion of truth: that these extraordinary events actually took place. This aim leads him to adopt an extreme form of realism, which may be called a *trompe-l'œil* technique. The *nouvelle* is related by Martin du Gard in the first person, as if he had direct knowledge of the series of events, and this impression is fostered by the prefatory note: '. . . quelques feuillets d'un ancien carnet de voyage. C'est une conversation,—une confidence, plutôt,—recueillie naguère sur un paquebot qui me ramenait d'Afrique. Ces propos, je les ai notés tels quels . . .' (p. 1107). But there can be no doubt that the story is entirely imaginary, although many readers were deceived; a note in his *Journal* in 1945 is explicit: '. . . on refusera sans doute (comme il est arrivé jadis pour *Confidence africaine*) de croire que cette aventure est intégralement inventée . . .'[1] Realizing that the full story, as he wishes to tell it, could scarcely stand without some preliminary explanation, he excuses this: 'Mais, au moment de les recopier, je m'aperçois qu'ils ne seraient guère intelligibles sans quelques préliminaires.' (p. 1107) Since he wishes to tell the story in the first person, he is obliged to introduce a second narrator: Barbazano himself, whom he is deemed to have met. This meeting is said to have taken place in a sanatorium at Font-Romeu, where Barbazano's nephew, a sickly boy dying of consumption, was a friend of Frantz H., a ward of Martin du Gard's. The latter struck up an acquaintanceship with Barbazano,

[1] *Souvenirs*, p. cxxv.

and after the death of the nephew, the friendship continued by correspondence. A few years later, says Martin du Gard, circumstances obliged him to travel to North Africa, and he was invited to stay with Barbazano in 'Y' for six weeks. After this stay they returned to Marseille together, and Martin du Gard wrote the story on the boat. The preliminary section of explanation ends at this point, and is followed by what purports to be an extract from Martin du Gard's diary, setting down Barbazano's story the day after he had heard it, in direct speech.

This technique enables Martin du Gard to set the scene and to describe directly some of his characters, twenty years after the original events. Thus we see Michele Luzzati, the ill-fated son of the incestuous relationship, shortly before he dies; Barbazano's sister Amalia, enormously fat, constantly eating, surrounded by half a dozen shouting children; Luzzati, her husband, also corpulent, but more sentimental than his wife. The contrast with the original events can thereby be rendered all the more striking. In addition, Martin du Gard can make psychological comments and value judgments without departing from his chosen method of narration: he describes Amalia's greed in terms which allow considerable psychological nuances, without detracting from the verisimilitude:

Je dois ajouter, pour être juste, que sa gourmandise avait un caractère impérieux, passionnel, qui l'empêchait presque d'être répugnante: cette voracité semblait être la revanche, le refuge, de toutes les ardeurs d'une femme; et cela n'était pas très loin du pathétique. (p. 1112)

The supposed diary extracts are intended to add to the illusion of veracity. The device of diary extracts is of course conventional in the novel and short story; here it is combined with another traditional cadre—Barbazano's account, in direct speech. This is some ten pages long, and Martin du Gard ignores the practical impossibility that, a day after Barbazano had been talking to him, he would be able to quote, word for word, even a quarter as much. This implausibility apart, the illusion of reality is maintained; Barbazano is made to address him by name: '"Tenez, monsieur du Gard, c'est bien la première fois que j'ai envie de raconter ça à quelqu'un"' (p. 1114). Finally, at the end of the story, Martin du Gard completes his *tour de force* by pretending, in a parenthesis, that if he were in fact writing a fictional account based on the same events, he would handle his material differently:

(Suivaient quelques notes, d'ordre professionnel, pour le cas où me viendrait un jour l'envie de tirer littérairement parti de cette histoire. Je ne vous les recopie pas, mon cher ami. J'en extrais seulement, pour terminer, ces quelques lignes:)
'. . . Il faudrait aussi changer la fin, à partir du retour de Sicile . . . Et surtout ne souffler mot des souvenirs que j'ai de l'adipose Amalia de quarante ans, trônant à la caisse au milieu de sa marmaille; ou bien, bâfrant sa bouillie de figues au miel; ou bien, à table, laissant couler hors du corsage son imposante mamelle, pour céder au caprice de son dernier-né, un crapaud joufflu qui avait atteint ses deux ans sans être sevré, qui mangeait déjà le couscous avex nous, et qui, le repas terminé, se hissait goulûment sur les genoux de sa mère pour téter quelques gorgées de vieux lait, en guise de dessert.' (p. 1127)

The reason for this passage is not only a desire to prolong the *trompe-l'œil* effect to the end of the story; he clearly believes that this ending is artistically superior to the neatly rounded one. As it is, he ends on a note of anticlimax, a static description which has no immediate logical connexion with the events previously narrated. This is the same device as that frequently employed in the *Thibault* series to bring a separate volume to a close. The effect is one of contrast, between the original events and the prosaic present, and is almost grotesque: Leandro's account of the depth and beauty of his passion for his sister, twenty years before—'. . . les quatre seules vraiment belles années de ma vie!' (p. 1121)—stands out in pathetic relief against her present state.

At the same time, however, it must be said that Martin du Gard lays himself open to the charge of implausibility here: if we can believe that the impetuous, passionate Leandro of twenty years ago could have turned into the philosophical and educated man who can now speak so dispassionately of his past, it is more difficult to accept that the young Amalia could have turned into this obese creature, that marriage and maternity could have so distorted her violent nature and dulled her sensibilities. As so often, when psychological explanation and motivation are insufficient to create full plausibility, the episode simply has to be taken for granted; but artistically this might be regarded as a flaw in the story.

The three different methods of presentation permit great stylistic versatility. The introductory section, although in the first person, is written in normal literary style: that is, the 'transparent' style of the *Thibault* series. The diary extracts are in an abbreviated 'notebook' style, with personal pronouns omitted: 'Serai à Paris ce soir, mais vendredi seulement à Bellême (pp. 1113-14). And the bulk of the story, Barbazano's narrative, is again told in the first person, in the conversational style of an educated man, with a certain intimacy of tone which does not conflict with intelligent description and analysis. Here, though, despite the somewhat colloquial note, the hand of Martin du Gard may occasionally be detected:

Souvent aussi, grâce à moi, ils se retrouvaient le dimanche au football, quand le père permettait à ma sœur de m'accompagner. Amalia n'avait pas de secrets pour moi. Le soir, dans la chambre, pendant qu'on se mettait au lit, et long-temps encore après qu'on était couché, on se faisait par-dessus la cloison de bois d'interminables confidences à mi-voix . . . (p. 1116)

Here the smooth run of the style betrays him, and the use of 'on' instead of 'nous' provides insufficient concealment. This section is mostly in the perfect tense, although some of the earlier events are narrated, as above, in the imperfect; possibly use of the dramatic present to achieve greater immediacy might have covered up better. But in any case, the story is being retold by Martin du Gard, in his diary; and after his experience with *La Sorellina*, he was probably not so much concerned with achieving complete stylistic illusion as with creating a general impression of verisimilitude.

The subject matter of the story deserves comment; he is interested in the extraordinary aspects of life, but is also keenly concerned with various aspects of human sexual behaviour. We have already seen in *L'Une de nous* and in *Les Thibault*, notably in *La Belle Saison*, how he is prepared to tackle, or at least to mention, certain rarely treated aspects of human behaviour. Here the same process is merely extended. An apparently irrelevant remark in the diary extract, which gives Barbazano the opportunity to begin his story, casts some light on this:

Avions échangé des propos décousus sur la littérature moderne: timides progrès de la psycho dans le roman français contemporain; hardiesses de certains auteurs étrangers, etc. Lui ai cité un récent article du *Temps*, qui accuse les jeunes romanciers américains d'aborder à plaisir des sujets 'scabreux' et parfaitement 'invraisemblables'. (p. 1114)

This passage appears to voice some of Martin du Gard's own opinions: he believes that the novel of psychological analysis, to be thorough, must deal with all facets of human personality. The same attitude must have been behind his choice of subject when he wrote his first serious play, *Un Taciturne*, although the manner of treatment is entirely different.

Irony, usually one of his most favoured weapons, is almost absent from the story, which is narrated without comment, as objectively as possible. The sharp final contrast, a deliberate anticlimax, might be regarded as irony of a sort, but the ironic aside and comparison so common in the *Thibault* series would conflict with the author's intention of creating the illusion of veracity. Nevertheless, occasionally he yields to the temptation of satire, as when he claims how difficult he found it to resist Barbazano's offer for him to give a lecture in North Africa:

Comme je lui affirmais que j'étais incapable de prendre la parole en public, et surtout que je n'avais aucun message à apporter ... (..) (il) me répondit avec une désarmante autorité: 'Eh! vous ferez comme vos confrères. Tous les écrivains qui passent ici font une conférence. Les historiens sur l'histoire, les poètes sur la poésie, les romanciers sur le roman. Ils parlent d'eux, de leur œuvre, et leur façon de travailler, de leurs manies, de leurs régimes. Et, quel que soit le stock dont ils ont eu la précaution de faire approvisionner nos librairies, en huit jours tout est enlevé!' (p. 1110)

And in addition to the irony, Martin du Gard is here explaining some of his reasons for normally refraining from such public demonstrations. Later, as a Nobel Prize winner in Stockholm, he will break his own rules, but only in the context of a vastly changed world political situation.

In relation to the whole of Martin du Gard's work, *Confidence africaine* is clearly not of cardinal importance. The tone and theme are closely reminiscent of the Hirsch episode in *La Belle Saison*; once again we see the identification of the erotic with the exotic, in the North African background to the story. The treatment is also typical, in that considerable attention is devoted to the aftermath of the relationship. In the depiction of Barbazano and Amalia years after the original incestuous episode, we see once again the destructive effect of time. *Confidence africaine* is certainly successful on its level; it is well told, with considerable psychological analysis and incidental description, and throughout bears the hallmark of craftsmanship and versatility. We may speculate that if Martin du Gard had chosen to write in the genre of the *nouvelle* or short story more often, he might well have gained his place as a master in the field. He considered writing short stories, in the financial difficulties which followed his decision to destroy *L'Appareillage*, and has stated: 'J'avais dans mes notes de nombreux projets de nouvelles',[1] and if Gallimard had not come to his aid, *Confidence africaine* might well be only one of a long series. However, he chose to put his major effort into his *roman-fleuve*, an effort on the grand scale, rather than disperse his creative genius in a number of lesser works.

In the *Souvenirs* Martin du Gard does not mention the composition of *Vieille France;* however, in a letter to Jean Schlumberger he described his intentions in some detail:

J'écris en ce moment une longue nouvelle, ou même un petit livre, qui met en scène, par petites touches objectives, les habitudes d'un minuscule village français. Vu évidemment sans la moindre indulgence. Collection de figures laides, de cœurs refroidis, stupides, cruels. Un monde indéfendable. Je procède d'une façon très neuve pour moi, par simples croquis juxtaposés. Arriverai-je, dans ces esquisses de quelques lignes, à créer un petit groupement humain vivant? C'est très difficile et je ne puis en répondre, mais je travaille certains jours avec assez d'entrain.[2]

The word 'croquis' recurs in the dedication of the book: 'ce simple album de croquis villageois' (p. 1015); this description is not entirely accurate, as we shall see, but *Vieille France* can only with difficulty be fitted into any accepted fictional genre. It

---

[1] Ibid., p. xcvii.   [2] Quoted in *N.N.R.F.*, 12/58, p. 1068.

consists of a number of vignettes or short sketches of village life, linked by the character of Joigneau, the village postman, whom the narrator accompanies on his round and who therefore provides a convenient means of describing many of the inhabitants of the village and much of village life.

It may be wondered why Martin du Gard should decide to compose these scenes of peasant life, a work apparently on a considerably lower level than *Les Thibault*. The title gives the clue: *Vieille France;* the sketches are intended to have a symbolic or representative value. The situation of the village concerned, Maupeyrou, is never indicated geographically, and might be almost anywhere in France where red wine is produced.[1] Similarly, the date is not specified; it is a few years after the First World War, possibly about the mid-twenties, since the War seems a more vigorous memory than it would have become by, say, 1932. The actual day when the action takes place is equally vague: it is any hot summer day. Thus the entire setting is typical and representative.

Since, however, the general tone of the book is distinctly pessimistic, practically all of the characters being presented in an unfavourable light, Martin du Gard received much adverse criticism, particularly from patriotic and Right-wing critics, to the effect that, even though his village, Maupeyrou, may be accurately portrayed, it is none the less not at all typical of France as a whole. He has attempted to evade this criticism by claiming that the title alone is at fault; if he had entitled the book *La Journée du Postier* the question would not even have been raised.[2] This explanation is a little disingenuous in view of his further remarks: that *Vieille France* was originally intended to be the first of two similar books, the second to be called *Jeune France*, presumably giving a brighter picture of French life. We can accept this as genuine, but it implies the same symbolic intention which he was previously trying to deny. And it is still true that *Vieille France* is the only one of the two

[1] Maupeyrou could not therefore be situated in Picardy or Normandy, as certain critics have suggested (cf. P.-J. Brodin, *Présences contemporaines*, vol. ii, Paris, 1955, p. 268).
[2] *N.N.R.F.*, 12/58, pp. 1068-9.

books which came to fruition: the pessimistic side was clearly uppermost.

The book gives a consistently depressing view of peasant life, relieved only occasionally by brutal farce. Only in one scene does a flash of hope break through: in Chapter XXIV, where the village youths express their contempt for the whole of country life. Joux puts their feeling into words: ' . . . ici tout est usé . . . Dans les grandes villes, quand même, le monde n'est pas retardé comme chez nous!' (p. 1093). The young men have no use for politics, but are convinced that they could do better themselves, and indeed with scarcely any effort could bring the whole social edifice crumbling down: 'Les vieilles noix sont mûres, à c't'heure . . . (..) N'y aurait qu'à gauler dans le tas. vous verriez si ça dégringole!' (p. 1094). In this episode, perhaps, we can see the other side of the picture, and what was intended in *Jeune France;* although it is not made clear what ideas the young men have, we can assume that their 'revolutionary' tendencies and disgust for the existing structure of society spring more from the political Left than the Right. *Vieille France* was written at the very time when, as we shall see, Martin du Gard's ideas were as close to Communism as they ever became.

For the remainder of the book, we might well take the thoughts of the schoolmistress, Mlle Ennberg, to represent those of the author:

. . . elle . . . (..) rêve à sa solitude, à la vie de ce village, à cette humanité animale qui rampe encore dans les bas-fonds. 'Pourquoi le monde est-il ainsi? Est-ce bien la faute de la Société? . . .' Et la question redoutable qu'elle s'est déjà posée souvent, l'obsède une fois de plus: 'Ne serait-il pas la faute de l'Homme? . . .' (p. 1102)

And again in the continuation:

Mais elle garde au cœur un tel besoin de confiance et tant d'ingénue ferveur, qu'elle ne se résigne pas à douter de la nature humaine. Non, non! . . . Que vienne enfin le règne d'une Société nouvelle,—mieux organisée, moins irrationnelle, moins injuste,—et l'on verra peut-être enfin ce que l'Homme peut donner!' (p. 1102)

The whole book is saturated with two vices: self-interest and sexual lust. Joigneau, who knows the entire village and whose character is the only one thoroughly drawn, is the finest example; but scarcely no one in Maupeyrou is exempt from them. Joigneau's occupation makes him the natural centre of village intelligence: he is the only man who knows the entire population, and he has no scruples about steaming letters open; indeed, his siesta hour is regularly devoted to this task. As he goes round the village no possible business transaction escapes him: early in the morning Flamart, the station porter, shares his breakfast with him in exchange for confidences about his wife's correspondence; later, he takes his two dogs with him on his round, thereby saving himself the cost of feeding them:

Il a compris depuis longtemps le parti qu'un facteur, s'il élève des chiens de race, doit tirer de la distribution des lettres ... (..) Son couple d'épagneuls connaît les habitudes de chaque ménagère et la place exacte de toutes les poubelles du pays. La tournée est à la fois leur exercice et leur repas journaliers. La vente des chiots est un profit presque net. (p. 1029)

Everything else is on the same level: Joigneau is prepared to do a service to Bosse, the café-owner, on condition that there is 10 per cent in it for himself; even to help La Mauriçotte to an inheritance, provided that she will sign over part of it to him. He is one of the key men in local politics, the chief supporter of Arnaldon, the *maire;* but this service is only performed for hard cash.

Joigneau's relations with his wife are also based on these two principles. He rarely exchanges an unnecessary word with her, refuses to allow her to have children as this would prevent her from running the post office, and merely eats her food and uses her body. No woman's modesty is safe from his gaze, and he satisfies his extra-marital lusts with La Philiberte, an unfortunate woman living miserably with two infants in a slum hut on public land—from which Joigneau, with his political influence, can have her expelled if she refuses his sexual demands. The ending of this episode is typically ironic:

D'ailleurs, il lui allonge toujours vingt ou trente sous: en somme, c'est vite gagné. Trente sous, ça fait deux jours de pain. Et puis, faut se faire une raison: ces histoires-là, ça ne durera qu'un temps. Dès que les gosses seront plus grandes, la Philiberte pourra les mettre à l'école et se louer pour les lessives: on a tant de mal, aujourd'hui, à trouver des femmes qui lavent. Alors, en six mois, elle aura économisé de quoi revenir s'installer à Roubagne, près de Narbonne! à Roubagne, où elle a encore sa tante infirme, à Roubagne, dont elle rêve chaque soir en s'endormant, et où les gens, je vous jure, ne sont pas comme ceux d'ici. (p. 1070)

The entire book is shot through with similar episodes: La Mélie, Joigneau's own wife, is strongly attracted by Joseph, the sixteen-year-old blacksmith's apprentice who lodges in the attic; although nothing actually happens on this day, it will obviously not be long before this potential passion bursts into full flame.

The treatment of the *mutilés de guerre* and of the war widows shows this satirical attitude at its clearest. The three wounded men are the laziest of the village, spending their time talking and fishing:

Pascalon boite, surtout quand il traverse le village. C'est le moins pensionné, le moins paresseux des trois. Il est fossoyeur et savetier. Il a su profiter de son retour au pays dès la première année de la guerre: le soir même de la réception municipale qui lui a été faite à la mairie, il s'est fait nommer par la commune gardien du cimetière, et loger sur place . . . (pp. 1070-1)

Nor do the war widows escape more lightly:

C'est le trio des veuves de guerre. Elles ont à peu près le même âge, et, toutes trois, un grand fils, pupille de la nation. D'autres liens encore les unissent; leurs robes noires, leur dévotion, leurs commérages, leur rancune contre les épouses pourvues, leur haine des embusqués—c'est-à-dire des hommes épargnés par la guerre,—leurs revendications de pensionnées, et la chasteté orgueilleuse qui détraque lentement leurs cerveaux après leur avoir déréglé le corps. (p. 1077)

Passages such as this, bordering on the cynical, could scarcely be better calculated to rouse the ire of the patriotic; but Martin du Gard has no time for sentimental glamorization of the war.

Cynicism is rarely to be found in the *Thibault* series, but it is very much in evidence here. Espérance, the daughter of the *épicière*, would gladly marry practically anyone in order to escape from her home. Her good looks, instead of facilitating matters, in fact reduce her chances: 'Vaine attente: Espérance est bien trop jolie. Elle est pauvre, et on la sait abonnée à un journal de modes. Tous les garçons lui tournent autour, mais aucun ne l'épousera' (p. 1033). This cynicism is itself only an expression of profound pessimism, Maupeyrou is clearly beyond hope of regeneration from within. The only inhabitants who are not perfectly satisfied with the state of affairs are those with some education: the priest and the two schoolteachers. But even they are powerless to effect any change. The priest has surrendered after thirty-five years of struggles against the general indifference and the ignorant prejudice of the faithful minority. The description of his efforts is typical of Martin du Gard's attitude to his material: an attitude which he scarcely troubles to conceal:

Il y a trente ans qu'il a débarqué à Maupeyrou, avec un zèle de jeune apôtre dans son bagage de séminariste. Les premières années, pour lutter contre la frigidité religieuse de ce vieux pays sclérosé, où chacun ne pense qu'à soi, à son petit commerce, à sa petite épargne, à sa petite sécurité, il a tout mis en œuvre pour créer entre ses ouailles un esprit d'entre-aide chrétienne. Peine perdue. Tous, même les pratiquants, se sont dérobés à ses initiatives. Le patronage, l'ouvroir, le comité charitable, qu'il a théoriquement fondés, n'ont jamais fonctionné, faute de recrutement. Impossible de réchauffer l'âme de ces travailleurs à petit profit. Depuis trop de générations, l'exercice quotidien d'une économie vitale a étouffé tous leurs instincts généreux. C'est maintenant une race méfiante, envieuse, calculatrice, que la cupidité ravage comme un chancre. En a-t-il toujours été ainsi? C'est une question que le prêtre se pose souvent, avec angoisse. Pendant des siècles, ce petit peuple de France est pourtant venu s'agenouiller dans cette église qu'il déserte aujourd'hui. Qu'est-ce qui l'y amenait? L'amour? La foi? Des besoins spirituels, maintenant atrophiés? . . . N'était-ce pas plutôt la crainte? La crainte de Dieu, la crainte du clergé? Le respect routinier de l'ordre établi? . . . L'abbé Verne sait bien que ces leviers-là sont cassés. D'ailleurs, il répugnerait à s'en servir. (p. 1040)

And, with a strange repetition of Candide's resolve, he has turned inward on himself, and spends the bulk of his time cultivating his garden. As a final irony, he grows vegetables and sells off what he does not need himself, affected by the same mercenary instincts as his flock.

M. Ennberg, the schoolmaster, has met with no more success, and indeed is worse off. He can hardly keep his fat, slovenly wife and their three children, and instead of devoting his evenings to further study, he is obliged to write copy for commercial laboratories. Education generally is as little welcome in Maupeyrou as religious guidance: the only child who shows any promise, the only 'nature capable d'un peu de générosité, désireuse de s'instruire, de s'élever' (p. 1101) is not allowed private tuition, even when offered gratis, by her parents, who sneer that she already knows more than she needs. Ennberg's political idealism is likewise unwanted: his position as school-teacher obliges him to act as secretary to the *maire*, and to see all his ideals, human dignity, equality, democracy, free thought and free speech, abused by Arnaldon.

Traditional politics comes in for short shrift in *Vieille France:* Joigneau claims that Maupeyrou cannot be backward when 80 per cent of the vote always goes to the Left, and Martin du Gard's condemnation of village life is directed against all sides. Further light on this is cast by Joigneau's conversation with M. des Navières, a retired bank clerk, living at starvation level. M. des Navières has a vague idea of the Soviet system in Russia, and describes an ideal society where money no longer exists, where everyone is provided for by the State. Joigneau has no time for this; despite his political affiliations, he is actuated in everything purely by motives of self-interest.

Technically *Vieille France* is excellent. The numerous episodes and sketches are written to a rigid plan: Joigneau's daily round. This necessarily leads to a certain symmetry and balance, which is maintained by limiting the amount of space devoted to each new character. Then, as night falls, at the end of the book, some of the sketches are briefly taken up again, almost as echoes. The final two sketches take us back again to the *curé* and the two schoolteachers, to emphasize the hoplessness of village life. The book ends on an indeterminate note, like *Confidence africaine:* Mlle Ennberg suddenly remembers her dream of the previous night: that her brother was silently strangling his wife with a clothes line. The memory is not enlarged upon or analysed: that is left to the reader, in fact almost forced upon him by the *points de suspension* at the end of the final sentence.

This technique of hinting, rather than direct statement, frequently noted in *Les Thibault*, is much used here. The Merlavigne brothers, the village bakers, and their debauched maid, burn what they say is a litter of kittens in their furnace, but no one believes them. Mme Loutre had a child by a German prisoner-of-war while her own husband was a prisoner in Germany, now all three live together in apparent amity, 'mais on n'a jamais su lequel des deux "hommes" partage le lit de l'enfant, ni si c'est toujours le même' (p. 1051). And the truth about the Pâqueux family, who keep their father as a prisoner in their farm, is never clearly stated. The reason for the constant use of this technique is of course that Martin du Gard is primarily concerned with creating atmosphere; deep analysis is unnecessary for this, nor is a complicated plot essential. Nevertheless, his method of careful documentation and preparation remains the same; he made a small map of the village to ensure that all topographical details would be correct,[1] while Schlumberger has remarked that each house in Maupeyrou has been given a different smell.[2] The scene at the smithy in Chapter X is clearly the result of keen observation; the best example of a vignette of village life in the book, it is largely a set-piece of description for its own sake.

The primary narrative tense is the present, for dramatic immediacy. At times the various past tenses are used for some past event needed to explain the present, but only briefly. In many ways, indeed, *Vieille France* resembles *Barois:* the constant dramatization, the almost mechanical scene-setting as Joigneau moves round the parish, indirect presentation of events through direct speech. This direct speech is constantly supplemented by *style indirect libre*, or a mixture of *style indirect libre* and straight-forward third-person narration.

Quérolle, silencieux, fait son calcul. La statue, compris le socle gravé, lui a juste coûté vingt sous: Mme Quérolle avait,—assez imprudemment d'ailleurs, —pris un billet à la tombola de la Sainte-Enfance, et elle a gagné pour deux cents francs d'achat dans une fabrique d'objets pieux. L'envoi était franco, mais il y a eu un verre de rouge pour le camionneur. Tout compte fait, ce n'est pas une matinée perdue . . . (pp. 1042–3)

Martin du Gard permits himself a fair degree of realism in his descriptions, but in reported speech compromises by only ocassionally departing from colloquial French:

---

[1] This sketch-map later appeared as the frontispiece of one edition of *Vieille France:* cf. *Bibliographie, Pléiade* ed., p. cxlvii.

[2] *N.N.R.F.*, 12/58, p. 1071.

'C'est rien que pour aller boire qu'il cherche à se lever, le salaud. (..) ...
Mais il n'y a plus une goutte de gniole ici; et, pour s'en aller au village, je
suis tranquille: il sera crevé dix fois, avant que d'arriver au bistro!' (p. 1057)

The contrast with the vigorous local dialect of the two peasant
farces is evident.

A comparison between *Confidence africaine* and *Vieille France*
perhaps helps one to arrive at a just evaluation of the latter
book. In the *nouvelle* Martin du Gard shows an essentially
humanist attitude, that of understanding and sympathy for a
situation which conventionally attracts only condemnation. In
Vieille France, on the other hand, he deliberately suppresses
almost all tendency to sympathy, preferring to depict his village
as populated by monsters. This is illustrated by his use of irony.
In *Les Thibault*, irony never prevents him from showing sympathy towards his characters, even the most unengaging, such
as M. Thibault. The note has now changed to one of bitter
satire. Many scenes which, with different treatment, could be
comical or even farcical, are deliberately made to leave an
unpleasant taste in the mouth: examples are the dispute between
Célestine and the Quérolles (Chapter VIII); and the episode at
the Pâqueux farm (Chapter XXI). The reason is clear: Martin
du Gard is not interested in the comic aspects of life in Maupeyrou
(and the comparison with the peasant farces is again instructive).[1]
'Pas de trêve, dans ces vies consacrées au gain', we read towards
the end of the book (p. 1095); *pas de trêve* is the keynote of his
own attitude to his characters. In 1932 Martin du Gard was at his
most pessimistic; his personal disappointment at the temporary
check in the *Thibault* series combined with political disillusionment. *Vieille France* is an expression of this pessimism, yet, as
satire, the work must be regarded as a distinct success. There is
no mixing of genres as in *Devenir;* within the strict bounds set,
he achieves his aims. *Vieille France* remained his favourite book:
'C'est le seul de mes livres que je consentirais à republier sans y
rien changer',[2] and has been widely popular in translation

---

[1] *Vieille France* approaches very closely in this respect to Zola's attitude to the peasants
in *La Terre*. In particular the priest here recalls Abbé Godard in Zola's novel.
[2] Quoted by Schlumberger, *N.N.R.F.*, 12/58, p. 1068.

abroad.[1] It is a measure of Martin du Gard's literary talent that he was able to transmute even his despair, his inability to reconcile his idealistic hopes about the future of man with the imperfect reality about him, into a successful work of art.

[1] In the U.S.S.R. and Central Europe *Vieille France* has been often taken as a typical picture of the decadence of French capitalist society. Since its first publication in 1954, the English translation, *The Postman*, has also sold extensively as a paperback, furnished with a lurid cover.

7

L'ETE 1914

No sequel to *La Mort du Père* appeared until the three volumes of *Eté 1914* came out in November 1936. The long interval requires some explanation. On finishing *La Mort du Père*, Martin du Gard immediately set to work on the succeeding volume, to be entitled *L'Appareillage;* by the end of 1930, not only was a first draft completed, but a good half of the manuscript was ready for the press. Then, on New Year's Day 1931, he and his wife were involved in a motor accident. Both were seriously injured, and spent two months recovering in a nursing-home in Le Mans. During this time he began to have serious doubts about the long-term plan of his novel: to carry out his original intentions, he would have to write at least fifteen more volumes, as only about a third of the total had so far been completed. He began to realize that the general tempo of his narrative had slowed down, and this might endanger the unity and balance of the whole series.[1] The most obvious solution, to prune the plan severely, was impossible: all the episodes planned would be necessary if the whole narrative were to hold together. It became clear that he would either have to persevere with his original plan in its entirety, or to make a complete change. He decided on the second course, and a rereading of the manuscript of *L'Appareillage* confirmed him in this:

Tout bien pesé, la seule solution raisonnable était de renoncer à terminer les *Thibault* comme je l'avais prévu; et d'enter sur le tronc des six parties déjà publiées *un autre dénouement,*—en m'efforçant de rendre la greffe aussi peu apparente que possible.[2]

This decided, he extracted from *L'Appareillage* certain material which he might use later, and burned the manuscript—'pour

---

[1] *Souvenirs*, p. xciv.   [2] Ibid., p. xcvi.

être dans l'impossibilité de revenir sur ma résolution'.[1] This rash act was, he states, made easier by the fact that he was already engaged on his first serious drama, *Un Taciturne;* possibly even his *Thibault* series was beginning to bore him a little. He had already, during 1930, written his *nouvelle, Confidence africaine,* which appeared in the *N.R.F.* of February 1931 (and therefore must have been submitted before the accident of January 1st), so it is reasonable to assume that the state of mind which caused him to change his entire plan had its origins in 1930 if not before.

He abandoned his original plan before working out a new one; indeed, the new plan was not finally settled until the end of 1933.[2] The rough outlines of this plan seem, however, to have been sketched out by February 1932: and entry in Gide's *Journal* mentions his 'immense joie de savoir R enfin délivré des *Thibault*—ou du moins résolu de réduire à deux le nombre des volumes qui lui restent à écrire'.[3] The surplus material would, according to Gide, be available for possible future works; and the condensed form of the *Thibault* series would permit him to 'se déclarer lui-même bien davantage'.[4]

The two volumes mentioned by Gide had grown somewhat by the time writing began, and Martin du Gard encountered numerous difficulties, financial as well as technical, before he finally finished the work, and at one time envisaged writing short stories purely to meet his financial needs; generous advances from Gallimard averted this.[5]

The original plan is of some interest:

Dans mon dessein initial, Jacques seul était tué à la guerre. Antoine revenait sain et sauf. Il épousait Jenny, et l'aidait à élever Jean-Paul, le fils de Jacques. Une fille, Anne-Marie, naissait du mariage. De nombreux événements, déjà imaginés, me servaient à mettre en relief, sur le fond si particulier de la France d'après-guerre, l'existence d'un grand praticien, l'évolution des caractères de Jenny et d'Antoine, les difficultés de leur vie conjugale, l'éducation et le développement de leurs enfants, etc . . . Un épisode, compliqué, particulièrement pathétique, et qui devait occuper l'un des derniers volumes en entier, se trouvait centré sur Jean-Paul. Héritier des natures ardentes de Jacques et de Jenny, il se lançait, à vingt ans, dans une folle aventure. Il séduisait la femme de

---

[1] Ibid., p. xcvi.   [2] Ibid., p. xcvii.   [3] Gide, *Journal 1889–1939*, p. 1112.
[4] Ibid., pp. 1112–13.   [5] *Souvenirs*, p. xcvii.

son meilleur ami; et, pour sauver l'honneur de sa maîtresse, se trouvait amené
à abattre d'une balle de revolver le domestique d'Antoine, un jeune maître-
chanteur, qui avait découvert la liaison, et menaçait de remettre au mari un
document volé et irréfutablement accusateur. Scandale parisien, cour d'assises,
etc . . . Tout était minutieusement agencé pour être d'un bel effet dramatique;
et, sur ces données de roman-policier, je me flattais d'écrire un ouvrage
purement psychologique . . .[1]

(As a result of this episode, Jean-Paul was to be convicted and
to serve a prison sentence.)[2] From this information alone it is
impossible to say whether his self-disparagement is justified; the
murder and subsequent trial are, however, interesting, since
they show the desire to incorporate into the *roman-fleuve* the
theme of violence and its psychological motivation. A similar
preoccupation with violent action and dramatic tension can be
seen in the new plan. More significant, as Borgal has remarked,
is the fact that Jean-Paul, born in 1914 or 1915, would not be
20 until 1934 or 1935. The novel series must therefore have
been planned, in the early 1920's, to extend forward fifteen
years into the future. This implies considerable self-confidence,
and also that these later volumes would be purely on the
psychological plane:

. . . en concevant l'histoire du fils de Jacques, l'auteur n'a pas tenu le moindre
compte du temps réel, tissu des incidences politiques ou internationales,
(comment eût-il pu les prévoir?) mais uniquement du temps psychologique,
particulier au personnage, indépendant, limité aux seuls points de sa naissance
et de sa mort . . .[3]

It may well be, as Borgal goes on to say, that realization of this
anomaly had something to do with the change of plan. However, when Martin du Gard made his original one, there was no
real reason why he should not extend it into the future. He was
still in his thirties, and wished to write a novel covering over
thirty years. He was therefore obliged either to make the novel
begin when he himself was a small child, or to make it end at
some point in the future. The first alternative would oblige him
to write about a period which he scarcely knew at first hand,
and so to have recourse to historical reconstruction; the second

[1] Ibid., p. xcv.   [2] From a conversation with Martin du Gard in June 1955.
[3] Borgal, op. cit., pp. 111-12.

would make him run the risk of inaccurately predicting the future. At the time, his interests were primarily psychological, as the correspondence with Margaritis shows; he wished to subordinate the highly documented novel of ideas to the novel of psychological observation. This aim he carried out in the earlier volumes: although Jacques becomes a revolutionary, he is clearly more interested in the psychology of revolution than in revolutionary ideas themselves. Similarly, problems of ethics and religion are seen largely in their effect on Antoine's personality. During the 1920's his interests had probably swung round again towards pure ideas and politics, so that he would tend to place less emphasis on the psychological aspects of his material. This is borne out by the fact that what ideas there are in the earlier volumes occur in *La Consultation* onwards—in the volumes written after 1926 (Martin du Gard's presence at the Pontigny *Entretiens* may have influenced this swing in his views, by involving him in friendship with writers like Malraux, who was not only keenly interested but also deeply immersed in politics; or Gide too, in his Communist phase). However, we cannot at present say with any precision what Martin du Gard's interests were in 1931, at the time of the change of plan, but by 1933 he had almost certainly evolved further towards political involvement; Hitler's accession to power no doubt hastened the process, which continued throughout the composition of the remaining volumes.

Of the destroyed volume, *L'Appareillage*, we know little. There was a long scene between Jenny and Gise at Hyères; and since, before burning his manuscript, he had '. . . détaché quelques bribes . . . (. .) certains détails de caractère, dont je me suis effectivement servi pour les rencontres de Jacques et de Jenny à la fin de *l'Eté 1914* . . .',[1] we may presume that Jacques and Jenny met again, and that Jacques's relationship with Gise was also further developed. The Hyères episode presumably followed this, as a *mise au clair* of the triangular situation. The title of the volume probably refers to Antoine's installation of a laboratory, which we see completed in *Eté 1914*. Antoine's liaison with Anne

[1] *Souvenirs*, p. xcvi.

de Battaincourt was also probably to begin in this volume.
The action must have taken place during the months between
M. Thibault's death in December 1913 and the summer of 1914;
more than this it is difficult to say.

Much of this volume must have been more or less transitional,
such as the description of Antoine's preparations to become a
grand praticien, leading up to a more important volume dealing
with the war. How large a part the war was originally intended
to play is doubtful; but in the new version it is central. Martin
du Gard's own attitude to the struggle of 1914–18 had evidently
changed; the initial numbing effect had died away and he now
felt able, even impelled, to use war as subject matter. Its effect
upon him possibly only became clear gradually: it is the complete disintegration of the whole of pre-1914 Europe. To
illustrate this is one of the main aims of *Eté 1914* and *Epilogue*.

The chief characters are now seen primarily against the background of the conflict which is about to sweep them away
from their former existences; alongside that conflict, they as
individuals have little importance. By the time it is ended,
Jacques and Antoine are dead; Daniel is maimed and envisages
suicide. With the deaths of the main characters the novel can be
brought to a close; the war merges their individual destinies
with that of the whole of Europe, giving the novel an altogether
wider significance.

This aim implies a completely new orientation of the narrative. The first six volumes of the series are primarily psychological; a number of characters are depicted against their own
background, and their relationships and problems are analysed
almost entirely in psychological terms (even the metaphysical
themes, time, solitude, and death, are treated as personal psychological problems); little attempt is made to relate the individual
characters and their environment to French or European society
as a whole (only in *La Consultation* was the date made clear).
Social questions, such as education and punishment, it is true,
were touched upon, but again only in individual terms; none
of the main characters was faced by physical, as opposed to
psychological, difficulties such as poverty. Their freedom of

choice was restricted only by their personalities. Their significance extended only to themselves as individuals, representatives
possibly of Man in general, but not of the totality of contemporary French society. All this now changes; European society
comes to the foreground, and the characters not only have to
become symbols of that society, but the significance of their
previous lives as individuals has to be integrated into that wider
context. The difficulty of this undertaking is not immediately
apparent; but in effect Martin du Gard had to write an entirely
new novel, yet without the freedom of spontaneous creative
activity, since he remained bound by the limitations of the
earlier narrative.

Eté 1914, the first of the two final volumes projected, extends
to some 750 pages of the *Pléiade* edition,—nearly as long as the
first six volumes combined. Yet the period covered is only some
six weeks, from June 28th until August 10th 1914. The narrative
can therefore only move slowly: the term *Sekundentechnik* again
comes to mind, as in *La Consultation*. Indeed, the direct action
covers an even smaller period than these six weeks. There are
several distinct sections of the volume. The first nine chapters
all take place in Geneva, where Jacques is now living, on June
28th, and consist mainly of static description of life among
revolutionary circles, with a great deal of political exposition,
ending with the news of the Sarajevo assassinations (once again
the *nœud d'événements*). Chapters X–XII take place on July 12th:
two weeks later. They are also largely devoted to political
exposition, and explanation of developments since the end of
June. Another week passes before Chapter XIII, and from that
point the narrative is more or less continuous, centred upon
the movements of Jacques. On July 19th he arrives in Paris,
returns to Geneva on the 21st, travels to Antwerp for the 22nd,
and is back in Paris on the 23rd. He remains in Paris, and we are
given day-by-day accounts until he leaves for Berlin on the
28th, returning via Brussels, on the 29th, to Paris again. On
August 2nd he leaves, for the last time, to Geneva, stays in
Basle from the 4th until the 9th, and the final episode takes
place with the retreating French troops in Alsace, on August 10th.

This continuous narrative occupies a total of seventy-two chapters.

The narrative focus thus swings sharply round again to Jacques. Although individual chapters deal largely with subsidiary themes, such as Antoine's affair with Anne or his discussions with Rumelles, it is never long before Jacques returns to the foreground. Antoine's less important rôle is inevitable in view of the principal theme: the approach of war and reactions to it. His attitude is essentially passive, since he has not been following the course of European politics with anything like the passionate interest of his brother. To dramatize his material Martin du Gard has to describe Jacques's efforts to avert the war, and he therefore makes Jacques a leading figure in Geneva revolutionary circles. The whole theme of the war naturally leads to a further complication: to a considerable extent *Eté 1914* must be an historical novel, with all that involves in historical research and accuracy.

There was already a basis for Jacques's life in Geneva, in the Lausanne scenes in *La Sorellina*. Two characters, Rayer and the Belgian albino Vanheede, were directly presented in the earlier volume, and several others mentioned by name (Paterson, Richardley, and Quilleuf). This does give some link with the past. Nevertheless, it scarcely touched the surface of revolutionary life and ideas, and so much of the early chapters of *Eté 1914* has to be devoted to careful exposition. The greatest problem is how to integrate political and documentary material without boring the reader, and despite efforts to make it more interesting by embodying it in colloquial speech, a heavy didactic note remains.

At this point we realize that Martin du Gard has abandoned the position he arrived at in 1918, and is once again writing a novel of ideas. The opening chapter foreshadows what is to come: long expositions of the European political situation, analyses of topical events, of the various diplomatic moves preceding the outbreak of war, and of the beliefs and motives of the different members of the Geneva revolutionary group.

Martin du Gard's correspondence with Marcel Lallemand

gives us a good deal of insight into his problems. Although the new plan for *Eté 1914* had appeared satisfactory, its execution involved him in unforeseen difficulties. In particular, he had been constantly troubled by the need for extensive documentation:

Je n'ai jamais, ni si douloureusement, senti mes limites que depuis ces trois ans que je travaille à cet achèvement des *Thibault*. Et si j'ai tant d'impatience à en avoir fini et à pouvoir travailler à des œuvres plus purement psychologiques, (c'est) parce que la sagesse, à mon âge, est de labourer *son* champ et d'en tirer le plus ample rendement, plutôt que de se heurter sans cesse à ses limites en cherchant à les dépasser toujours.[1]

A later letter to Lallemand describes some of his difficulties in more detail: all are basically connected with the need for historical accuracy, especially as far as the Socialist movement is concerned:

J'ai trouvé à peu près l'essentiel à Bibliothèque, et dans les livres de Zévaès sur le Socialisme français de 1912. J'ai refait de bout en bout la scène à la Parlote de Genève, qui ne me satisfaisait pas. Je vous enverrai un de ces jours les pages du laïus de Meynestrel, pour que vous me disiez si je n'y ai pas laissé des bourdes de profane . . . (..)

Je ne suis pas sans inquiétude sur ce que j'ai pu faire des milieux socialistes de *L'Humanité*, et j'aurai besoin que votre œil parcoure cela, avant de publier. Quelle folle entreprise, cher ami! Personne ne saura le mal que je me suis donné pour tramer tous ces fils, vie politique française, vie politique européenne, et vie personnelle de mes personnages . . .[2]

Thus we see that Martin du Gard not only had to put in detailed research, but also was obliged to submit his first draft to an expert as a check upon accuracy. Not only this: we also discover that the whole character of Meynestrel was altered upon Lallemand's advice. Meynestrel was originally intended to play roughly the same rôle, but was to be a straightforward pacifist, intent, like Jacques, on preventing the war at all costs. Lallemand put forward the objection that the true revolutionaries, such as Lenin, in fact welcomed the outbreak of war, since they hoped this would lead to social disintegration and the necessary conditions for revolution. Martin du Gard at first found it difficult to accept this change,[3] but on further thought, he came round

---

[1] *N.N.R.F.*, 12/58, p. 1138 (letter to Lallemand, 29/8/35).
[2] Ibid., p. 1140 (letter to Lallemand, 18/1/36).
[3] Ibid., pp. 1138-9 (letter to Lallemand, 17/9/35).

to Lallemand's view. The idea would also tend to lend greater psychological depth to the volume.[1]

Some months later, he received Lallemand's comments on the second volume of *Eté 1914* Chapters XXVI to LVIII). Although Lallemand still regarded Meynestrel as not historically convincing, he decided to make no more changes, since he had promised Gallimard his manuscript by the same Spring (1936), and the changes Lallemand thought necessary would mean a delay of at least a year.[2] Once again his reply to Lallemand is revealing:

Comment voulez-vous que je renonce à faire de Meynestrel un type solitaire, capable de détruire des documents à l'insu de tous ses meilleurs camarades et collaborateurs? C'est tout le personnage!

Comment me tirer de cette contradiction? J'ai construit tout mon livre sur le pacifisme de Jacques; c'est ça qui le conduit jusqu'à ce raid ridicule où il trouve la mort, en voulant semer sur le front de bataille des tracts pacifistes, pour arrêter la tuerie . . .

Si Meynestrel était pacifiste, il serait historiquement faux. Et, si Jacques était d'accord avec Meynestrel, rien de ce que je lui fais faire et penser ne serait plus possible.

Je vois bien l'erreur initiale.

J'ai combiné tout mon livre sur cette idée fausse que les révolutionnaires de 14 étaient du type Jaurès, résistance coûte que coûte contre la guerre. J'avais conçu Meynestrel comme Jaurès. Puis, en cours de travail, mis en éveil par vous, par d'autres lectures, j'ai vu l'erreur. Alors j'ai fait de Meynestrel un cynique, qui désire la guerre parce qu'il y voit le début de la révolution. Ça m'a tout désaxé, déséquilibré mon œuvre. Et pourtant il le fallait bien. Et maintenant je n'arrive plus à en sortir. Tout reste boiteux. J'aurais peut-être mieux fait de persévérer dans mon erreur et de faire, du moins, une œuvre qui se tienne? . . .[3]

This difficulty with the character of Meynestrel arises, thinks Martin du Gard, out of a fundamental mistake made when he decided to change the plan:

Ce qui me frappe si fort, c'est que toutes vos critiques portent justement sur tous les points où je suis un incompétent, où je pensais avoir tant bien que mal camouflé mon incompétence. De sorte que je ne vois pas d'issue. Je traite un sujet auquel je n'entends rien, auquel je n'entendrai jamais rien, à moins de revivre une seconde vie dans la peau d'un révolutionnaire. *Cela n'est pas*

---

[1] Ibid., pp. 1140-1 (letter to Lallemand, 28/1/36).
[2] Ibid., p. 1142 (letter to Lallemand, 16/5/36).
[3] Ibid., pp. 1142-3 (letter to Lallemand, 16/5/36).

réparable. (..) J'avais commis la faute majeure, impardonnable: vouloir parler de ce qu'on ne sait pas . . . De ce qui ne s'apprend pas. Mon travail est vain; raté dès l'origine, dès le départ.[1]

Martin du Gard's comment about his new plan, in the *Souvenirs,* now seems something of an understatement: 'Un nouveau plan était greffé sur l'ancien tronc. Je n'avais plus qu'à le suivre, et à composer mes quatre derniers volumes . . .'[2]

Martin du Gard's problems all spring basically from his conception of what *Eté 1914* must be: Jacques faced with the prospect of a European war, doing his utmost to prevent it, and finally being destroyed by it. All others themes are subservient to this one, with its many implications.

The war, or rather the threat of war, itself becomes a protagonist, and the whole novel becomes an historical novel, since Jacques's fate is inextricably bound up with the outbreak of war. This immediately implies a considerable narrowing of scope, since narrative topics can no longer be selected freely. Martin du Gard has not only to show how the outbreak of war affects Jacques and Antoine, but also Jacques's actions as they affect the outbreak of war. Therefore Jacques cannot passively await events in Geneva, much less ignore their existence like Antoine; he has to rush all over Europe in vain attempts to avert the catastrophe. The effort is doomed, through historical necessity.

This marks a major difference between the historical method in *Barois* and *Eté 1914.* In the earlier novel he had availed himself liberally of documentary and historical sources, but the historical events narrated did not affect the essence of the plot. The course of the Dreyfus Case was common knowledge, and any reader naturally knew the outcome beforehand. But the core of the plot is Barois's struggle to achieve complete freedom of thought, to shake off the influences of his childhood; and his crusade in *Le Semeur* and involvement in the Dreyfus Case, are only a means of illustrating that struggle. The outcome of the case merely marks the high tide of his achievement; but this could have been represented by some other event, fictional or not, and it has no direct bearing upon Barois's later decline. In

[1] Ibid., p. 1142 (letter to Lallemand, 16/5/36).   [2] *Souvenirs,* p. xcvii.

Eté 1914, however, Martin du Gard has deliberately deprived himself of most of his means of creating suspense: the reader knows from the outset that Jacques's actions cannot make the slightest difference to the historical fact of the outbreak of war.

There is a further difference. In *Barois* research was comparatively simple: there were ample documentary sources for the whole of the historical section in contemporary newspapers. Although much of the Dreyfus affair was still controversial in 1910, there could be little disagreement about the evidence, say, in the Zola trial, which was fully reported in the Press. In *Eté 1914*, however, the research is into a complex question: the exact causes of the war; a question on which there was—and is—enormous disagreement, and on which professional historians had been working for years without a conclusive answer. Martin du Gard found it almost impossible to find out what really happened in any one episode:

Je cherche des renseignements sur ce qu'on a appelé la *Semaine rouge*, les grèves italiennes de juin 14. Les écrits de ceux qui y ont été mêlés sont un inextricable enchevêtrement d'allusions à des faits précis et d'élucubrations doctrinaires. Et les livres ou articles des défenseurs du capitalisme sont les seuls à exposer des faits, donner des bases précises. Mais comment croire qu'ils ne dissimulent pas une partie de la vérité? Entre ces deux sources, l'humble historien que je voudrais être s'arrache les cheveux![1]

Small wonder that he added the wry comment:

. . . j'étouffe (pourquoi ne pas l'avouer?) dans cette époque où il n'y a plus que des 'mystiques' métaphysiques, politiques ou sociales . . .[2]

In addition, he never held the Central Powers entirely responsible. As early as 1915, he had been one of the few Frenchmen to welcome *Au-dessus de la mêlée* (as reprinted in Massis's pamphlet: *Romain Rolland contre la France*[3]), and he wrote to Rolland as follows:

La première bouffée d'air pur, je puis bien dire la seule depuis un an, si j'excepte quelques lettres de très rares amis, me sera, encore une fois, venue

---

[1] *N.N.R.F.*, 12/58, p. 1149. G. Sneyers, (*Romanciers d'entre deux guerres*, Brussels, 1941, p. 185), has criticized Martin du Gard for having documented *Eté 1914* too exclusively from Left-wing journals such as *L'Humanité*, *La Bataille Syndicaliste*, and *La Guerre Sociale*.

[2] *N.N.R.F.*, 12/58, p. 1149 (letter to Lallemand, 19/2/36).

[3] H. Massis, *Romain Rolland contre la France*, Paris, 1915.

de vous . . . (. .) J'éprouve à vous l'écrire ainsi, sur-le-champ, sans réfléchir, une joie profonde: une joie d'autrefois![1]

This would seem to show that he was not so much engaging in objective research as seeking factual justification for his long-standing opinion, that the responsibility of the war was shared, to a greater or lesser degree, by all the major powers. Although Germany and Austria were more to blame, if the Allied governments had kept their heads war might have been avoided, and with it the shattering of European civilization. This view, if frequently advanced by historians, was bitterly disputed in nationalist circles in France, and Martin du Gard came in for some violent attacks after the publication of *Eté 1914*.[2]

This alone does not entirely explain his choice of plot in the later volumes. There can be little doubt that throughout the thirties—until war actually broke out—his political attitude was one of extreme pacifism, and he made this clear on several different occasions. Shortly after the outbreak of the Spanish Civil War in 1936, at the very time when the International Brigade was being formed, he was writing to Lallemand:

Suis dur comme fer *pour la neutralité*. Principe: tout, *plutôt que la guerre!* *Tout*, *tout!* Même le fascisme en Espagne! (. .) même le fascisme en France! *Tout:* Hitler, plutôt que la guerre![3]

This attitude directly influenced his choice of plot, as he freely admitted in his Nobel Prize speech at Stockholm. He remarked that possibly the Swedish Academy had awarded him the Prize for these qualities, and continued as follows:

. . . permettez-moi d'avouer, combien il me serait doux de penser que mon œuvre (. .) peut servir, non seulement la cause des lettres, mais encore la cause de la paix. Dans ces mois d'anxiété que nous vivons; alors que, déjà, le sang est répandu aux deux extrémités du globe; alors que, déjà, presque partout, dans un air vicié par la misère et le fanatisme, les passions fermentent, autour des canons braqués; alors que, déjà, trop d'indices nous révèlent le retour de ce lâche fatalisme, de ce consentement général qui, seul, permet les guerres; en ce moment exceptionellement grave que traverse l'humanité, je souhaite—sans vanité, mais de tout mon cœur rongé d'inquiétude—que mes livres sur

---

[1] Quoted in R. Rolland, *Journal des Années de Guerre*, Paris, 1952, p. 504.
[2] E.g. a polemical review of *Eté 1914* by Massis (*Revue Universelle*, 1/2/38, pp. 354–61).
[3] *N.N.R.F.*, 12/58, p. 1149 (letter to Lallemand, 19/2/36).

L'été 1914 soient lus, discutés, et qu'ils rappellent à tous, (aux anciens qui l'ont oubliée comme aux jeunes qui l'ignorent, ou la négligent), la pathétique leçon du passé.[1]

He could scarcely have been more explicit.

In view of this open admission of *engagement* we may well pause to consider his political standpoint. All his life he had had definite political beliefs of a Left-wing nature, but had held aloof from actual participation in politics. His Left-wing sympathies became more pronounced in the early thirties, but he did not follow Gide's example and join the Communist—or any other—party, partly, no doubt, because of his distaste for public life, and partly because of a deep-seated conviction that politics and art do not mix. In 1934 he wrote to Lallemand:

Pour l'instant, je suis l'homme qui tourne le dos. Je me répète que j'ai passé trente ans et plus à lutter contre les croyances et à me défaire de toute conviction passionnée . . . (. .) . . . prendre parti est une nécessité *de l'action*, mais nullement *de la pensée*, ni *de l'art*.[2]

His political actions went no further than, for instance, associating himself with Gide's idea of obtaining a chair for Einstein at the *Collège de France* in 1933, or than signing petitions for humane treatment of prisoners in the Spanish Civil War.[3] By 1936, any enthusiasm he had had for the U.S.S.R. was fast evaporating: 'Et vraiment le régime de l'U.R.S.S. me tente de moins en moins, après l'infâme procès de Moscou'.[4] Nor could he see much likelihood of Communist success in France:

Plus je vais et plus je me convaincs que le programme réel du P.C. est, à l'heure actuelle, et pour longtemps encore peut-être, inacceptable à la France, qui est foncièrement *bourgeoise*, du plus petit manœuvre au magnat des 200 familles . . .[5]

---

[1] Quoted in *Les Prix Nobel en 1937*, pp. 69–70. Immediately after the award of the Nobel Prize, Martin du Gard is reported as saying almost the same words in a press interview: 'J'ai surtout le secret espoir que le Prix Nobel contribuera à la diffusion de mes derniers volumes, cet *Eté 1914*, où j'ai tenté, selon mes moyens, de travailler pour la paix, en tirant example du passé, en ressuscitant les jours d'angoisse qui ont précédé la mobilisation, en montrant l'absurde inertie des masses pacifiques devant la menace de la guerre . . .' (quoted by Lucien Vermont in *Les Nouvelles Littéraires*, 20/11/37).

[2] *N.N.R.F.*, 12/58, p. 1146 (letter to Lallemand, 26/11/34).

[3] Cf. Gide, *Littérature engagée*, Paris, 1950.

[4] *N.N.R.F.*, 12/58, p. 1150 (letter to Lallemand, 9/9/36).

[5] Ibid., p. 1151 (letter to Lallemand, 8/4/37).

He also recognized the fundamental contradiction between Communism and individualism: Gide noted in his diary that Martin du Gard chaffed him about this.[1] Another letter to Lallemand clarifies this attitude: he feels in himself a profound *dédoublement* and his intellectual Left-wing beliefs are balanced by his bourgeois heredity.

> ... je crois que vous avez tout à fait raison de souligner ce que mon atavisme bourgeois a laissé d'éléments en moi ... (..) On ne change pas de peau ... (..) J'ai toute ma vie lutté contre ces éléments, et, à la fois, *composé avec.* Vieillissant, et devenu beaucoup plus indifférent et sceptique, je me retourne vers mon passé, je regarde cette vie qui n'a cessé d'osciller entre deux pôles, et je ne regrette rien. Plus équitable que jadis pour le poids de bourgeoisie que je traîne collé a ma peau, je crois pouvoir penser que c'est à ce poids que je dois, en grande partie, mon équilibre. Je veux dire un certain sens de la mesure, l'horreur des extrêmes et, si je dis toute ma pensée, une certaine disposition à la justice, une certaine aptitude à faire, toujours et en tout, la part de César et la part de Dieu ... Je me désole de moins en moins d'être tel, quand je vois, dans le monde contemporain, les dérèglements, les sottises, voire les crimes, dont s'accompagne presque toujours l'esprit partisan ...[2]

Later, writing *Epilogue*, his pacifist hopes had given way to a bitter irony. Indeed, in the depressing days of 1941, he appears to have given up all hope of reforming the world through political action:

> ... Plus je vais, plus je me persuade que c'est le bonheur qui compte, et qu'on ne l'atteint pas dans l'anormal ... (..) ... je n'ai plus le fétichisme de la Porte étroite et des Voies difficiles.[3]

We can now see more clearly what he was trying to do in *Eté 1914.* The idea of transforming the ultimate meaning of the novel, combining the personal tragedy with the destiny of the whole of Europe, has an immediate political objective: to prevent another war. Here again we may profitably make the comparison with *Barois.* In *Barois* there is no doubt where the author stands in relation to his theme: firmly on the side of free thought, in permanent opposition to religion; Martin du Gard himself did not hesitate to call his book a *roman à thèse.* But he

---

[1] Gide, *Journal 1889–1939*, p. 1293.
[2] *N.N.R.F.*, 12/58, p. 1152 (letter to Lallemand, 8/7/37).
[3] Ibid., p. 1155 (letter to Lallemand, 10/8/41).

carefully refrained from overtly loading the scales against the Church, and so achieved a considerable degree of objectivity. In *Eté 1914* he not only returned to the novel of ideas, but also neglected the lesson of balancing the two sides. *Eté 1914* is a *roman à thèse*, not in the same sense as *Barois*, but in the more serious sense that a large part of the novel is basically concerned with a *demonstration* of the thesis that the First War, and all the misery caused by it, were avoidable. Into that demonstration the earlier volumes in the *Thibault* series have to be dovetailed as best they can.

Since the narrative now has to conform to historical events, it can, to some extent, be called an historical novel. The historical technique followed is the normal one, and that of *Barois*. The fictional narrative is grafted on to actual historical events, either directly or indirectly, with occasional presentation of historical characters. But these characters always remain unimportant, in the context of the novel, and are subordinated to the fictional characters. Thus, in *Eté 1914*, the Sarajevo assassination is indirectly narrated (Chapter IX), while the Brussels Congress (Chapter LIII), demonstrations in Paris (Chapter XLVII), and, above all, the assassination of Jaurès (Chapter LXIII), are directly presented. The remaining events are fictional although conforming to actual dates and happenngs.

The chief need is to dramatize. Only by constant dramatization can *Eté 1914* gain anything of the same consistency as the earlier volumes, narrated largely in dramatic tableaux. The action is made to take place all over Europe: Jacques spends the six weeks before the war dashing from country to country, in intelligence missions for the Geneva revolutionaries. At the same time this is an attempt to lift the novel geographically on to the European plane, and it means the creation of large numbers of very minor characters. To enliven his material, Martin du Gard invents the character of Meynestrel, one of the most interesting in the whole series; yet Meynestrel as we know him owes a great deal to Lallemand; since the original conception of this character was very different. He also has to reintroduce the leading characters of the earlier volumes, an easier task. Jacques can easily be made to return to Paris, and be brought into contact with Antoine again; while Jérôme's death provides a *nœud d'événements* to link up with the Fontanin family. As we have seen, Jacques's affair with Jenny and Antoine's with Anne de Battaincourt was almost certainly taken over from the original plan. The events leading up to the war are exhaustively discussed by the various revolutionaries, whose sharpened awareness of political happenings makes them fully conscious of the issues involved; while the scenes in Paris, in Antoine's circle, show the effect of these same events on a selection of Frenchmen: Rumelles, Studler, Roy, Jousselin, Philip, and Antoine himself.

The most original episode is no doubt the *dénouement:* the suicidal flight above the lines in Alsace. But perhaps the most interesting invention is the Stolbach episode. Colonel Stolbach, of the Austrian General Staff, makes a special journey to Berlin to put the final touches to plans for co-operation between Prussia and Austria should war break out. Immediately before Stolbach's return to Vienna, his briefcase is stolen, and Jacques acts as a courier, bringing the stolen documents, proving Austro-Prussian collusion, back to the Socialist leaders in Belgium. But Meynestrel, under the emotional shock of Alfreda's departure to England with Paterson, destroys them, and with them the possibility of preventing the war by publishing them in the international Press. Since this episode is purely invented, it seriously weakens Martin du Gard's claim to historical accuracy, and renders him vulnerable to the charge of fabrication for propaganda purposes.

The episode, however, does have the merit of readability: it is naturally dramatic and is one of the highlights of the volume. Much of the material is less rewarding. The endless discussions of the revolutionaries are arid and fail to hold the attention. Despite Lallemand's advice, the scene at the *parlote* in Geneva (Chapter V) is not completely successful, and indeed throughout we have a sense of futility in all the different revolutionaries, which can only be dispelled by the further reflection that in 1914 Lenin was just such a man. The scenes of exposition tend to get out of hand: thus Jacques's exposition of the current international situation in Chapter XV is tedious, despite attempts to break up the mass of facts with colloquial speech.

At the same time, there are too many minor characters, who confuse the reader. Here of course there is the Tolstoyan model: but Martin du Gard is not Tolstoy, and finds himself in difficulties when he attempts to paint characters with whom he is not immediately familiar. We have already seen that, for example, Gregory is not nearly so convincing as Vécard: in *Eté 1914* some dozens of shadowy figures flit through the narrative, of whom only very few make any permanent impact. The group of revolutionaries in Geneva is best handled: Meynestrel, Paterson, and Alfreda play a large enough part in the plot to be adequately drawn and differentiated from the other characters; while Vanheede, the albino, so devoted to Jacques, also appears successful. But the others are more doubtful, and the confusion is only increased by the numbers of revolutionaries and Socialists, historical and fictional, whose names are mentioned but who are never actually introduced. Mithoerg, Charpentier, Monier, Boissonis, Guérin, Charchowsky, Zelawsky, Périnet, Saffrio, Skada, Quilleuf, Trauttenbach, Julian, Emilie Cartier, Richardley, the two Prezels . . . This is merely the list of the characters who take part in the *parlote;* and one may well wonder why Martin du Gard attached so much importance to this scene, with its only too apparent technical problems of differentiation and dramatization.

The reason for this scene can probably be glimpsed in another letter to Lallemand, commenting on the relationship of Jacques to the other revolutionaries:

Pour l'instant, ce que me rendrait le plus service, ce serait que vous m'écriviez (..) ce que vous entendez plus précisément quand vous parlez du 'point central', *l'angoisse de Jacques devant l'action révolutionnaire.* Je vois assez bien— esthétiquement—une sorte de méditation de Jacques au début de ce second volume (Chapter XXVI). Une méditation où, s'analysant, il se dirait: 'Jusqu'ici mon adhésion au parti révolutionnaire n'a été qu'un jeu, malgré tout. Un jeu intellectuel, auquel m'a poussé mon désespoir devant la misère de la condition faite aux hommes. Mais, depuis cette menace de guerre, il y a quelque chose de complètement changé en moi . . . '

Mais c'est là où moi, R.M.G., je ne vois plus clair. Les éléments, l'expérience *me manquent.* Pas de bases au travail de l'imagination. Vous dites: 'Jacques forcé par les événements . . . Agir les idées . . .' Je vois bien ce que vous voulez dire, mais trop confusément pour emboîter le pas. Vous dites: 'Jacques se trouve tout à coup *devant la Révolution.*' Non . . . C'est plus simple que cela. *Devant la menace d'une guerre* européenne, qui hérisse en lui son pacifisme naturel, son humanitarisme de jeune bourgeois tendre. Ça lui donne un but d'action: lutter contre la guerre, éviter l'hécatombe, à tout prix. Il y a du flou dans l'intelligence de Jacques. (..) C'est un intellectuel, par formation et par goût naturel. Et un fils de famille, quoi qu'il fasse! (..) Il ne peut pas devenir tout à coup semblable à un enfant du peuple, qui, par sa naissance même et sa jeunesse, s'est trouvé 'nourri' dès le berceau et n'a eu qu'à grandir parmi les siens. Il a une nature *révoltée*, mais compliquée et *incertaine* (à cause de la multiplicité de tendances, hérédités, éléments contradictoires, qui sont en lui). Capable d'*enthousiasme*, mais guère de foi. Perpétuel décalage en lui, flottement. Trop raisonneur, trop habitué à voir le pour et le contre de tout. Il est frère d'Antoine, par le sang! par son passé!

Ne pas faire de lui un personnage à la Jules Romains, aux contours nets, symbolisant une idée claire. C'est un refoulé. Énergique, courageux, mais hésitant toujours, par intelligence. Répugnant aux extrêmes. Se refusant à la violence. Etc.
Tout l'opposé d'un vrai révolutionnaire!

Si vous pouviez, en tenant compte de tout ça et de tout ce que vous savez de Jacques, me dire *comment vous imaginez* ce choc qu'il reçoit en juillet 14, lorsque, cessant d'être un sympathisant intellectuel, il est pris par le besoin d'agir *pour épargner à des millions d'innocents les massacres* des champs de bataille, —peut-être que je finirais moi-même par y voir plus clair . . .[1]

Several points arise out of this lengthy quotation. The central drama of the volume consists in Jacques's struggle against the threat of war: he, in fact, could be said to symbolize Martin du Gard's pacifist instincts. But at the same time he is no true revolutionary. As a Belgian critic has pointed out:

Jacques (..), au milieu de l'action collective reste un individualiste: l'action n'est pour lui qu'un moyen, non un but. Et c'est en quoi d'ailleurs il affirme les droits de l'esprit.[2]

Martin du Gard wishes to contrast Jacques's own reactions to the threat of war with those of a selection, on the one hand, of other revolutionaries, and, on the other hand, of ordinary people. The obvious way to achieve this contrast is by means of the group discussion, a technique used in *Barois* and even in *Devenir.* It is noteworthy that the chapter immediately preceding

---

[1] Ibid., pp. 1143–5 (letter to Lallemand, 19/5/36). A comparison may be drawn here with Malraux's similar analysis of revolutionary mentality in *Les Conquérants.*
[2] Sneyers, op. cit., p. 187.

the scene at the *parlote* is devoted to an analysis of the revolutionary mentality, in which Martin du Gard distinguishes between the *apôtres* and the *techniciens*. On the whole, Jacques is an *apôtre*, with his 'native sensibilité à l'injustice' (p. 33), an idealist, as opposed to the *techniciens*, the realists and practical politicians of revolution. The leaders of the movement, such as Meynestrel, combine both aspects; perhaps Jacques too, but he is handicapped by his bourgeois heredity. His individualist approach is emphasized, and we recognize Martin du Gard himself behind him. His description of Jacques:

Lui, il ne parvenait pas—bien qu'il fût, autant que ses camarades, persuadé que, dans le domaine de la civilisation, la bourgeoisie avait atteint le terme de sa mission historique—il ne parvenait pas à accepter la suppression systématique et radicale de cette culture bourgeoise dont il se sentait encore tout pénétré. (p. 35)

This identification is perhaps essential for Martin du Gard's aim of what we may as well call pacifist propaganda: only by giving Jacques some of his own feelings can he achieve adequate psychological profundity. But at the same time he does not forget that Jacques is a Thibault, and makes him, if not a leader, a confidant, with 'un manifeste ascendant moral' (p. 35) over the others. An interesting passage (p. 53) deals with Mussolini, at the time of course one of the leading Italian Socialists. Martin du Gard introduces this passage for ironic reasons, making use of his knowledge of post-war history, a technique we shall meet again in *Epilogue*. There is something of the same irony in the next passage, where Prezel indulges in a panegyric of the German Social Democrats, who would see to it that the Pangermanists would have no chance of plunging their country into a war.

Jacques's attitude to violence is brought out clearly in Chapter VIII, in his discussion with Mithoerg and Meynestrel. He sees in the concept of revolutionary violence an appeal to the baser instincts of man (p. 73), and he follows this up with the prophecy that when revolution eventually comes the revolutionaries themselves will institute their own tyranny: a thought perhaps inspired by the French Revolution, but more probably by Martin du Gard's own reflections on the aftermath of the Soviet revolution. Mithoerg is given a fanatical, Sorelian belief in the *mystique* of violence, and the contrast underlines one of the fundamental problems of revolutionary mentality: the difficulty for a man like Jacques, whose revolt arises out of his assertion of the rights of the individual against society, to reconcile his individuality with the need for submission to another absolute—the dictates of revolutionary action. Martin du Gard's position is clear, and Jacques is given the best of the argument:

Exalter la violence et la haine pour instaurer le règne de la justice et de la fraternité, c'est un non-sens: c'est trahir, dès le départ, cette justice et cette fraternité que nous voulons faire régner sur le monde! ... (..) ... la vraie révolution, la révolution qui mérite qu'on lui voue toutes ses forces, elle ne s'accomplira jamais dans le déni des valeurs morales! (p. 77)

Underlying the surface disagreement there is a strange psychological similarity: in both cases the ideas are more determined by psychological revolt against society than rationally, objectively worked out. Meynestrel does not take sides in this argument: Martin du Gard is carefully preparing the aura of mystery around him, and he contributes only a somewhat cryptic prophecy about the possibility of a complete regeneration of man (p. 78). But even in the case of Meynestrel, idealistic faith in the possibility of changing human nature is not strong enough to conquer his purely personal problems, as we shall see. The argument itself is only saved from becoming an actual quarrel, with Mithoerg hurling insults at Jacques: 'Un dilettante rationaliste! ... (..) un protestant! Tout à fait un protestant!' (p. 82)—by the news of the assassination at Sarajevo. The epithet of 'protestant' is interesting: both for its implications of freedom of thought—'le libre esprit d'examiner, le libre jugement de la conscience ...'—which Mithoerg appears to resent, and also for the contrast, within the fabric of the novel between Jacques or Antoine, with whom he shares this trait, with the actual Protestants—the Fontanins, Jérôme and Daniel, whose egoism is of the body, not of the mind.

These first nine chapters might be called the *exposition* of the volume: some eight pages are devoted to an analysis of the revolutionary mentality *before* the threat of war. The only link

with the earlier volumes lies in the presence of Jacques (and
Vanheede), and in brief allusions to past events, while the
narrative tempo has obviously been greatly reduced.

The next three chapters are taken up with an *exposé* of the
Austro-Slav political situation by Boehm, and the criticism may
fairly be levelled that they are tedious going; more so, than the
earlier chapters, which are of considerable interest as an examination of the revolutionary mentality. This psychological problem
is still of great relevance today, but the diplomatic nuances of
Sarajevo have at best only limited interest. Nevertheless, for the
future development of the plot, there is Meynestrel's elliptical
comment on the events at Sarajevo: 'Prématuré!'; the idea that
the world was not yet ripe for revolution:

La révolution ne peut sortir que d'une crise violente; la guerre est, dans
l'état présent de l'Europe, l'occasion la plus probable de cette crise . . . (p. 97)

This is, as we have seen, the expression of Lallemand's conception
of how Meynestrel ought to think and act, and from the brevity
of the concluding chapter of this section (XII)—a scene between
Meynestrel and Alfreda—we may surmise that it was inserted
after the rewriting of the *parlote* episode, in order to elucidate
Meynestrel's thought. He is made to think that the very idea of
the proletariat's being able to prevent the outbreak of war is absurd
(p. 105), but, for reasons of his own, keeps this belief to himself.

There follows a natural break in the narrative, and the scene
changes to Paris, one week later. The chapter heading reveals
its content: 'L'après-midi d'Anne de Battaincourt'. The tone is
one of ironic contrast between the impoverished revolutionaries
in Geneva and the idle *femme du monde* in Paris, and the fact
that the former are fully aware of the possibility of war while
Anne is completely ignorant of what now lies only a fortnight
ahead. The deeper implications concern Antoine, whose life
since his father's death has become completely worldly. The
hollowness of his life is symbolized by the description of his
waiting-room, with its formal, inhospitable furniture:

. . . rien n'était plus impersonnel que cette salle, fastueuse et nue. Antoine n'y
travaillait jamais: il ne s'en servait qu'aux jours de visite. Les murs étaient

cachés à mi-hauteur par des bibliothèques, dont on devinait les rayons vides derrière les vitres voilées de soie chinoise. Au centre, trônait un bureau d'apparat où, sur la surface inhospitalière d'une glace sans tain, s'alignait une garniture en maroquin,—classeur, sous-main, tampon-buvard, chiffrés d'un monogramme. Pas un dossier, pas une lettre, pas d'autre livre qu'un *Annuaire des Téléphones*. Dressé comme un bibelot près de l'encrier de cristal vierge d'encre, un stéthoscope d'ébonite évoquait seul la profession du propriétaire; encore cet accessoire ne semblait-il pas avoir été placé là par Antoine, pour un usage médical mais par la main anonyme d'un décorateur, soucieux de pittoresque. (p. 109)

Passages such as this, where the contrast is implicit, are perhaps just as effective as those where the comparison is made openly, as in Chapter XXV, where Anne makes Antoine drive her to a restaurant forty-five kilometres from Paris, for a caprice, and then has a scene with the waiter for not having brought her Pekinese exactly what she orders.

Antoine's relationship with Anne is confidently handled, and is closer to the tone of the earlier volumes than most of *Eté 1914*. Presumably this relationship was taken over from the original plan. The episode fits in well with Antoine's development, and provides an antithesis to his love for Rachel. In the present volume it is equally an antithesis to Jacques's relationship with Jenny: both, in different ways, are finally ended by the war. Anne symbolizes utter social uselessness, with distinctly unpleasant overtones (her deliberate neglect of her invalid daughter, or her relationship with Goupillot, whom she had not murdered, as scandalous gossip believed, but had robbed, in case his will should not be made in her favour). Nevertheless, the portrait of her is not unsympathetic; the reader is not automatically made to feel hostile towards her, and can fully understand her attraction for Antoine, especially in his frame of mind before the threat of war becomes serious. The description of her affair with Antoine adds to the general picture of sexuality in the novel series as a whole; she represents not so much the amoral, completely free woman, like Rachel, but the empty-headed socialite who is a complete slave to sensual pleasure. An aura of voluptuousness surrounds her every action, even when buying provisions (p. 112). Still, the affair does no credit to Antoine, who knows perfectly well the character of his mistress, her drug addiction, and her Lesbianism. The relationship is based on a mutual egoism: Antoine refuses to go further than a 'compagnonnage amoureux' (p. 218), although he could, if he wished, influence Anne into turning her energies into something more socially useful. Later, in Chapter LVII, he decides to break with Anne, and this itself is a symbol of his desire to return to a fully realistic life. The break itself is most effectively motivated by Simon de Battaincourt's visit, which gives Antoine a more profound insight into Simon's character, which previously he had only known superficially, or distortedly through Anne's eyes. This episode is a good example of the technique of indirect presentation of character, so that the total portrait is a composite one. The break with Anne is directly connected with the purifying effect of the threat of war, and later in the novel the point is driven further home: Antoine's situation is made typical of what is happening throughout Europe:

Il croyait son cas particulier. Il ne se doutait pas qu'il avait obéi à un phénomène très général. Le frisson qui secouait l'Europe ébranlait les vies privées; de toutes parts, entre les êtres, les liens factices se desserraient, se rompaient d'eux-mêmes; le vent précurseur qui passait sur le monde faisait tomber des branches les fruits véreux. (p. 570)

Here however the effect is less powerful: in order to make the individual case symbolical of all Europe—a general aim in *Eté 1914*—Martin du Gard is obliged to be too explicit, and the moralizing generalization is too obvious, couched as it is in a semi-biblical cliché: *les fruits véreux*. He is on more plausible ground when he makes Antoine go back to Anne, for one last embrace, on the eve of mobilization.

Antoine's rôle in *Eté 1914* is essentially passive. In the three previous volumes he was in the foreground, but now, with Jacques in the active rôle, he is shown as the average man, aware of the threat of war too late, and swept away passively by the flood of events. The contrast with Jacques is obvious. One consequence is that there is a steady development in Antoine, in keeping with his character throughout the series, his portrayal as if in a *Bildungsroman:* from the *Pénitencier* onwards he is forced, by events, out of his natural egoism into greater awareness of the different problems of life. Previously he has taken little interest in politics, and at first even now resists Jacques's attempts to enlighten him. But gradually he becomes involved, in spite of himself, and is transformed from the rich bourgeois, 'Tony', with his *garçonnière* and expensive mistress, his manservant, 'le cœur pur de toute haine de classe' (p. 110), and his team of assistants, into a drafted soldier compelled back into the fold of common humanity. The contrast with Jacques is extended. Although, in *La Belle Saison*, it had been Antoine who sneered at his father's adoption of the name Oscar-Thibault, and Jacques who had defended him, Antoine himself now has a plaque outside the house: *Laboratoires A. Oscar-Thibault* (p. 117). The new installation of the former Thibault home is extensively described, with Antoine's underlying thought: 'consacrer sa fortune à accélérer son ascension professionnelle' (p. 120). The irony is sharpened by Jacques's unvoiced opinion after Antoine has shown him round with naïve pride: 'Un gosse de riche, qui montre ses joujoux' (p. 121). Later reflections turn from irony into bitterness, and Jacques directly attacks his brother's luxury:

La vanité de Père . . . La vanité aristocratique du bourgeois! . . . Quelle race! . . . On dirait, ma parole, qu'ils prennent pour une supériorité, non seulement leur fortune, mais leur habitude de bien vivre, leur goût du confort, de la 'qualité'! Ça devient pour eux un mérite personnel! Un mérite qui leur crée des droits sociaux! Et ils trouvent parfaitement légitime cette 'considération' dont ils jouissent! Légitimes, leur autorité, l'asservissement d'autrui! Oui, ils trouvent tout naturel de 'posséder'! Et ils trouvent tout naturel que ce qu'ils possèdent soit inattaquable, protégé par les lois contre la convoitise de ceux qui n'ont rien! Généreux, oh! sans doute! Tant que cette générosité est un luxe de plus: une générosité qui fait partie des dépenses superflues . . . (p. 123)

This time the irony turns against the younger brother, who, despite the mental tirade above, cannot resist a faint tinge of envy when he sees Antoine's luxurious bathroom and compares it with his own miserable hotel room.

Antoine's basic attitude to politics is one of indifference, and, to his own thinking one of independence. His beliefs are outlined in a fine analytical passage:

Il n'avait jamais eu le temps de s'intéresser à la politique; ni l'envie. La discipline scientifique l'avait habitué à penser que, dans le monde social, comme dans celui de la vie organique, tout est problème, et problème difficile; que, dans tous les domaines, la recherche de la vérité exige l'application, l'étude, la compétence. Il considérait donc la politique comme le champ d'une activité étrangère à la sienne. A cette réserve raisonnée, s'ajoutait une naturelle répugnance. Trop de scandales, d'un bout à l'autre de l'histoire des Etats, l'avaient persuadé qu'une sorte d'immoralité suintait naturellement de l'exercice du pouvoir, ou, du moins, qu'une certaine rigueur d'honnêteté, qu'il avait coutume, lui, médecin, de tenir pour primordiale, n'était pas de règle, n'était peut-être pas aussi nécessaire, sur le terrain de la politique. Aussi suivait-il avec une indifférence méfiante la marche des affaires publiques; sans plus de passion qu'il n'en apportait à voir fonctionner le service des Postes ou des Ponts et Chaussées. Et si, dans une conversation de fumoir . . . (..) . . . il lui arrivait, comme à tout le monde, de risquer un jugement sur les actes d'un ministre en place, c'était toujours d'un point de vue précis, terre à terre, volontairement simpliste: à la manière d'un voyageur d'autobus qui, pour louer ou critiquer le chauffeur, s'inquiète uniquement de la façon dont celui-ci manie le volant. (p. 128)

These ideas may be based on Martin du Gard's own distaste for active politics, at least before the thirties, but Antoine himself is gradually forced into involvement, which reaches its height in *Epilogue*.

We have already commented on the over-long exposition by Jacques to his brother, repeating in fact much of what Boehm had already said, at equal length, in Chapters X and XI. However, this conversation does act as a means to recall Gise, Mlle de Waize, and other minor characters, and to introduce Jérôme's attempt at suicide. By this means the Fontanin family are brought back into the narrative: an object which might otherwise have been difficult to achieve.

After this episode, Antoine drops out for the most part. In Chapter XXXV, there is a rather contrived group scene, where Jacques has lunch with Antoine and his assistants, Studler, Jousselin and Roy, a simple means of describing different reactions to political events. Roy takes the Nationalist view: as Antoine comments, he is a faithful *Action Française* reader (recalling Tillet and Grenneville in *Barois*). Jousselin takes a middle view, but says very little, since he represents very much the same position as Antoine; while Studler, a Jew, has ideas fairly close to those of Jacques. A similar technique is employed in Chapter XL, where Thérivier and Philip are also brought into the discussion. Studler and Roy amplify their previous arguments, and in the character of Roy, who is not unsympathetically handled, space is given to the opposing view. The attempt can scarcely be said to be successful. Not only are numbers against Roy, but Studler, with whom he is arguing, outweighs him without any help from Jacques. This particular scene is more important for the appearance of Philip, who becomes what one might call a father figure, against whose wisdom the other characters can be judged, rather like Luce in *Barois* (although Philip is much more convincingly portrayed). He is no idealist, like Luce, but a thoroughgoing sceptic, almost a cynic, and it is certainly in his words that Martin du Gard expresses his own thoughts most clearly:

. . . le comique, c'est que, parmi tous les vrais, les urgents problèmes qui se posent actuellement en Europe, et dont la solution exigerait de patientes études, je n'en vois pas un, pas un seul, qu'on puisse espérer trancher, à la manière du nœud gordien, par une guerre . . . (. .)

Vue avec quelque recul, il n'y a pas une guerre moderne qui n'aurait pu être évitée, semble-t-il, très aisément: par le simple bon sens et la volonté pacifique de deux ou trois hommes d'Etat . . . (pp. 343-4)

Philip makes a good contrast with Rumelles, the politician, who is useful technically, since he can give confidential information about the progress of events and the real opinions of the French Government, as opposed to its public statements. But since Rumelles is entirely fictional, historical veracity is again weakened.

Antoine's further appearances are rare, and subject to the needs of the plot. There is another chapter (XLI), with Rumelles, then another scene where Antoine goes to the *Quai d'Orsay* to give Rumelles his injection, a device permitting a glimpse of the general anxiety and panic prevailing there, together with some more confidential information. There follows the scene with Simon de Battaincourt; and there is another lunch with Jacques and the assistants, during which Antoine fully realizes the implications of war for the first time:

Le moral, cette fois, était sérieusement touché. La tourmente faisait chanceler les bases sur lesquelles il avait précisément construit sa vie: la science, la raison. Il découvrait soudain l'impuissance de l'esprit et, devant tant d'instincts déchaînés, l'inutilité des vertus sur lesquelles son existence laborieuse s'appuyait depuis toujours: la mesure, le bon sens, la sagesse et l'expérience, la volonté de justice . . . (p. 516)

Here again the discussion tends towards tedium, and Studler's analysis of the situation surely owes much to *post-war* beliefs when he says that 'nous avons tous *besoin* de croire que l'Allemagne est coupable . . .' (p. 524). This is where Martin du Gard puts into Jacques's mouth the same words as in the letter to Lallemand: 'Tout, tout,—plutôt que la guerre' (p. 525). He is an absolute pacifist first, and only then a Socialist: '. . . je ne vois rien—exactement *rien*!—qui puisse être pire, pour un peuple, que la guerre!' (p. 526). The episode develops into a confrontation of attitudes towards mobilization: Antoine would obey the call, but Jacques would do anything rather than join up. The question here is the social one of conscientious objection (the principle of conscientious objection has never been accepted in France). Antoine hits at one of his brother's main weaknesses: he is unlikely to prevent the war before it begins, but once it has started and is moving with its own momentum, he has even less chance of influencing events.

There is one more group scene, where both Jenny and Philip join Antoine and his team; this is notable for Philip's pronouncement, *ex cathedra* as it were, about the three most important events of his life:

J'aurai eu trois sombres dates dans mon existence . . . (..) La première a revolutionné mon adolescence; la seconde a bouleversé mon âge mûr; la troisième empoisonnera sans doute ma vieillesse . . . (..)

La première, c'est quand l'enfant provincial et pieux que j'étais, a découvert, une nuit, en lisant à la file les quatres Evangiles, que c'était un tissu de contradictions . . . La seconde, c'est quand je me suis convaincu qu'un vilain monsieur, qui s'appelait Esterhazy, avait fait une saloperie, qui s'appelait 'le bordereau', et que, au lieu de le condamner, on s'acharnait à torturer à sa place un monsieur qui n'avait rien fait, mais qui était Juif . . . (..)

La troisième, c'est il y a huit jours, quand les journaux ont donné le texte de l'ultimatum, quand j'ai vu dessiner la partie de billard . . . Quand j'ai compris que c'étaient les peuples qui allaient faire les frais du carambolage . . . (pp. 596–7)

This passage, justly famous, can reasonably be taken as representing Martin du Gard's own views, not, indeed, of the events which had most influenced his own life—he is at least thirty years younger than Philip—but of the events which had most profoundly affected the whole climate of European civilization in his epoch. He had tried to deal with the first in *L'Une de nous*, had successfully treated the first two in *Barois*, and is at present attempting the third. (It is a measure of his artistic ambition that he chose as subject matter these three crucial topics.) Philip goes on to prophesy the destruction of civilization as he knows it; the future may belong to men like Jacques, despite the irrational and emotional origin of their beliefs:

Toute mystique est légitime . . . (. .) . . . légitime, et peut-être nécessaire. (. .) A la base de toutes les grandes modifications sociales, il a toujours fallu quelque aspiration religeuse vers l'absurde. L'intelligence me mène qu'à l'inaction. C'est la foi qui donne à l'homme l'élan qu'il faut pour agir, et l'entêtement qu'il faut pour persévérer. (. .)

Peut-être que ceux qui pensent comme votre frère sont des précurseurs ? Peut-être que cette guerre fatale, en déséquilibrant à fond notre vieux continent, prépare une floraison de pseudo-vérités nouvelles, que nous ne soupçonnons pas ? . . . (. .) C'est un phénomène sans précédent. Les conséquences son imprévisibles . . . Qui sait ? Tous les élements de la civilisation vont peut-être se trouver refondus, dans ce brasier ! (p. 598)

Although Martin du Gard here is showing perhaps a deeper understanding of the true significance of the war than many of his fellow-Europeans, there can be no doubt that once again he is using hindsight, attributing opinions to Philip which were only commonly current after the war, not before it. This brings us to a basic confusion in the novel. At one moment he is trying to reconstruct the events of 1914, and their immediate effects; at another he is attempting an analysis of those same events in the light of the war itself and its aftermath; behind this there stands the aim of preventing a further war by means of one or both of these methods; and throughout he is doing his best to weld the entire narrative on to the earlier volumes by reintroducing minor characters such as Chasle and Gise.

Jérôme's suicide is on the more simple level of straightforward psychological narrative. This episode is deliberately melodra-

matic, and evidently Martin du Gard had a weakness for this
type of episode, which recalls his original plan, where Jean-Paul
was to become involved in a murder. It provides an opportunity
for another description of an operation, as well as reintroducing
the theme of Death, if in a distinctly perfunctory manner. The
effect on Mme de Fontanin is more important, and there is an
excellent passage of psychological description (p. 191) when
she looks at her dead husband, as handsome in death as he was
in youth. His life was a lie—'un mensonge amusé, insouciant,
incorrigible'—but the true pathos of the situation is in the
stunting of her natural instincts caused by her marriage to this
worthless charmer:

Jérôme . . . Tout ce que sa vie de femme avait connue de l'amour était là, sur
ce lit . . . Elle qui s'était dit, depuis tant d'années déjà, que sa vie amoureuse
était révolue! Voici qu'elle comprenait soudain qu'elle n'avait jamais cessé
d'espérer . . . C'était maintenant, c'était seulement cette nuit, que tout allait
être fini, à jamais. (p. 191)

And her thoughts, despite herself, slip back to the last time
Jérôme had made love to her, at Maisons, after his return from
Amsterdam. In one important respect, however, she is fortunate,
since she has a powerful and effective religious belief. She is
therefore spared one of the main terrors of the materialist human
condition: fear of death, and her final state of mind, that of
'renoncement et résignation', is described sincerely and without
irony. Thus she is largely redeemed from the apparent tragedy
of her situation; indeed, in *Epilogue*, as matron of a hospital,
she draws new strength from her widowhood and the war, and
is one of the few characters who survive successfully the totality
of events.

Daniel makes only very brief appearances. This is probably
to simplify the narrative; since he was in any case doing his
military service in *La Mort du Père* he can easily be kept out of
the way, and in fact only comes briefly on leave at the time of
his father's death. He is chiefly important in relation to Jacques,
whom he is now meeting for the first time for four years. The
old relationship has almost completely disintegrated, and Daniel
is unable to make any real contact. This is an important scene,

which emphasizes one facet of Jacques's character: he has now no friends, only comrades, since he has deliberately cut himself off from his former friends. Ultimately he suffers from solitude just as much as Antoine, who regrets in *Epilogue* that he has never had any real friends, only acquaintances. The theme of isolation recurs when Jacques visits Daniel's studio (Chapter XXXI). Daniel states that the worst thing he feels about his father is that 'Il est mort sans que nous ayons jamais eu ensemble le moindre abandon, le moindre échange' (p. 271). Yet this is by no means entirely Jérôme's fault, partly because Daniel shares many of his weaknesses, and partly because he has built his life on a deliberate self-isolation, plunging himself into art as a means of escaping the common misery of mankind: 'plus que jamais, il se sentait attaché à ce merveilleux refuge où il avait eu le privilège de pouvoir installer sa vie' (p. 276). By an ironical twist Jacques and Daniel each think that the other has missed his real vocation, distorted his true destiny, by not having developed in the way that he himself has developed. Daniel thinks that Jacques has 'trahi sa mission naturelle' (p. 276) in abandoning his writing for political action; Jacques, that Daniel has divorced himself from reality for his own pleasure: '. . . quand une fois on a pris contact avec la misère universelle, alors, mener la vie d'un artiste, non, ça n'est plus, absolument plus, possible . . .' (p. 276). Since each of the two is funda- mentally determined by his particular combination of heredity and environment, the egoistic gap between them is unbridgeable.

Daniel's isolation is brought out in the scene where he is alone with his mother, in Chapter XXXIII. Again no real contact is possible between them, even with the heightened emotional stress of Jérôme's funeral. Mme de Fontanin's sadness is tinged with egoism:

Sans qu'elle se l'avouât, la disparition de Jérôme éclaircissait l'horizon. Dorénavant, elle serait seule et libre, entre ses deux enfants . . . (p. 286)

(In this passage we see an ironic reflection of Jérôme's own feelings after the death of Noémie, in *La Belle Saison*.) She finds herself forced to defend her husband from her son's accusations out of loyalty, and the result is similar to that in Daniel's meeting with Jacques.

One of the key themes of the volume is the relationship between Jacques and Jenny, and it is one of the least satisfying. In *La Belle Saison* the developing relationship was outlined with considerable subtlety, but Jenny was rather colourless, probably because of her introverted nature, rendering an adequate portrayal difficult. The episode of Jérôme's death renews the relationship, which ripens into a love affair. The threat of war acts as a catalyst, bringing the relationship to fruition almost immediately, just as it ends that of Antoine and Anne. There is something basically implausible here: it is reasonable enough that the threat of war should heighten emotional and sexual tensions, but not to the extent of making Jacques, in the midst of his frenzied efforts to prevent the war, wish to unite himself and Jenny permanently in marriage. However, implausible or not, the whole theme has to be taken at face value. To some extent, Martin du Gard avoids the imputation of implausibility by allowing Antoine to criticize his brother, and it seems certain that Antoine's words echo his own ideas:

Laisse-moi dire la vérité: tu es foncièrement inapte à faire le bonheur d'un autre être . . . Foncièrement! Donc, même en d'autres circonstances, jamais tu n'aurais pu rendre Jenny heureuse. Et, en aucun cas, tu n'aurais dû . . . (. .)
En aucun cas! Mais, en ce moment, moins que jamais! . . . La guerre . . . Et avec tes idées! . . . Qu'est-ce que tu vas faire, qu'est-ce que tu vas devenir? C'est l'inconnu. Un inconnu terrible! . . . Libre à toi de courir tes risques. Mais lier un autre être à ta destinée, en un moment pareil? C'est monstrueux . . . (pp. 601–2)

Mme Magny has made the point that Jacques and Jenny could in any case never have been happy together if they had survived the war and married;[1] although this type of conjecture is to some extent academic, in this case it seems perfectly true. Jacques's revolt against his family and society is fundamental to his whole character, and for him to settle down into a happy marriage would strain the bounds of credulity still more. Jenny represents, for Jacques, an ideal, to be equated with the ideal

[1] Magny, op. cit., p. 339.

society which he hopes will replace the decaying capitalist world:

Pour cet amour, qui engageait toute sa vie, il avait plus que jamais besoin d'un monde nouveau, de justice et de pureté. (p. 325)

There is an intense irony in the disproportion between the ideal nature of this love, in theory, and the practice of it: Jenny trailing round Paris with Jacques, dazed, almost hypnotized, from one futile meeting to another. And at the same time there is something naïve about the entire episode. Mme de Fontanin is made to go to Vienna, rather implausibly, to attempt to disentangle Jérôme's affairs; her absence is necessary for the affair between Jacques and Jenny to develop. Jacques spends most of his visit to Jenny explaining Socialism to her, since she has absolutely no idea of his new way of life; the reader can hardly forbear to smile on seeing passages like this:

Elle avait soudain conscience—et elle en était confuse—d'avoir atteint sa vingtième année sans rien savoir du labeur et de la misère du monde. Entre la masse des travailleurs et elle, jeune bourgeoise de 1914, les cloisons de classes étaient aussi étanches que celles qui séparaient les castes de la civilisation antique . . . 'Tous les riches que je connais ne sont pourtant pas des monstres,' se dit-elle, naïvement. Elle pensait à ces œuvres protestantes auxquelles participait sa mère, et qui 'faisaient la charité' à des familles nécessiteuses . . . Elle se sentit rougir de confusion. La charité! Elle comprenait maintenant que ces miséreux, qui sollicitaient une aumône, n'avaient rien de commun avec les travailleurs exploités, qui revendiquaient le droit de vivre, et leur indépendance, et leur 'dignité'. Ces miséreux-là n'étaient pas le peuple, comme elle l'avaient cru sottement; ils n'étaient que les parasites du monde bourgeois; presque aussi étrangers du monde ouvrier évoqué par Jacques, que ces dames patronnesses qui les visitaient! Jacques venait de lui révéler le prolétariat. (p. 371)

Although this passage is in *style indirect libre*, presumably to represent Jenny's own thoughts as much as the narrator's analysis, it cannot escape the charge of ingenuousness. And behind it there lies a deeper fallacy, that of making the characters too conscious of the final significance of events. Only by their being fully aware of events can the drama of the situation be brought out; yet in actual fact few people had any idea of the possibility of a war until it was upon them, and it appears that Martin du Gard himself was not one of those few.

This fallacy is closely bound up with the technique of the double level, which, as we have seen, stands at the very basis of *Eté 1914:* the fusion of the destinies of the individual characters with that of the whole of Europe. We can now see more clearly why Martin du Gard was so dissatisfied with the volume even before it was published, and why he wished to return to 'des œuvres plus purement psychologiques'. Indeed, those episodes of *Eté 1914* which are on a simple psychological plane are on the whole the most effective: the scene where Jacques and Jenny for the first time make love is both much more sensitive and much more convincing than, say, the scene at the Montrouge meeting.

Another important element in the volume, consciously or not, is the desire to exhibit technical skill, the *tour de force*, which has already found expression in *La Consultation*, with its limited narrative *durée*, and the use of Jacques's *nouvelle* in *La Sorellina*. Several examples can be identified in *Eté 1914*. There is something of the detective novel, or rather the novel of violence, possibly influenced by American models, in Jérôme's death and the Stolbach episode, and in the description of the assassination of Jaurès. This last scene is not essential for the development of the plot; but naturally it is dramatic for its own sake, and it is also a *tour de force*,—of historical reconstruction from various contemporary newspaper reports.

The best example is the account of Jacques's death with the retreating French troops in Alsace. This is an exercise in irony, and is largely written in a different style from the rest of the volume. (It is typical of Martin du Gard's attitude that the one war scene extensively treated should be one of retreat, of defeat, and not of victory.) Now it is Jacques who has cut himself off from reality, carried away by the mystical dream of stopping the war by dropping pamphlets over the front line. The narrative becomes almost a 'stream of consciousness' technique, in the present tense, which is especially suited for the effect desired —the semblance of delirium. Already, in the chapters before the flight, while Jacques waits at Basle, the descriptions give a sense of his not being entirely lucid: 'Son obsession le ronge . . .';

'... comme un intoxiqué à sa drogue ...'; '... son regard d'ensorcelé ...'; 'ce travail fiévreux' (pp. 703-4). He intends a complete abandonment of his ego to his mystical aim, a complete abnegation of self. His death is, therefore, suicide; and a further passage makes it clear that it is intended as a gesture, which is still worth while if it achieves nothing. Only by such an action can Jacques resolve the contradictions of his nature and attain true peace of mind. Clearly at this point Jacques is not entirely sane. This is only one more confusion in the general aim of the volume: both Jacques and Meynestrel act for decidedly personal reasons, their deaths are not historically inevitable. Because of this, the tragic effect is weakened, and the aim of preventing another world war has nothing to do with the manner of Jacques's death. It is probable that this part of the plot belongs to Martin du Gard's original plan; Jacques's death is another important aspect of the theme of death, and fills out the psychological picture of his life, without needing to have any connexion with the general European situation. This seems, at any rate, to be the explanation of such passages as these, written in a mixture of *style indirect libre* and interior monologue:

Par quels chemins, quels détours, la destinée a-t-elle conduit jusqu'à ce dernier soir l'enfant de jadis? Suite de hasards? Non. Certes, non! ... Tous ses actes se tiennent. Cela, il le sent, il l'a toujours confusément senti. Son existence n'a été qu'une longue et spasmodique soumission à une orientation mystérieuse, à un enchaînement fatal. Et maintenant, c'est l'aboutissement, l'apothéose. Sa mort resplendit devant lui, semblable à ce coucher de soleil glorieux. Il a dépassé la peur. Il obéit à l'appel, sans vaine crânerie, avec une tristesse résolue, enivrante, tonique. Cette mort consciente est bien l'achèvement de cette vie. Elle est la condition de ce dernier geste de fidélité à soi-même ... de fidélité à l'instinct de révolte ... Depuis son enfance, il dit: non! Il n'a jamais eu d'autre façon de s'affirmer. Pas: non à la vie ... Non au monde! ... Eh bien, voici son dernier refus, son dernier: Non! à ce que les hommes ont fait de la vie ...
(p. 717)

The final irony of the last chapter must be viewed in the light of this decision of Jacques to sacrifice himself in one ultimate heroic gesture. The irony is thereby redoubled. There is nothing heroic about the eventual manner of his death: (Martin du Gard has himself declared that Jacques 'a vécu et est mort comme un imbécile . . .'[1]). Not only have all his efforts to prevent the war come to nothing, the last desperate venture above the lines ends in disaster before he has had time to drop a single leaflet. He is badly hurt, cannot speak, is suspected of being a spy, and is finally shot in the French retreat, too much of a burden to the men in whose hands he has fallen, and dies a miserable death to the echo of the shout 'Fumier! Fumier!'. The gesture is completely wasted, a futile flourish of egoism which stands no chance of resisting the egoism of the retreating troops. And in his dying moments it ceases to matter even to himself: 'Mais il souffre trop; rien d'autre ne compte . . .' (p. 733). The key word in connexion with Jacques is *absurde:* an epithet frequently applied to him, usually by Antoine. This is not so developed a concept as the *absurde* of Camus (or Kafka), although it tends in the same direction. It essentially is utter pointlessness, the hopeless disproportion between aim and result which we see here, and is a necessary element in Martin du Gard's tragic conception of life. For the absolute materialist, everything is ultimately pointless, since life comes to an end with death; and this is expressed by bitter irony. The pointless end of Jacques' life is symbolical of the pointless end of the pre-1914 era.

The last chapter is almost entirely written in the same mixture of interior monologue and *style indirect libre*, with continual extracts of conversation presumably audible to Jacques as he lies on his stretcher. Through the whole texture of this narrative the reader is given a fragmentary picture of the French retreat, confused and incoherent as it is. This is another technical *tour de force:* the combination of a battle description, in the tradition of Stendhal's Waterloo (from which Tolstoy's battle-scenes also derive), with Jacques's dying delirium, to extract every ounce of bitter irony from the total situation.

In *Eté 1914* Martin du Gard's style has reached its full maturity; the aim is still that of transparency, but he is able to make free use of different methods. Stream of consciousness technique has been added to interior monologue; *style indirect libre* is used with supple mastery. (There is one excellent example of this

---

[1] *N.N.R.F.*, 12/58, p. 1145 (letter to Lallemand, 1/2/45).

(p. 141), where Antoine's reactions to Jacques's political analysis betray their unconscious origin by the use of the Maurrasian word *métèque*.) Once again there is an example of affective memory, leading to introspective insight, when Jenny is in the lumber-room (pp. 264-5); Martin du Gard deliberately makes this scene recall the parallel scene in *Le Cahier gris* when Mme de Fontanin had a closely similar experience. The *trouvaille*, the significant detail, is no less in evidence; notable examples are Antoine's recognition of his father's forced laugh in his own throat (p. 222); the image of the telephone as a dead snake (p. 534); his first realization of the full meaning of mobilization, when his trunk scratches the paint on the door (p. 633). (There is also one of the author's rare slips; whereas Mlle de Waize is 78 in *La Mort du Pére* (p. 1354), she is now only 68 (p. 150).)

Yet despite this evidence of technical ability *Eté 1914* is not a complete success; it is often considered the weakest section of the *Thibault* series. Since, as we have seen, Martin du Gard himself was aware of its faults even before publication,[1] this is not altogether surprising; he must, indeed, have been somewhat astonished at receiving the Nobel Prize in 1937.[2]

The reasons for this comparative failure are complex. He was, as we have seen, striving to achieve several different objects, some of which were probably incompatible. The essay at accurate historical reconstruction is unsuccessful, not so much because his sources were biased, as because he inserted purely imaginary scenes, such as the Stolbach episode, which distort the presentation of the actual historical events. Whether, in any case, such a reconstruction belongs to the novel genre, may be regarded as doubtful. The attempt to use *Eté 1914* for propa-

---

[1] C . Note 17 above.

[2] Maurice Martin du Gard (op. cit., pp. 464-5) rather maliciously suggests that Valéry was a candidate for the Nobel Prize in 1937, but his works had unfortunately not been translated into Swedish. Thereupon Gide was unofficially asked to make a recommendation; unable to recommend himself, he put forward Martin du Gard's name, fully expecting—and hoping—that it would be turned down on the grounds that he himself was much more distinguished than Martin du Gard. This would then open the way to his own nomination. The story is no doubt apocryphal; and is another example of the spite which the award of the Nobel Prize to a French writer seems inevitably to arouse among his colleagues (cf. the cases of Prudhomme, Rolland, and Camus).

ganda purposes, for this is what it amounts to, was not only
lamentably misguided, on the political plane, but also, on the
artistic one, exceedingly naïve. In depicting the chain of events
leading to the 1914 War he is trying to convice his readers,
rationally, of the horror and pointlessness of that war; yet
precisely those readers open to influence on a rational level
would scarcely be restricted to reading novels in their search for
evidence; works of historical scholarship presenting more or
less the same case as Martin du Gard's had been in circulation
for over a decade (and had he himself not drawn on them?).
But, in any case, to convince readers of the horrors of war is
primarily a task on the emotional plane, and one which had
been admirably carried out, years before, by Barbusse or
Dorgelès, to mention only two French writers. Although Martin
du Gard wished to break new ground, it remains undeniable
that the emotional effect of *Eté 1914* is pale in comparison with
Le Feu or *Les Croix de Bois*.

More important is his inability to achieve the synthesis of
experience he wished to communicate. *Eté 1914* is too much a
roman à thèse; another Belgian critic has put the point succinctly:

Un roman à thèse est toujours un mauvais roman si la thèse n'y demeure pas
implicite, si elle s'étale et se développe en théories au lieu d'émaner simplement
du drame ou de la psychologie des personnages.[1]

The application of this is apparent. The fusion of the destiny
of the individual characters with that of the whole of Europe
is only partially successful; what tragedy there is exists only on
the personal level, not the international one. The novel lacks
an essential element, tension, because the reader knows what is
going to happen, that war is unavoidable, whatever the individual
characters may do. It is also too long, weighed down by tedious
didactic passages; the balance of the earlier volumes is largely
destroyed by this. To some extent the subject-matter actually
consists of the passing of time (just as it had in *Barois*); by dwell-
ling on the events of six weeks in 1914 in a volume which almost
equals in length the six preceding ones, he reduces his ability to

---

[1] N. Cormeau, *Physiologie du roman*, Brussels, 1947, p. 141.

deal with time satisfactorily. The *Sekundentechnik* which had had a limited success in *La Consultation*—although even there it weakened the general balance—here merely produces the effect of inflation with superfluous matter.

Above all, the characters are inadequate symbols of European society; there is a double motivation of the *dénouement*, which is brought on by the weaknesses of the protagonists, as well as by impersonal external forces. Meynestrel is no Lenin, no man of iron, despite his intuition that the war will provide the opportunity for revolution. It is made to appear that the whole course of history might have been changed if Alfreda had not left Meynestrel to flee to England with Paterson, and if Meynestrel had not therefore destroyed the Stolbach documents before his attempted suicide. Jacques's death is not caused by external events, since he could have remained peacefully in Switzerland throughout the war like Romain Rolland—or the other revolutionaries. His own unbalanced character is quite sufficient motivation for his suicide, which indeed has been prepared in earlier volumes; the outbreak of war is the occasion of his death, not the cause of it. Antoine, the passive figure in the drama, is perhaps in a more truly tragic situation, since he is swept away by events, which his conception of duty do not permit him to escape, yet because of this even he is to some extent responsible for his fate. Martin du Gard needed to give his characters consciousness of the meaning of political events, but that consciousness immediately implies choice, and the dilemma is never satisfactorily resolved.

Yet despite these weaknesses, *Eté 1914* contains much that is of value. Above all, the portrayal of Jacques, the psychology of a bourgeois revolutionary, is probably one of the most effective ever achieved. The obvious comparison is with Kyo Gisors and Garine; and although Martin du Gard had time to make use of Malraux's work in his final conception of Jacques, his creation need yield nothing to the younger writer in depth or accuracy of observation. Antoine's affair with Anne is successfully described; also the Paterson-Alfreda-Meynestrel triangle. Most of the passages of dramatic narrative, as opposed to those of political explanation and dialogue, are of the same standard as those in the earlier volumes; and stylistic virtuosity solves many difficulties. Eté 1914 provides an object lesson in Martin du Gard's abilities and limitations, which he had already indicated, with some perspicacity, to Margaritis in 1918. Straightforward psychological narrative is perfectly adequate; but he cannot properly graft a mass of new ideas on to the framework of the existing characters.

8

EPILOGUE

A<small>LTHOUGH</small> the final volume of *Les Thibault* was completed in the spring of 1939, the outbreak of war interfered with publication, so that *Epilogue* first appeared in January 1940. These dates are important; some critics have professed to see in *Epilogue* ironic references to the Second World War: there is some ironic intention, but, at the time of writing, war, if threatening, was not inevitable.

The volume is constructed in two distinct sections, linked by a series of letters. The first fourteen chapters are written in normal narrative, centered once again upon a *nœud d'événements*. After the letters the remainder of the volume is taken up with Antoine's diary, begun after his realization that he is doomed. The last entry, written when he has taken the conscious resolution to anticipate his approaching death, ends the novel series.

The opening chapters give little indications that *Epilogue* is the ultimate volume. The *nœud d'événements* is built round the death of Mlle de Waize. This provides an opportunity to bring together the surviving characters in Paris. A telegram informs Antoine, a patient at a *Clinique des Gazés* in Provence, of his aunt's death; its wording is skilfully designed to hint at the basic developments since Jacques's death, and to indicate the time gap:

La buraliste avait déjà commencé à dicter:
— 'PARIS—3 MAI 1918—7 H. 15—DOCTEUR THIBAULT—CLINIQUE DES GAZES—
LE MOUSQUIER PRES GRASSE—ALPES-MARITIMES—Vous y êtes?'
— 'MA-RI-TIMES', répéta le planton.
— 'Je continue: TANTE DE WAIZE . . . W comme Wladimir, A, I, Z, E . . .
TANTE DE WAIZE DECEDEE—ENTERREMENT ASILE DIMANCHE 10 HEURES—
TENDRESSES—Signature: GISE. C'est tout. Je relis . . .' (p. 759)

EPILOGUE 165

The basic technique is once again to dramatize; and only when the third-person narrative ceases does it become obvious that all loose ends have been neatly tied. The *nœud d'événements* in fact provides a tableau in which all the remaining characters of any importance are represented or mentioned. They are all described in a passive state: although they may, like Dr. Philip, play some part in the action, it is not focused upon them but upon Antoine. The volume begins when he receives the telegram in hospital; he decides to return to Paris, for the first time since the declaration of war, for the funeral; we see him with Gise, then Rumelles, Daniel, Jenny and her (and Jacques's) son, Jean-Paul, Mme de Fontanin, and finally with Philip. Thus when the method of narration changes to a simple reproduction of Antoine's diary, there is no great change in the focus of interest, only in technique.

This tableau technique has the great advantage that it provides a convenient means of disposing of all characters except Antoine, but it has corresponding disadvantages. Perhaps the greatest is that, although enormous psychological changes have taken place in certain characters, there is not enough space for thorough analysis of them. Nor could they be prepared in earlier volumes; firstly, because these changes were probably not anticipated until the change of plan, and secondly, because the changes came, like the war, as something completely unforeseen and shattering. As a result we have to take at face value the transformation of Mme de Fontanin into an efficient, authoritative hospital matron, of Jenny from an introspective, neurotic girl into a clear-headed, blunt-spoken 'new woman', or of Daniel into a stolid, easy-going idler, if bitter underneath. In the last case, it is true, there is ample motivation, in his wound, which had not only lost him a leg, but also emasculated him. But this type of disability was, by the late 1930's, almost a cliché of war novels, and the sensitive handling of the psychological issues involved, identifying Daniel's whole artistic and creative urges, indeed his whole interest in life, with his virility, is scarcely sufficient to redeem the portrait entirely.

Here we touch upon one of the incidental drawbacks of the

subject-matter of *Epilogue*. Whereas, in *Eté 1914*, whatever its faults, the material was at least more or less new to the novel, here he is handling stock themes which had appeared in book after book from the twenties on: the fact that atrocities were committed by both sides, the emptiness of the cry 'A war to end wars', and the meaningless waste of human lives. An example is the episode where Rumelles invites Antoine to dinner at Maxim's. Irony is evident in the pointed contrast between the life of the frontline soldier and that of the man living in security behind the lines. The general picture of the expensive restaurant, crowded with gay staff officers, has a certain staleness. (Not that Martin du Gard makes the common mistake of over-simplifying. The sketches of Rumelles is by no means one of a typical *embusqué:* although he has been in perfect safety throughout the war, he is worn out and ageing rapidly.)

The war is of course one of the primary themes of the series; but it is noteworthy that, apart from the episode in Alsace at the end of *Eté 1914*, direct descriptions of violence are avoided. In the present volume, we see at first hand Antoine's hospital in Provence, and various places in and around Paris, but all battle episodes are fragmentary, seen through the eyes or memory of one of the characters, as if Martin du Gard were only concerned with the holocaust for its implications. These implications are the desire, common to many war novelists, to give a realistic picture of the horrors caused by war, unrelieved by any idealistic view; and the propagandist aim, as in *Eté 1914*, of preventing the resumption of hostilities. These two aims cannot entirely be separated; and there is the further complication that Martin du Gard is writing some twenty years after the events he is describing. The temptation to use knowledge of future events is consequently very strong, especially in passages where characters themselves are looking into the future. The general effect is that, although the passages of straightforward description are unexceptionable, where Martin du Gard's own comments are introduced, where he allows Antoine to indulge in speculation about the League of Nations, the impact of the volume is weakened, just as similar preoccupations had detracted from *Eté 1914*. The thesis does not arise out of characters and events, but is imposed upon them.

Thus the hospital scenes are effective; and the basic narrative of Antoine's few days in Paris would be equally acceptable but for the fact that his experiences are used partly as vehicles for Martin du Gard's own reflections. The Rumelles episode, for instance, turns into a general discussion of the political background of the war. These long political passages, like those in *Eté 1914*, do not adequately hold the reader's attention. At times Rumelles is even made to condemn himself out of his own mouth, as when he admits to Antoine that all means of winning the war are good, even lying propaganda (pp. 810–11). That a highly-placed civil servant should have had such a cynical view is possible, but it is more likely that Martin du Gard is attributing to Rumelles a view of the war which only became popular some time afterwards, when there was time to see events in proper perspective, with full knowledge of hitherto secret matters.

A similar flaw occurs throughout the volume: in Philip's prophecy about future dictatorships, accepted by the people, in Studler's prediction that war will inevitably lead to revolution; in Antoine's fears, in his diary, that Wilson's idealist plans might turn out to be futile.

All in all, however, the theme of the war and hopes for the future are subordinated to the principal theme: once again that of death. The volume opens with a death, that of Mlle de Waize, which is not only a useful technical device, but foreshadows Antoine's own. The shadow of death is never absent: Antoine is continually recalling, in disjointed snatches of war memories, wounded patients who died, or his former assistant Roy, killed in 1914, while around him in hospital fellow-officers are constantly dying. The theme is further stressed by the frequent memories of his own father—even before his own realization that he cannot recover—and by the re-introduction of Rachel, in the narration of her death from yellow fever in Guinea.

The crucial episode is the meeting between Antoine and Philip. Hitherto, Antoine has regarded his eventual recovery as certain, if slow; and while discussing his symptoms, he allows himself to be convinced only too easily, that 'le fond est solide, malgré tout . . .' (p. 893). Only when, turning his head suddenly, he catches Philip's expression—which he himself has seen so often in the past when examining patients together— does the realization strike him that he is doomed. Philip's previous behaviour now all becomes apparent: attempts to gain time and avoid the issue. After this, there is nothing further to be said; and as Antoine leaves, Philip makes the same 'bruit mouillé' (p. 902) that we heard when he left Héquet's dying child in *La Consultation*.[1]

The chapter which follows describes Antoine's wanderings in the Champs-Elysées while he attempts to come to terms with the certainty of his approaching death. Throughout the whole *Thibault* series the theme of death has become more and more central, until in *La Mort du Père* we had one of the most effective treatments of the subject ever written. But the subject was not yet exhausted. Most of the horror of M. Thibault's illness and death was *external*, seen from outside; until almost the end the dying man was unaware of his condition. Now Martin du Gard wishes to portray the reactions of a man who is fully aware of his fate months before his death, a man moreover who is a doctor, who cannot be deceived; and to treat the subject from the inside. This explains the change of narrative technique to a reproduction of Antoine's diary.

All this implies a return to the basic metaphysical themes—the theme of the war, and the future of Europe, is at best no more than contingent. There is a contrast with M. Thibault, who eventually recovered his faith and serenity: Antoine has to face death alone, without either friends or spiritual guides, and with no hope of immortality. This merges into another theme: that of metaphysical solitude. Antoine in fact dies in just as great solitude as his brother and his father, but without any form of consolation.

At this point the continuous narrative ceases, and is followed by a series of letters: from Daniel to Antoine, avowing his impotence; from Jenny to Antoine, anxious about his health

---

[1] *La Consultation*, p. 1070.

(and supplying an opportunity to reply at some length); from Antoine to Jenny; and, finally, the letter recounting the death of Rachel. Antoine's letters are the most powerful expression of his anguish, much more so than the diary entries which follow, which are something of an anticlimax. There are several reasons for this. In the first place, the internal portrayal of the reality of death is too difficult an aim—perhaps even is inherently impossible. 'Il faut être passé par là pour comprendre', explains Antoine in his first letter (p. 910). The inevitability of imminent death may well be such a shattering emotion that it cannot be grasped by anyone who has not undergone it. The anguish of such an experience, the utter panic of fear of death, may well be inexpressible in language. In fact no direct description is attempted. The chapter where Antoine wanders, half-distracted, through Paris in the air-raid, is narrated in the third-person and in *style indirect libre;* in his letters to Jenny, he writes about his 'paroxysme de détresse et de révolte' (p. 912) in retrospect; the diary entries, for the most part, scarcely mention his state of mind.

The description of Antoine's last months is less effective than the comparable scenes concerning M. Thibault. Martin du Gard has deliberately chosen a method of narration which deprives him of practically all dramatic effect, once the scene with Philip is over. Furthermore, he is preoccupied with using the diary to express the various philosophical and other ideas which Antoine is supposed to have had while dying. This in fact is almost certainly an error of judgment, since Martin du Gard thereby weakens his main theme.

The diary form naturally lends itself to the introduction of diffuse ideas, and may have been tempting because of this. Nor should we forget that he had been keeping a diary himself since the First War, used the diary technique in *Barois* and *Confidence africaine*, and was thoroughly familiar with Gide's *Journal;* while his pride in technical virtuosity may also have had some bearing. The essential theme of the diaries is really the future of Europe, the end of the war, Wilson's proposals and other contemporary political events. Again and again Antoine comes back to this subject. Here once more Martin du Gard seems to have embarked upon a doubtful course. In Antoine's first letter to Jenny, there is the significant passage already partly quoted:

Il m'est arrivé cette chose terrible: j'ai appris, j'ai compris, que j'étais *condamné*. Sans retour. Cela traînera sans doute quelques mois. Quoi qu'on fasse, *je ne peux pas guérir*.

Il faut être passé par là pour comprendre. Devant une pareille révélation, tous les points d'appui s'effondrent.

Excusez-moi de vous dire cela sans ménagements. Pour celui qui sait qu'il va mourir, tout devient si indifférent, si étranger. (p. 910)

It is the last sentence which is important: it expresses again an idea from *La Mort du Père*: 'Tout lui était égal: définitivement, totalement égal' (p. 1267), which itself, bears a close correspondence to Martin du Gard's own letter, just before his death, to Marcel de Coppet.[1] In view of this state of *belle indifférence*, it seems a little strange that Antoine should later take such a keen interest in political matters. Admittedly Antoine achieves a state of relative calm afterwards, in which '(il) renoue contact avec le monde' (p. 912), but he says that he has only reached this state by means of an 'usure de sensibilité', 'créant un état de moindre réaction, un commencement d'indifférence, ou plus exactement d'anesthésie'. And throughout the diary, although it is possible that a dying man could take the interest in contemporary events which Antoine does, we are left with a rather uneasy feeling of implausibility.

The theme of death is treated especially in terms of survival. The desire for survival had already been treated several times, in connexion with M. Thibault; and certain incidents are now recalled—and rejudged—by Antoine. His father evidently had a profound emotional need for survival, going beyond religious belief. Whereas Jacques intuitively understood this, it is only now that Antoine softens his judgment of his father, realizing that bourgeois vanity was only partly responsible for his change of name to Oscar-Thibault:

Beaucoup réfléchi a mon père. Désir, qui le hantait, de donner son nom: à ses œuvres, à des prix de vertu, à la grande place de Crouy. Désir, qu'il a

[1] *N.N.R.F.*, 12/58, pp. 1162-5 (letter of 18/3/58).

réalisé, de voir son nom (*Fondation Oscar-Thibault*) gravé au fronton du
pénitencier. Désir d'imposer son prénom (le seul élément qui, dans son état
civil, lui était personnel), à toute sa descendance, etc. Manie de coller son
monogramme partout, sur la grille de son jardin, sur sa vaisselle, sur ses
reliures, jusque sur le cuir de son fauteuil! . . . Beaucoup plus qu'un instinct
de propriétaire (ou, comme je l'ai cru, un signe de vanité). Besoin superbe
de lutter contre l'effacement, de laisser son empreinte. (La survie, l'au-delà, en
fait, ne lui suffisaient pas.) Besoin que j'ai hérité de lui. Moi aussi, secret espoir
d'attacher mon nom à une œuvre qui me prolonge, à une découverte, etc.

On n'échappe pas à son père! (p. 921)

This tenacious clinging to the idea of survival explains Antoine's
interest in Jean-Paul. Even Antoine's proposal of marriage to
Jenny is also connected: with no children of his own, he is subconsciously attempting to find a substitute in Jean-Paul and his
anxiety to legitimize him is no more than a rationalization of
this.

The desire for survival is closely linked to Antoine's determination to assert his own will until the very moment of death,
in fact, to choose that moment himself. He has fought against
sickness and death all his life; they have been the concrete
expression of evil. Now, as a last symbol of his struggle he
decides that he will kill himself as soon as his grip on his mind
and consciousness weakens. One of his first diary entries is:
'Organiser ma mort' (p. 919); and he does so systematically.
Immediately after the fateful interview with Philip, he obtains
the drugs necessary for a rapid, painless death—a fine stroke of
dramatic irony. The problem of euthanasia first appeared in *La
Consultation*, in connexion with Héquet's baby; it recurred, at a
more personal level, in *La Mort du Père*, where Antoine thought
he had satisfactorily resolved it. That it should now affect him
personally is a bitter irony typical of Martin du Gard, and
although in his original plan Antoine was not intended to die,
we may well believe that something of the sort was already in
mind.

Another manifestation of Antoine's desire to survive is his
very resolve to keep his diary, with medical notes about the
progress of his illness and his thoughts as he approaches death.
It is naturally in keeping with his whole character that he should

wish to retain power over his will: he has always been a believer
in strength of will and energy. He manages to retain sovereignty
over his will to the end: 'Mener jusqu'au bout l'analyse' (p. 954);
his last thoughts are a stoical analysis of his feelings in the face of
death. In *Epilogue*, Antoine has, in fact, become a witness of
events, and no longer participates in them. Quite apart from
reflections about the war and its aftermath, the volume, seen
almost entirely through his eyes, gives ample opportunity for
final judgment on the various characters. Some of these judgments
are illuminating, since they make explicit certain matters which
had previously been no more than suggested. Jacques is a case in
point. The utter pointlessness of his death, although obvious,
was never definitely stated in *Eté 1914;* now Antoine sees it
quite clearly as *absurde* (p. 769). Later, when he meets Jenny
again, the word is repeated: 'cet absurde sacrifice' (p. 838); and
Antoine is moved to consider the fundamental contradiction in
Jacques's revolutionary ideas (p. 838). He extends his examination of Jacques to take in the latter's love for Jenny, and the word
'absurde' is deliberately introduced once more, while his final
judgment is even more strongly phrased:

Je pense à Jacques . . . *Juvénile:* épithète qui lui convenait si bien! N'a jamais
été qu'un adolescent. (Voir dans le dictionnaire les caractères typiques de
l'adolescent. Il les avait tous: fougue, excessivité, pudeur, audace et timidité,
et le goût des abstractions, et l'horreur des demi-mesures, et ce charme que
donne l'inaptitude au scepticisme . . .)
Aurait-il été, dans son âge mûr, autre chose qu'un vieil adolescent? (p 931)

Another facet of this is seen when Jenny's feelings for Jacques
are analysed. Despite his enormous posthumous influence over
her, her only real memory of him is Paterson's portrait; time
has destroyed her old feelings: 'Elle venait d'imaginer que
Jacques était brusquement de retour: et, ce qu'elle avait éprouvé,
c'était autant de gêne que de joie . . .' (p. 880) These passages
can be compared with a letter to Lallemand, in which Martin
du Gard complains that many readers believe:

. . . parce que j'ai peint le personnage avec tendresse, que Jacques jouit de ma
prédilection particulière, qu'il est, à mes yeux, un modèle . . . (. .) . . . je porte
sur Jacques à peu près le même jugement qu'Antoine, qui aime profondément

son frère, mais qui déclare, je crois, quelque part, que, tout compte fait, Jacques a vécu et est mort comme un imbécile . . . (. .) . . . Jacques, avec tout son cœur, sa générosité, son intelligence, avec tout son charme personnel, est, sur le plan intellectuel et social, un 'esprit faux', irrémédiablement faux; et sur le plan de la vie, un 'velléitaire' sans consistance.[1]

Antoine's revaluation of his father has already been mentioned. The relationship between them is in fact stressed several times. The ghost of M. Thibault could almost be said to haunt the book. When Antoine returns to what is now his apartment, completely refurnished after his father's death, he nevertheless has the impression of returning not to his own home, but to his father's (p. 784). The room where he sleeps is his father's old room, and the circumstances of his death there are intentionally recalled (p. 813). The greater part of Chapter VI is devoted to an account of Antoine's strange dream of domination by his father. This is a curious episode, which probably owes much to the post-Freudian interest in dreams, and its purpose remains puzzling. From the point of view of plot development, it is not really relevant; furthermore, the italic passage seems somehow out of place in its context. It is introduced in the pluperfect tense: 'Voici ce qu'il avait écrit' (p. 816), yet the final (unfinished) sentence is followed by the remark: 'La rédaction s'arrêtait là. Antoine n'avait plus envie de poursuivre' (p. 818). This confusion of tenses suggests, apart from carelessness, that the episode was artificially inserted in its present position. It may, indeed, have formed part of the diary section in the first instance, and have been transferred to this point for its note of mystery, almost of presentiment. It may also have been rescued from the original plan of the novel series, which would again account for its apparent inappropriateness here. (The same can be said of other episodes of *Epilogue*. The relationship between Jenny and Gise is given considerable attention (pp. 795-7 and 841-3), not essential for the development of the plot—or the themes—of *Epilogue*, but which does recall the scene between the two at Hyères which occurred in *L'Appareillage*.[2] The emphasis on the obstinate, rebellious nature of Jean-Paul is a similar case: he is

---

[1] Ibid., pp. 1145-6 (letter of 1/2/45).   [2] Cf. *Souvenirs*, p. xciv.

even more self-willed than Jacques— '. . . le refus d'aliéner la moindre parcelle de son indépendance, pour quelque motif que ce soit . . .' (p. 870). This portrait of Jean-Paul would fit excellently into the psychological background of the wild 20-year-old driven into murder in the original plan.[1])

The final picture of Daniel is decidedly pathetic. He has always been a complete sexual egoist, and this egoism, as represented by Jérôme, has already been shown to be unable to resist the ravages of time. In some ways Daniel is more stable than his father— he has had his art to fall back on; but his art is so intimately connected with his virility that it cannot exist without it. He is maliciously perverse, with his defence of war profiteers: '. . . les seuls qui ont su ramener les événements à la mesure de l'homme' (p. 844). Though completely idle, he will not help in the hospital, and the reader tends to sympathize with Jenny's view, that he has no right to indulge in self-pity, for at least he is still alive and out of danger. The truth is that he is still essentially an egoist, with no real interest in anyone outside himself; and his spiritual resources are too slim to allow him to recover from his loss of virility. His intention, at some future date after his mother's death, to 'disappear', contrasts sharply with Antoine's decision to exert his individual liberty to the ultimate moment.

The greatest revaluation Antoine makes is of his own character and pre-war life, with his shame at his 'glissement vers la vie facile' (p. 818), after his father's death. On the material side he had squandered, in a matter of months, his father's laboriously accumulated fortune, with his *laboratoires* and refurnishing of the entire flat; while what remained of the money he had invested—the irony is evident—in Russian securities.[2]. He realizes that 'il était engagé dans une fausse route' (p. 819), and discovers the cause of this failure in 'l'empoisonnement par l'argent' (p. 820). This is the final aspect of the theme of ambi-

[1] Cf. ibid., p. xcv.
[2] Martin du Gard probably had a personal memory in mind here: after the death of his own parents, he too had spent a good deal of his inheritance in buying and furnishing his country house at Bellême. (*Souvenirs*, pp. xcvi–xcvii).

tion: in the face of death, ambition is an empty ideal; fifteen years of efforts by Antoine to 'arrive' have turned to ashes in his mouth. In a minor key Daniel reflects the same theme.

In *Epilogue* Antoine finally reaches maturity. His life, throughout the novel, has been developing towards greater social feeling: the first step away from egoism occurred when he succeeded in taking Jacques in his own charge; his affair with Rachel taught him the value of love on a higher plane than the merely sexual one; and now the war, and the sentence of death hanging over him, destroy the last elements of egoism, and bring his views firmly over to the ideal of social co-operation. (It is one of the ironics of the novel that he only reaches this stage shortly before his death.) He now fully realizes how limited his attitude to life has been: no more than '. . . une philosophie élémentaire d'homme d'action, basée sur le culte de l'énergie, l'exercice de la volonté . . .' (p. 947). In any case his philosophy had scarcely been sufficient to deal with all circumstances, since he acknowledges that many of the crucial decisions of his life have in fact been in contradiction with his supposed principles, which evidently did not express his 'nature authentique' (p. 948). Thus the final treatment of the Barresian themes of energy and ambition implies the destruction of Antoine, just as Jacques and Daniel are destroyed by their own forms of egoism.

The problem of ethical responsibility, which had occupied him so much in *La Consultation*, now crops up again, in connexion with Darros, one of the patients at the hospital who is apparently shamming in order to avoid being sent back to the front. Antoine cannot bring himself to condemn Darros, and discovers that he has arrived at an extreme position on the general ethical question: he no longer believes in human responsibility (p. 958). The notion of the universe as 'un ensemble de forces aveugles, qui s'équilibrent par la destruction des moins résistants' is ethically unbearable to him, but he cannot accept the traditional distinction between good and evil either. He eventually concludes that this distinction is 'un instinct, qui s'est perpétué en nous à travers les millénaires, et grâce auquel la société humaine s'achemine vers son perfectionnement' (p. 962). (In this passage Martin du Gard has slipped over from psychological self-analysis by Antoine to metaphysics, and the dramatic interest is small. These are probably his own views, rather than Antoine's and are by no means original, being the common currency of late nineteenth-century rationalism such as that of Le Dantec. Antoine is rather feebly made to parry this criticism: 'J'invente peut-être à mon usage une explication archiconnue. Peu importe. Nouvelle pour moi' (p. 962). And when Le Dantec is actually quoted (p. 964), the artifice is only too apparent.)

Another regret of Antoine's is that he never enjoyed himself enough while he had the chance. The memory of Rachel constantly haunts him, and his final judgement is that this 'pauvre aventure est, malgré tout, ce qu'il y a eu de meilleur dans ma vie' (p. 997). He enjoins Jean-Paul: 'gaspille tout de même un peu de ta jeunesse' (p. 975). This self-analysis acts as a jumping-off point for precepts for Jean-Paul. There are numerous examples of these, and put together they could almost be said to form Antoine's—and Martin du Gard's—spiritual testament:

'Ne pas se laisser aveugler par l'individuel' (p. 920).
'On n'échappe pas a son père' (p. 921).
'. . . on est toujours seul pour sa fin' (p. 930).
'Rien de pire que d'entrer dans la vie sans une vocation forte . . . (. .) . . . méfie toi de la fausse vocation' (p. 949).
'. . . méfie-toi de tes inclinations . . . (. .) Tâche de découvrir, peu à peu, ta personnalité réelle. (. .) Accepte-toi, avec tes bornes et tes manques . . . ' (pp. 950-1).
Sauvegarder son être. Ne pas craindre de se tromper. Ne pas craindre de se renier sans cesse. Voir ses fautes, pour aller plus avant dans l'éclaircissement de soi-même et la découverte de son devoir propre.
(Au fond, on n'a de devoir qu'envers soi (p. 967).)
Devenir un homme de valeur. Développer en soi une personnalité qui s'impose. Se défier des théories en cours. (. .) *Ne te laisse pas affilier!* (pp. 981-2)
Cultive ta volonté . . . (. .) Si tu es capable de vouloir, rien ne te sera impossible. (p. 991)
Pas de vérité, que provisoire. (. .) Se guérir jeune du goût de la certitude. (p. 994)

The generalization has always been a common feature of the French psychological novel, and Martin du Gard is doing no more than following in this tradition. But at the same time, it is perhaps a failure of his indirect method that he needs to state these precepts so directly, and so obviously to make his final volume carry a message.

This theme of vocation is constantly emphasized in Antoine's diary, and it probably was to be an essential element in the original plan for his later volumes; one which he was not prepared to sacrifice completely. It had in any case been already treated incidentally in *La Belle Saison* and elsewhere, much more effectively than in the bald exhortations here, where once again ideas have been inadequately assimilated into psychological reality.

Martin du Gard seems more at ease in *Epilogue* than in *Eté 1914;* possibly because of greater familiarity with his material. The characterization of minor figures gives him little difficulty: instead of the Geneva political exiles, he only needs to introduce a few fellow-patients and doctors at Antoine's hospital; only one of these, Dr. Bardot, is treated at all extensively. Other characters, such as Chasle or Philip, can be taken up again from earlier volumes; and the scenes—in Provence, Paris, and Maisons-Laffitte—present few problems. There is naturally a wealth of medical material, again no novelty; despite the complications of Antoine's case, descriptions are again highly accurate.

The diary extracts are relatively simple to compose:[1] the topical references to the war, political speeches, and so on, could easily be inserted in correct chronological order by judicious use of contemporary newspapers. They also provide a basis for Antoine's musings, a starting-point for whatever Martin du Gard wishes to stress. The terse diary style—'Après le déjeuner, crise d'étouffement. Piqûre. Chaise longue, sous les oliviers. Trop fatigué pour cette lettre à Jenny . . .' (p. 925)—is easily achieved, by simple suppression of verbs, articles, and personal pronouns.

He also produces considerable effects by heightening the perceptions of the dying man, who suddenly begins to pay attention to the beauties of the Provençal landscape (p. 942). Then as Antoine's condition deteriorates, his thoughts turn

[1] Ibid., p. cxxii.

more and more from their previous strictly logical and practical
pattern. In an almost Pascalian passage (pp. 968–9), he compares
the minute size of the earth with the infinity of stars and solar
systems in the heavens. Like M. Thibault before him, his
thoughts constantly swing back to events from his past—to his
youth as a medical student, to war memories, to Rachel. In the
last days of his life, he becomes haunted by peculiar metaphysical
preoccupations which indicate that his mind is becoming warped
under the strain (pp. 1002–3).

From all this we can see that craftsmanship remains at a high
level. The diary section is not merely a means of solving technical
difficulties, but is as carefully planned as any other episode in
the series, and from the point of view of pure technique shows
high qualities.

One element in *Epilogue* is more important than in earlier
volumes: the use of irony. A note of bitter irony runs through
the entire volume: the disproportion between Antoine's hopes
in 1918 and the reality of European politics in the 1930's. The
same quality pervades in the book. The series of wounds and
circumstances which lead to Antoine's death are ironic; his
death is ultimately just as meaningless and ridiculous as Jacques's.
If he had not received a wound earlier—comparatively harmless
in itself—the gassing would not have been serious; if he had
taken the proper precautions, the same precautions which he
was supposed to be making sure that others were taking, he
would have escaped; if, afterwards, he had taken the most
elementary prophylactic measures, the infection would not have
taken hold.

There is a fine scene of irony where the very victims of German
gas, many like Antoine, actually dying, gloat at the rumour that
the Allies have discovered a new gas which (rather like the gas
described by Malraux in *Les Noyers de l'Altenburg*) destroys all
vegetation for years. And, at the end of the volume, the chaplain's
visit to Antoine provides another opportunity for irony. (It is
noteworthy that religion receives very summary treatment here,
despite the theme of death. Antoine's materialism and agnosticism are unassailable.)

In *Epilogue* Martin du Gard makes the same mistake as in *Eté 1914:* he attempts to weld together the novel of psychological analysis and the novel of ideas, without entirely succeeding. In *Epilogue*, the dichotomy is even more marked, since the novel falls naturally into two halves, illustrating the two conflicting tendencies. The first section of the volume is in many ways admirable; Martin du Gard narrates incident in much the same style as in the earlier volumes, and is able to link present events with past memories through reintroduction of old characters. In this way he is able to achieve the *unité romanesque*, and largely re-establishes the balance destroyed in *Eté 1914*. But Antoine's diary takes the novel on to an entirely different level, and the unity is again broken. Whereas the bulk of the novel series consists of psychological themes worked out in individual destinies, described objectively in third-person terms, Martin du Gard is now analysing and interpreting ideas, through a first-person narrator. The marriage between what are in essence two entirely separate literary genres is doomed to failure; and Antoine's diary, which might have been successful as a separate work, as the confession of faith of a humanist, is inadequately integrated into the objective narrative.

9

THEATRE AND MAUMORT

MARTIN DU GARD's major work is undoubtedly in the field
of the novel; but he also wrote three plays, and was
tempted by the theatre throughout his life.[1] As a school-
boy, he was already an enthusiastic matinée-goer, familiar with
all the popular plays of the period; above all, 'j'avais presque vu
naître le *Théâtre-Libre*, et j'assistais régulièrement, de saison en
saison, à toutes les créations d'Antoine et de Suzanne Desprez'.[2]
Later, in 1913, acceptance of *Barois* by the *N.R.F.* group put
him in contact with Jacques Copeau; on October 22nd of that
year he was present at the inauguration of the *Vieux-Colombier*.
Already in the previous August he had written his first peasant
farce, *Le Testament du Père Leleu*, which Copeau put on at the
Vieux-Colombier in February 1914. This play, a farce in three
acts, published in 1920, was widely successful, and later entered
the repertoire of the *Comédie Française*. A second farce, *La
Gonfle*, was drafted in 1922, completed two years later, and
published immediately after *La Sorellina* in 1928; but *La Gonfle*
has never yet been staged.

In both these plays, Martin du Gard was striving for originality no less than in his novels. This originality was to take the
form of a renewal of the peasant farce which had died out in
the seventeenth century, and critics have claimed to see in them
the spirit of the medieval *fabliau*. This has received convincing
proof by Guichard, who has shown that sixteen of the anecdotes
related by Andoche, the hero of *La Gonfle*, have been taken
from a play of 1610, *Le Moyen de Parvenir*, commonly attributed

---

[1] He confessed to the present author in 1955 that he would have liked to write more
plays, since he thought his technical abilities lent themselves to the drama, but 'il m'a
manqué les sujets'.

[2] *Souvenirs*, p. lviii.

to Béroalde de Verville.[1] Both Martin du Gard's farces were originally written in popular dialect, that of Berry, although to improve comprehension by a sophisticated Parisian audience, *Père Leleu* was rewritten in a less naturalistic form of peasant speech, with instructions to the actors about phonetic changes: 'eil' to be pronounced 'èle', 'oi' as 'oué', 'moyen' as 'mâu-yen', and so on. The result is certainly convincing to any reader except a professional dialectologist, and less difficult to the eye than, say, Shaw's attempts at phonetic rendering of Cockney English, as the following example shows:

La Torine. Héï! J'sais-t-y sculement tout ce qu'il disait, moi? De toutes sortes! Et d'autres, mêmement! Il savait bien que vous fricassiez avec moi, pardine ... Il me disait que vous étiez trop gnamolli pour faire un bon coq de volailler ... Puis, que vous étiez plus ralu qu'un échardon, et plus grigou qu'un puits séché ... Puis, que j'étais bien sottisière de croire vos paroles de promesse, et que jamais j'entendrais sonner les écus de mes treize années de gages, qui ont point encore été payés! ... (p. 1146)

Père Leleu is based on the time-honoured, but simple and effective device of a reversal of rôles—'the biter bit'. In Act I Père Alexandre, an old, sick man, is dying, while his housekeeper and mistress, La Torine, attempts to persuade him to make a will in her favour, since her wages have never been paid in her thirteen years with him. (The cry of 'mes gages!' runs through the play, and clearly recalls Molière's *Don Juan*.) Despite her entreaties, Père Alexandre refuses to call the *notaire*, hinting that if he makes a will it will be in favour of Père Leleu, the neighbour. At this La Torine describes how Leleu had made Alexandre a cuckold before his wife's death. This news leaves him unmoved, so she goes on to relate how Leleu had made advances at herself, which finally succeeds in infuriating the old man. But before calling the *notaire*, Alexandre persuades La Torine to bring him a bottle of *marc* hidden under the woodpile, drinks from it, and falls back dead. La Torine, frustrated in her intentions, immediately abandons her coaxing tone and the act ends on the cry of her true feelings for Alexandre—'Vieux

---

[1] L. Guichard, *Revue d'histoire littéraire de la France*, 10/60, pp. 559–62. The comparison may also be drawn between Martin du Gard's peasant farces and those of Jules Romains.

crapule!!!' (p. 1151). Act II shows the dead man still on stage, hidden under a blanket; La Torine shows Leleu the corpse, and explains her situation—thirteen years without pay, and now possibly being forced to beg on the streets. Finally she comes to the point—Leleu is similar enough in appearance to Alexandre to be able, wrapped up in blankets, to impersonate him in front of the *notaire*, and to make a will in La Torine's favour. Act III shows this plan being put into effect: Leleu, prompted by La Torine, runs through the list of his goods and properties, but, at the crucial moment, instead of naming La Torine as sole legatee, he names himself—'mon vieil ami, le père Leleu'. After the departure of the *notaire*, La Torine's fury is short-lived; the play ends as she reconciles herself to her fate, which is to be Leleu's servant and mistress, again presumably without pay.

Although the farce is too flimsy to withstand profound analysis, some comments may be made. First, the play is successful on its level. The methods of achieving comic effect are traditional—earthy references to cuckoldry and fornication, satire on the priest, complete and unashamed egoism by all the characters without exception—in fact, the world of *Vieille France* seen in its purely comic aspects. The tone is one of macabre humour, which could no longer be sustained if the moral implications of the characters' behaviour were ever examined. They are shown as acting with animal cunning: no other psychological traits are allowed to temper their greed and selfishness. The subject, viewed rationally, is not really a cause for laughter, but is well suited for the farce where the spectator's reaction is never allowed by the swift movement of the action to allow time for reflection. The simplicity, both of the plot and of the emotions, and the dramatic irony of the ending give the play a timeless quality: once again Martin du Gard has accomplished a *tour de force*.

During the winter of 1913–14, the author spent much of his time at the *Vieux-Colombier*, and accompanied the *troupe* on their English tour in March 1914. But despite the intimacy with Copeau, no further play emerged at this stage. Martin du Gard had indeed dramatic projects in mind, especially his new

Commedia dell'arte, to be called the *Comédie des tréteaux*—inspired by Copeau's pre-war production of *Les Fourberies de Scapin*.[1] The principle idea behind the *Comédie des tréteaux* was to play farces on a simple trestle stage, 'presque sans accessoires et sans aucun décor'. (Despite the naturalistic dialogue of *Père Leleu*, this farce was also intended to be played with no more than a few pieces of furniture as the set.) In these farces, 'ce théâtre de foire', the characters were to remain constant: 'un ménage de bourgeois adipeux et cossus', *Monsieur* and *Dame Punais*, two sly valets, *Fric* and *Miette*, a gangster, *Monsieur Malandrin*, and so on. These characters were to be invariable under all circumstances, and highly stylized:

Je voulais qu'ils fussent reconnus dès leur premier bond sur le tréteau. Je m'étais persuadé qu'ils seraient vite aussi populaires que Polichinelle, Arlequin, don Quichotte ou Monsieur Prudhomme; et je m'imaginais déjà composant pour le Vieux-Colombier, avec le concours de Copeau, une série de courtes comédies satiriques, où nous aurions, de concert, allégrement fustigé les travers de nos semblables et les mœurs du temps.[2]

But this striking project, in which not the least interesting feature is its avowed ambition, rapidly came to nothing after Martin du Gard's demobilization in 1919. Copeau was a changed man; in any case the most important task at hand was to reopen the *Vieux-Colombier* and make the *troupe* financially viable once again; Martin du Gard had plans, admittedly vague, for a *roman-fleuve;* and, we may surmise that, although he had a clear picture of what his *Comédie des tréteaux* was to be like, with its fixed characters, he was less certain about the exact nature of the satires he wished to present. Copeau himself has hinted at another possibility: 'He began to dislike this too human instrument, this medium which is too much exposed to weakness and accident, which sooner or later escapes from the strict control of the artist, whose work it deforms and betrays. He wanted to keep everything in his own hands and let nothing slip from them.'[3] From this it seems that what possibly attracted

---

[1] I am indebted to *Souvenirs*, pp. lxxvi–lxxvii for the whole of this section.

[2] Ibid., p. lxxvii.

[3] Quoted in H. C. Rice, *Roger Martin du Gard and the World of the Thibaults*, New York, 1941, p. 16.

Martin du Gard to the theatre in the first place—the opportunity
of working with a team, of escaping from the tension of solitary
creative composition—was, when once the novelty had palled,
exactly what sent him back to his solitude. Certainly his methods
of work, in lonely country retreats, with his careful researches
and documentation, had little in common with the gregarious
life of the theatre.

It is not known whether Martin du Gard intended his second
peasant farce, *La Gonfle*, for the stage. In the stage-directions, it
is true, we do find the note: 'Dans la pensée de l'auteur, la
pièce doit être jouée par trois hommes et un jeune garçon';[1]
but at the same time the inherent difficulties in any production
must have been evident to him. The play is subtitled: 'Farce
paysanne fort facétieuse, sur le sujet d'une vieille femme
hydropique, d'un sacristain, d'un vétérinaire et d'une pompe à
bestiau' (p. 1165). *La Gonfle*, like its predecessor, has three acts,
and the action all takes place on one day. The action is, however,
reduced to a minimum, and that mostly in the third act; the
main interest lies in the charcter of Andoche, the sexton, and
in his ceaseless monologues. La Bique, his mistress, who owns
the farm on which they live, is suffering from acute dropsy;
La Nioule, a semi-idiot adolescent girl, is pregnant either by
Andoche, or by M. Gustave, a vet and La Bique's nephew. The
dénouement is brought about by Andoche's successful scheming
to make M. Gustave deliver La Nioule of her child and La
Bique of her dropsy, by means of an anaesthetic and the 'pompe
à bestiau'. But whereas Martin du Gard had been highly sensitive
to dramatic necessities in *Père Leleu*, here he neglects them almost
entirely. The dialogue is not only naturalistic, but phoneticized
and difficult to reproduce; while the part of Andoche is so long
that it would provide a formidable task for even the most
talented actor. Above all, the farce is not basically comic: the
animal instincts of the peasants are even more evident here than
in *Père Leleu*, while the chief effect of the dialogue is to create
atmosphere, and an effect of horror or disgust in the audience.

---

[1] This desire to have the play performed by male actors only may possibly have some
connexion with the 1610 play.

The tone is, indeed, much closer to *Vieille France* than to the earlier farce, and the author's dislike for his creations is barely concealed. The roots of the play have been exposed—the play of 1610; the chief targets for satire are doctors (and vets), priests, and the mercenary and savage egoism of the peasants.

Fundamentally, *La Gonfle* is a play to be read, not performed. In *Père Leleu* (which is incidentally referred to in *La Gonfle*, hinting at a possible linked series of peasant farces), the rapidity of the action had prevented any but comic reactions by the audience; here the lack of action forces the reader to reflect on the subtle implications of Andoche's monologues—a cerebral reaction which automatically excludes the normal response to a farcical situation. It is difficult to resist the conclusion that once again Martin du Gard was aiming at the *tour de force;* as a stage-play, *La Gonfle* fails, despite any intellectual interest it may present to the reader. Andoche's monologues are skilful attempts to introduce something new into the stage-farce, but weigh down the play too much—it is two and a half times as long as *Père Leleu.* It is primarily a literary exercise, not a dramatic work.

Martin du Gard's third and final play, *Un Taciturne*, is of a very different type. This play, subtitled 'Drame en trois actes', was conceived during Martin du Gard's stay in hospital after his motor accident in 1931, and written later the same year, before being produced by Jouvet at the *Comédie des Champs-Elysées* in October of that year. Despite the brilliant cast—Jouvet himself, Pierre Renoir, Lucienne Bogaërt, and Valentine Tessier—*Un Taciturne* was not a success, while even Gide and the *N.R.F.* group were cool towards it.[1] Nevertheless, the play has definite qualities, and it seems probable that a simple refusal to accept the theme—homosexuality—as suitable for the stage, was principally responsible for its failure.[2] At the present day, as Borgal has suggested,[3] it might meet with more luck: one need only think of the international success of *Tea and Sympathy.*

[1] Cf. Julien Green's interesting comments to this effect: *Journal I*, Paris, 1938, p. 68.
[2] The audience's reaction to certain lines of the play was apparently so violent that Jouvet was forced to make cuts on successive nights.
[3] Borgal, op. cit., p. 99.

The plot of the play is complex. Act I presents the main characters,—Thierry, a middle-aged business man, unmarried, who lives with his sister, Isabelle, in her late twenties: Armand, Thierry's partner, sceptical, even cynical, with a dry sardonic wit; Wanda, Isabelle's friend from schooldays; and finally Joë, who bluffs his way into Thierry's office and persuades him to give him a post as personal assistant. In the second act, the intrigue is developed: Joë and Isabelle have fallen in love, although Isabelle refuses to admit this because of her past, since she had been sent to a reformatory for having stabbed Wanda in a fit of Lesbian jealousy. In the third act, she has finally decided to marry Joë, but Thierry refuses to accept this. When he realizes that he is in fact a homosexual, and has been in love with Joë from first meeting, he commits suicide by shooting himself. The plays ends with Armand's shouted comment: 'L'imbécile!'.

The principle theme closely parallels that of *Confidence africaine:* homosexuality, like incest, is not unnatural, but has to be accepted by the homosexual as a fundamental *donnée* of his existence. As Armand says: 'Ça peut arriver ces choses-là ... Ça peut arriver ... à des gens ... très bien ...! (p. 1346); and it is Thierry's refusal to accept this which precipitates the tragic ending. Thus the play fits into the Naturalist and post-Naturalist tradition of the problem play; homosexuality, which is seen as both a personal and a social problem, is isolated, and the crisis of the problem presented on the stage. Failure to surmount the crisis leads to the destruction of the protagonist, and the didactic lesson is thus made clear. In this framework Armand plays the rôle of the *raisonneur*, though he is saved from the worst faults of moralizing by his constant irony. The theme is once again closely related with the theme of vocation, so important in *Les Thibault:* to accept one's own limitations is a primary condition of a happy life, or even of life at all. Isabelle comments to Armand in Act I: 'Non seulement tu ne changes pas, (..) mais, plus tu vas et plus tu t'installes dans tes défauts.' He retorts, complacently: 'Oui. Exprès. C'est assez curieux. (..) Je m'y abandonne maintenant avec volupté et ça me permet de faire bien meilleur ménage avec moi-même ...' (p. 1257). Later,

Armand stresses the point again: 'on ne se refait pas, on ne se sépare pas de son ombre (p. 1299).

Although the acceptance of homosexuality as perfectly natural was undoubtedly what disturbed the audiences of 1931, the play has numerous faults. There are implausibilities: it is a little hard to accept that Thierry is prepared to employ Joë as his personal *aide*, in the circumstances of their meeting; it is only plausible if we accept that Thierry has fallen in love with Joë at first sight, and there is no other evidence for this. Act III is constructed in the form of a series of *tête-à-tête* interviews between various pairs of characters, and some of these are engineered a little clumsily. The final revolver-shot offstage, if striking at the time of *Hedda Gabler*, had become a cliché of the theatre by 1930, and it is arguable that Martin du Gard is too closely tied to the conventions of the neo-Naturalist school, following in the footsteps of Antoine and the *Théâtre-Libre*. (The interminable stage directions are another indication of this.) More important, perhaps, is the fact that Martin du Gard was attempting to compress too much into the narrow compass of the three-act drama. Although Martin du Gard's narrative technique in *Les Thibault* is best characterized as 'dramatic', this is not to say that episodes could be transferred to the stage without any difficulty. The conventions of the stage are much more circumscribed than those of the novel: character has to be presented more rapidly, with broader and inevitably coarser traits: the 'réticences, demi-aveux, et sous-entendus révélateurs' of the novel would tend to mystify the audience, or even to pass unnoticed. It is precisely this which mars *Un Taciturne*. The theme is presented in a subtle way which would probably be successful in the novel, with its greater leisure between reading and reaction, but which obscures comprehension in the play. It is not evident until close to the end of the final act that Thierry is in love with Joë; previously, it might equally be an incestuous love for Isabelle which provokes his violent opposition to the proposed marriage. There are also too many other emotional relationships in the play, not all of them relevant: Isabelle's Lesbian love for Wanda as a schoolgirl, Armand's hopeless love for Isabelle, or Thierry's old passion for Wanda. The total effect of the spectator is more one of confusion than of subtlety. Whether or not Martin du Gard realized this, he never entered into direct contact with the theatre again.

After *Epilogue* appeared in 1940, Martin du Gard published little: indeed, only his *Notes sur André Gide* (1951), and his *Souvenirs* in the *Pléiade* edition of his works (1955), together with a translation of Dorothy Bussy's novel *Olivia* (1949). Of these not much need be said. The book on Gide, composed entirely of extracts from Martin du Gard's diaries, has already taken its place as one of the shrewdest and most revealing estimates of Gide, both as man and as writer; the *Souvenirs* form a literary autobiography of considerable merit. Both books are indispensable to any serious study of Martin du Gard's work, and illustrates the same fundamental qualities of honesty, frankness, and integrity. *Olivia* is interesting both for its theme, Lesbianism, and for his methodical technique in translation. Since his knowledge of English was limited, he worked from a literal translation provided for him. (He also made translations from Chekhov in the same way, although these have not yet been published.) The peasant farces were also composed in a similar fashion: written originally in ordinary colloquial French, and afterwards 'translated' into the appropriate *patois*.

Most of Martin du Gard's creative activity after 1940 was in fact concerned with another projected *roman-somme*, *Le Journal du Colonel de Maumort*, of which a two-volume edition is now being prepared for publication by Pierre Herbart. There are numerous rumours that this novel was intended as a final *tour de force*, a posthumous work, a *roman d'outre-tombe*. As a last defiant gesture in the face of death, it was to be Martin du Gard's last word on life and mankind: he talks of *Maumort* in the *Souvenirs* as 'une figure exemplaire, qui serait comme un testament'.[1] Above all, the theme of death was again to be central, with Martin du Gard drawing on his own experiences

---

[1] *Souvenirs*, p. cii.

and feelings as death approached: 'le livre du vieillissement, du suprême découragement, du repliement sur soi . . .'.[1] The comparison with Antoine writing his diary in *Epilogue* is evident; but only the appearance of the novel can justify any judgments on it.

Ibid., p. xcix.

10

CONCLUSION

UNTIL *Maumort* appears, Martin du Gard's reputation as a novelist must rest, essentially, upon *Barois* and *Les Thibault*. *Devenir* is in no way contemptible as a first novel, but if it has a freshness and spontaneity absent from the later works, it also betrays unmistakable signs of unevenness and immaturity. *Vieille France* at times recalls *La Terre* in its implied attack on peasant life; but we have only to place the two side by side to be in no doubt about the minor proportions of Martin du Gard's book. As a *nouvelle*, *Confidence africaine* is excellent; but it stands alone, and the reputation of a short-story writer depends, much more than that of the novelist proper, not on an individual success but on a solid body of work. Indeed, both *Vieille France* and *Confidence africaine* give hints of what Martin du Gard might have produced, if he had set himself to write separate works instead of his *roman-fleuve;* but in a final estimation of his achievement they must remain definitely *en marge*.

Barois has been one of the outstandingly successful French novels of the century, but the reasons for its success are complex. Basically it is a *tour de force*, which is not to detract from its quality; but, like all such works, it is largely unrepeatable, since its best features are those which are unique in it: firstly, the attempt to embody in dramatic form the two major intellectual crises of the era, and, secondly, the experiment in dialogue technique. Any continuation in the same vein would have met with great difficulty, as the historical themes of the rationalist crusade and of the Dreyfus Case would have already been fully treated, and the stylized technique would have lost its novelty and originality. Moreover, the appeal of *Barois* has always been to some considerable extent a result of its relevance to political emotions in France, to the conflict between Nationalists and Dreyfusists which has persisted, in different and confusing forms, until the present day. This continued relevance to a political context is largely fortuitous, and it is possible to imagine a situation in the next few decades which might deprive the novel of this specialized appeal.

Les Thibault, much more than *Barois*, lies in the main stream of the French and indeed European novel, and it should be judged against that background; more specifically, it must be examined in the light of the concept of the *roman-somme*. There seem to be two principal elements in the *roman-somme*, which we may define as the single work which summarizes its writer's total contribution to literature. Firstly, there is the hope of making the novel into the prime literary form, a rather grandiose aesthetic idea akin to Schlegel's idea of *Universalpoesie* or Wagner's concept of the poetical music-drama. This idea gained force with the success of Balzac's *Comédie humaine:* the title indicates the universal scope of one single work, rather than a series of disconnected individual novels. Flaubert too was affected with the urge to write a work on the universal scale: Gide was later to quote, with approval, his wish: 'Publier d'un seul coup ses œuvres complètes'.[1] Zola's *Rougon-Macquart* series gave the concept pseudo-scientific backing, which the *roman-somme* and more particularly the *roman-fleuve* with its multiple heroes, often spanning several generations, have never since entirely lost. More immediate predecessors of the *roman-somme* can be found in Barrès's two trilogies, *Le culte du moi* and *Le roman de l'énergie nationale*, or in Anatole France's *Histoire contemporaine;* while even in Huysmans's preface to *A Rebours* the concept is clearly present:

. . . ce besoin que j'éprouvais (..) de briser les limites du roman, d'y faire entrer l'art, la science, l'histoire, de ne plus se servir, en un mot, de cette forme que comme d'un cadre pour y insérer de plus sérieux travaux.[2]

[1] Gide, *Journal 1889–1939*, p. 437.
[2] J.-K. Huysmans, *A Rebours*, new ed., Paris, 1947, p. xviii. Extensive bibliographies of the sequence novel can be found in H. Gmelin, *Der französische Zyklenroman 1900–1945*, Heidelberg, 1950, p. 6, and in J. W. Beach, *The Twentieth Century Novel*, New York, 1932, p. 246.

The second main influence is that of the German *Bildungsroman*, in which the biographical (or pseudo-autobiographical) form was used as a vehicle for the writer to express his total experience of life and his *Weltanschauung*, usually with a semi-didactic purpose: as Heller has put it: '. . . *Wilhelm Meister* has set the whole genre *Bildungsroman* on that course which invariably leads from the solitary excesses of sensibility to the nobly restraining acceptance of social purpose'.[1] The influence of the *Bildungsroman* in France was powerfully reinforced by the work of Tolstoy, who combined its social and metaphysical pre-occupations with a vast fresco of society, widely extended in both space and time. We have seen that already by the turn of the century Martin du Gard was an admirer of Tolstoy; then, at the threshold of his career as a writer, Rolland's *Jean-Christophe* began to appear. Rolland, although himself greatly influenced by Tolstoy, had once more narrowed the focus of the novel to the traditional biographical form, but the desire to use this form to embody a 'sum' of life and experience was explicitly stated in the preface to the closing volume:

J'ai écrit la tragédie d'une génération qui va disparaître. Je n'ai cherché à rien dissimuler de ses vices et de ses vertus, de sa pesante tristesse, de son orgueil chaotique, de ses efforts héroïques et de ses accablements sous l'écrasant fardeau d'une tâche surhumaine; toute une *somme* du monde, une morale, une esthétique, une foi, une humanité nouvelle à refaire.[2]

Jean-Christophe—and its wide success—could not have failed to impress Martin du Gard, and both *Une Vie de Saint* and *Marise* were conceived in precisely the same form—the biographical novel in several volumes—, while *Barois* too, although more restricted in length, conforms to this general pattern. The *dédoublement* of Barois and Luce parallels that of Christophe and Olivier; and the idea of a *somme* was in Martin du Gard's mind when he wrote *Barois;* he comments, in a letter to Margaritis: 'J'avais la folie de vouloir mettre là-dedans tout ce que je savais, tout ce que j'avais appris sur les religions, sur tout'.[3]

---

[1] E. Heller, *The Ironic German*, London, 1958, p. 140.
[2] Preface to *La Nouvelle Journée*, Paris, 1912.
[3] *N.N.R.F.*, 12/58, p. 1131 (letter of 1/9/18).

By 1920, at the time of the genesis of *Les Thibault*, the further example of Proust could not have escaped Martin du Gard— although he did not greatly like Proust's work—and at this same time Gide was also interested in the concept; in the early stages of *Les Faux-Monnayeurs* he wrote of his hope to 'grouper dans un seul roman tout ce que présente et m'enseigne la vie'.[1] By now, indeed, the *roman-somme* had become a common idea, particularly in the circle of the *N.R.F.*; the actual term had been used as early as 1913 by Rivière in his long article on the *roman d'aventure*.[2]

The attraction of the *roman-somme* as a literary form is evident. Yet, although it has remained vigorous to the present day, if we except Proust, no *roman-somme* has received universal acclaim. The essential reason would appear to be that those novelists who, like Martin du Gard, Duhamel, and Romains, took up the form, were confusing an extremely ambitious aim with a technique. The fact that they wished to undertake a *roman-somme* did not mean that they had selected an infallible method of achieving their best work; on the contrary, the problems of the conventional novel were thereby doubled. Once the novelist had resolved to convey in one single vast work his total apprehension and experience of life, he was immediately faced with many of the difficulties of the Naturalist writer, with the difference that the 'slice of life' had been replaced by the whole of life. The basic problem was that of the unity of the work as a whole, the integration of a huge quantity of material into a single novel. The normal solution to this problem had always been to use the biographical, or, better, the autobiographical form, so that unity could be imposed upon the totality of events by the presence of the hero or the personality of the narrator. Especially with a first-person narrative, it is possible in this way to incorporate a great deal of more or less subjective material directly into the novel, since the author's reflections and ideas can be directly transformed into those of the hero or narrator. (This is, of course, Proust's method; and, to a lesser degree, that of

---

[1] Gide, *Journal des Faux-Monnayeurs* (*Œuvres complètes*, vol. xiii), p. 8.
[2] Cf. L. Morino, *La Nouvelle Revue Française*, Paris, 1939, pp. 75–77.

Duhamel in the *Pasquier* series.) The disadvantage of this method is that the narrator himself, being seen from within, cannot be so sharply drawn as from outside; while the events narrated can only be described and analysed from his point of view. The possibilities of dramatic presentation are thereby reduced, unless the narrator is made to be present during all the events, a course which often involves excessive coincidence.

Martin du Gard's talents, as he himself realized, lay much more in the line of dialogue and dramatic presentation, and he therefore chose a third-person narrative, with an apparently omniscient observer. Nevertheless he felt unable to deprive himself of the right of comment entirely, and therefore compromised (like Tolstoy before him), by using a privileged character, Antoine, whose special position is made apparent by stylistic devices such as reported thought and interior monologue. At the same time he widened his focus from the simple *dédoublement* of *Devenir* and *Barois*, to take in a number of important characters (again in the Tolstoyan manner). In the early volumes (and no doubt in the original plan for the entire series), his themes are set in the form of personal relationships. The general plot is fairly loose, allowing the introduction of a wide choice of events, together with some material, particularly in *La Belle Saison* and *La Consultation*, which has on first sight little connexion with the main intrigue. The use of an omniscient observer gives an opportunity for more profound psychological analysis than had been possible in *Barois*, with its *style notatif* and strictly external description.

Martin du Gard was, initially, in no way attempting to include the whole of life in his novel; his comment in the preface to *Confidence africaine*: 'Tout ce que j'ai à dire passe automatiquement dans mes *Thibault*', must be taken to mean that only the essence of his experience of life and his view of man was being embodied in his novel-series. Only later, in the changed mood of the 1930's, did he strive to open his novel to take in a vision of the whole of Europe—indeed his total apprehension of the impact of war upon European society, the catastrophe which led to the destruction of an epoch. It is this more ambitious aim which is at the root of the comparative failure of *Eté 1914* and *Epilogue*. No novel has as yet satisfactorily treated the totality of war (as opposed to fragmentary episodes in it); and it was too much to expect that *Les Thibault*, a vehicle not primarily intended for this purpose, could be successfully adapted to it. The political overtones of *Eté 1914*, the pacifistic desire to prevent the outbreak of another war, merely made the effect worse; in general, it is unlikely that any novel with an immediate political aim will achieve a lasting aesthetic success, since the necessarily didactic note will tend to discourage later readers, and the mass of political material will largely be contingent, not essential, and will rapidly lose its appeal. To some extent *Barois* bears this out—the section on the Dreyfus Case is by general agreement too long; *Eté 1914* reinforces the lesson (while in *War and Peace* the didactic historical sections are looked at askance by even the most favourable critics). As an example of the integration into the novel form of a vast bulk of material—the 'whole of life' at one point of time—*Eté 1914* fails; and the entire *Thibault* series is marred by this failure.

There are also important practical reasons why the *roman-somme* as a whole has fallen short of the hopes of its creators. The difficulties caused by sheer length are well-nigh insurmountable. In the first place, the writer must be able to find a public for his novel, and that public tends to be repelled, rather than attracted—particularly in the mid-twentieth century—by the demands made upon him by the length of the novel. After working through *Jean-Christophe* and *A la recherche du temps perdu*, the average reader may well baulk at undertaking *Les Thibault*, let alone Duhamel's two novel-series, Romains's *Hommes de bonne volonté* and other lesser known works. As a result, some of Martin du Gard's best stylistic resources lose much of their effect. The density of a good deal of *Les Thibault* means that the novel yields much on a second reading which had previously escaped even the attentive reader; but who, specialists apart, has the time and energy necessary to undertake a second reading of a novel of such length? The practical handicaps of the *roman-somme* more than outweigh its theoretical advantages.

The length of the novel provides difficulties for the writer no less than for the reader. In a short novel, written in six months or a year, the author can appear impartial, entirely unconnected with the events he is narrating. Nevertheless he is in fact involved in them, to a greater or lesser degree; and over the period of twenty years during which Martin du Gard was writing *Les Thibault*, his attitude to his material changed considerably. We have seen how, in 1920, he projected a novel whose time-scheme extended into the 1930's, with full confidence in his ability to incorporate possible future events—presumably including alterations in his own attitude. Yet this was rash in the extreme; it might have been justified for the nineteenth-century novelist, who had not such a keen apprehension of the rapid effect of time upon his environment, but one which Martin du Gard should certainly have avoided. The destructive effect of time had been one of the key themes in his earlier work, and it was foolhardy to expect that he would himself be immune to it. (We may note in this respect the advantages of the first-person novel in coping with possible differences in the writer's attitude to his novel: Proust succeeds in turning the effect on himself of events not foreseen in the early stages of composition—such as the effect on society of the 1914–18 war—into almost a structural theme of his work.) In the event, Martin du Gard had greatly altered his attitude towards both contemporary events and his novel-material by 1932 or 1933, and, faced with the choice of abandoning *Les Thibault* or of making radical changes in its structure, he determined on the latter course as a *pis-aller*. If, on the other hand, he had restricted himself to several separate novels in the 1920's, all on a much smaller scale, he might have been better able to adjust to this change in attitude, instead of struggling with the rigid necessities of his single novel-series. Furthermore, instead of wishing to incorporate political matter in his novel, he might have decided to use it in an avowedly didactic manner, in a pamphlet or short collection of essays. Indeed, his determination to avoid direct involvement in politics may have done him a disservice. Although it enabled him to escape Gide's rash enthusiasm and somewhat humiliating *volte-*

face over Communism, it might have been better for his art if he had purged himself of political matter in works outside his novels, and thus remained within the realm of the purely psychological—as in fact his letters to Lallemand admit.

The contrast may profitably be made between Martin du Gard's work and that of three greater nineteenth-century novelists: Tolstoy, whom he always proclaimed as his master, and also Flaubert and Zola. Balzac may seem a surprising omission, but apart from the idea of the *roman-somme*, which in any case reached Martin du Gard through several intermediaries, there is little echo of Balzac to be found. The reason is almost certainly a stylistic one: Balzac's predilection for static description is the antithesis of Martin du Gard's own belief in dramatic presentation. (He disliked Balzac's work, as a comment in Gide's *Journal* indicates.[1])

This same question of style is the chief point of contact between Martin du Gard and Flaubert. The insistence upon the separation of form from content and the ideal of transparency are common to both; Martin du Gard's method of conceiving the events and, perhaps months later, transmuting them into clear prose is entirely Flaubertian. Auerbach's analysis of Flaubert's attitude to style can be applied almost without change to Martin du Gard:

His role is limited to selecting the events and translating them into language; and this is done in the conviction that every event, if one is able to express it purely and completely, interprets itself and the persons involved in it far better and more completely than any opinion or judgment appended to it could do. Upon this conviction—that is, upon a profound faith in the truth of language responsibly, candidly, and carefully employed—Flaubert's artistic practice rests.[2]

The similarity is too striking to be fortuitous, even if we did not know that Flaubert's *Correspondance* had been one of Martin du Gard's *livres de chevet* from 1897 to 1905.[3] He has in fact employed Flaubertian techniques more than any other modern French novelist. *Style indirect libre*, reported thought, and flexibility in

---

[1] Gide, *Journal 1889–1939*, p. 876 (entry of 10/3/28).
[2] E. Auerbach, *Mimesis*, paperback ed., New York, 1957, p. 429.
[3] R. Lalou, *Roger Martin du Gard*, Paris, 1937, p. 14.

the use of tenses, notably the imperfect, are the most common examples; but the entire method of dramatic presentation and the *tour de force* descriptions—of Amsterdam, Le Havre, Lausanne, Geneva, Packmell's, or the operation on Dédette—are all in the Flaubertian manner. The result, in both writers, is the achievement of solidity and density (Martin du Gard's dislike of preciosity is in accordance with this); a density illustrated by the use of the significant detail, the dramatic image, and on a larger scale the *nœud d'événements*. It is true that Martin du Gard also uses stylistic devices which had not been evolved in Flaubert's lifetime, above all interior monologue, but the final aim of transparency is the same; all techniques—the use of documents, lyrical passages, the dramatic present, *style notatif*, even occasional hints of collective motivation or *unanimisme*—are valid means to that end. (There is another important result of 'transparent' style: it enables the novelist, while remaining on a high artistic level, to reach a larger circle of readers than a more complex or artificial style would afford him.) Yet despite stylistic affinities there can be no doubt that Martin du Gard falls short of Flaubert's extreme density of narrative. The reason is that the ideal of density is in conflict with one of the basic elements in the *roman-somme:* the desire to incorporate vast amounts of material in a single narrative. In *Eté 1914*, especially, this conflict is not resolved, and only on comparatively rare occasions does the narrative there rise to the stylistic level of the earlier volumes, which approach more closely to Flaubert's achievement.

Martin du Gard also shares with Flaubert a tragic and pessimistic conception of man; it is not by accident that the theme of failure is predominant in the novels of both. This tragic view of man is at the root of another common element: the irony which pervades their work. Martin du Gard's use of irony is complex. In the first place it is used as a defence against sentimentality, and as a means to achieve apparent detachment from the characters in the novel, but this is not its only function. A savage irony is used to strike down his own heroes; essentially the irony of fate, showing his creations as insignificant individuals powerless against the chance forces of their environment.

The symmetry of Barois's life as he weakens in old age, Antoine's death exactly a week after the end of the war, André Mazerelles' own talents causing his destruction—all these betray a fundamental pessimism, much more deep-seated than any slender hope in the perfectibility of man.

Flaubert's influence is reinforced by Maupassant's. In the latter we find not only the ideal of craftsmanship, and certain stylistic traits which recur in Martin du Gard, notably the apparently inconclusive ending to a chapter or volume; there is again the pessimistic attitude and the obsession with the theme of death. Maupassant's artistic *credo* in the preface to *Pierre et Jean* could be wholeheartedly subscribed to by Martin du Gard: the belief in hard work—'le talent n'est qu'une longue patience';[1] in the typical rather than the exceptional:

Le romancier (..) qui prétend nous donner une image exacte de la vie, doit éviter avec soin tout enchaînement d'événements qui paraîtrait exceptionnel. Son but n'est point de nous raconter une histoire, de nous amuser ou de nous attendrir, mais de nous forcer à penser, à comprendre le sens profond et caché des événements.[2]

in the value of the significant detail—'L'habileté de son plan . . . (se trouvera) . . . dans le groupement adroit de petits faits constants d'où se dégagera le sens définitif de l'œuvre';[3] in the suppression of subjectivity: 'L'adresse consiste à ne pas laisser reconnaître ce *moi* par le lecteur sous tous les masques divers qui nous servant à le cacher'.[4] *Vieille France* is where Martin du Gard approaches closest to Maupassant in form; but the two writers shared throughout a common attitude to art.

His relationship to Zola (and to Naturalism) is fairly clear. We have seen the connexion between the *Rougon-Macquart* series and the *roman-somme;* and we can also detect the same fascination—if in a more sophisticated form—with the apparent achievements of positivistic science. The predilection for the character of the dotor or scientist is a significant expression of this; while Le Dantec's theory of heredity and environment—

---

[1] Preface to *Pierre et Jean*, 61st ed., Paris, 1897, p. xxx (Buffon's phrase, repeated to Maupassant by Flaubert).

[2] Ibid., p. xi.   [3] Ibid., p. xiii.   [4] Ibid., p. xxv.

A × B—is directly developed from Zola's more rigid determinist theories, although it differs in allowing much more latitude to the novelist, who can thus avoid Zola's worst excesses. Martin du Gard's method of composition also closely follows Zola's—although the passion for documentation must be traced further back to Flaubert. Massis has in fact claimed that Martin du Gard's entire technique was based upon his own book, *Comment Emile Zola composait ses romans*, which appeared in 1906.[1] This claim is doubtless exaggerated: Martin du Gard's interest in the dialogue technique, and his Chartist training, antedate Massis's book. Nevertheless this direct evidence of Zola's methods would have been unlikely to escape an avid reader of Flaubert's *Correspondance*, and would certainly have reinforced his belief in methodical composition.

One document reproduced in Massis's book is of undoubted relevance to Martin du Gard's work: that section of Zola's *Notes générales sur la nature de l'œuvre* which deals with the *général* (or Flaubertian) and *exceptionnel* (or Goncourtian) character.[2] Zola states that in the *Rougon-Macquart* series he must necessarily create 'exceptional' characters, thus following Stendhal rather than Flaubert, and that his work would thereby gain in artistic power, since the exceptional is always more noteworthy than the normal or general case. In *L'Une de nous*, the most derivative (and by far the weakest) of Martin du Gard's works, he follows Zola on this point: the interest in the grotesque and the macabre, in the pathological case, is evident; and the scene of Raymond's stroke during sexual intercourse could be taken directly from, say *La Terre*. This aspect finds expression, to a greater or lesser degree, in all Martin du Gard's later work: we need only mention the medical scenes of *Les Thibault*. A special case of the same phenomenon is to be found in both writers' interest in the more unusual manifestations of sexuality, such as incest or homosexuality, and their amoral treatment of these themes.

[1] H. Massis, *Bulletin de Lettres*, 15/10/52, p. 334. Thus claiming indirect credit for Zola's influence on Martin du Gard has not however prevented Massis from being one of Martin du Gard's severest critics.

[2] H. Massis, *Comment Emile Zola composait ses romans*, Paris, 1906, pp. 21-22.

On the other hand, after *L'Une de nous*, Martin du Gard abandoned the idea of the exceptional hero: Barois, Antoine, and Jacques are essentially representatives of Man rather than extreme, non-typical cases. A note in Gide's *Journal* touches on this point (and underlines an important difference between himself and Martin du Gard):

Roger, pour n'importe quelle question psychologique, (et même, ou surtout, en tant que romancier), élimine volontiers l'exception, et même la minorité. De là certaine banalisation de ses personnages. Il se demande sans cesse: que se passe-t-il, dans ce cas donné, le plus généralement? Le 'un sur mille' ne retient pas son attention . . .[1]

Although this is not true of many minor characters (we need only think of Gregory, or Hirsch), it certainly applies to the leading figures, and the stature of Antoine, for instance, is a question of some importance in a final evaluation of the novel.

In other respects Martin du Gard owes much less to Zola. He shows few of Zola's dynamic qualities, little of his epic force or zest for crowd scenes on the grand scale (except in *Eté 1914*, where they are far from successful). Their characterization has little in common; Martin du Gard treats his characters much more as independent individuals, while his psychology is much more subtle, deriving more from Tolstoy or even post-Naturalist novelists such as Barrès or Bourget. Nor does the Naturalist concept of the novel as a deliberately conceived sociological document find much echo in Martin du Gard. *Barois* is a special case, but it is more a document of the history of ideas than of sociology proper. Martin du Gard's social focus is throughout deliberately narrow, since he restricts himself largely to that small segment of upper-middle-class French society which he knows at first hand. (Once again, *Eté 1914* is the exception whose failure might be said to prove the rule. The greater use in this volume of basically uncongenial neo-Naturalist techniques partly explains its comparative failure.) The themes of *Les Thibault*, as originally conceived: vocation, adolescence, time, death, are primarily psychological or meta-

[1] Gide, *Journal 1889-1939* (p. 1259, entry of 2/10/36).

14

physical, not social. The novel-series is not even, in its final form, a complete family chronicle, since the entire action covers only fourteen years, from 1904 to 1918 (although the original plan would have extended it by at least one generation). There is of course a fair amount of documentary material in the novel —particularly the medical material—but its introduction is incidental, not structural.

The relationship between Martin du Gard and Tolstoy is basically that between disciple and master. Martin du Gard wished to emulate the gigantic achievement of the Russian; he was inspired by the panoramic qualities of *War and Peace* in his formative years, while Tolstoy's artistic and intellectual integrity (which had also attracted Rolland) was the cause of further admiration. Yet this influence is essentially of a general nature and shows little direct trace in Martin du Gard's production—if not in his ambitions—before *Les Thibault*. In *Barois* the linking of the novel to the historical context is perhaps a point of contact with *War and Peace*, but only with *Eté 1914* does this similarity become apparent, when Martin du Gard attempts to combine his apprehension of the historical situation in 1914 with his panoramic psychological novel. Yet even here his aim is radically different from—if not opposed to—that of Tolstoy. Whereas the latter, in the didactic historical sections of *War and Peace*, had striven to expose the great illusion that 'individuals can, by the use of their own resources, understand and control the course of events',[1] Martin du Gard is trying to show that the First War was not inevitable and that individual action might have prevented it (if Meynestrel had not destroyed the Stolbach papers; if Jaurès had not been assassinated, etc.).

It is in fact in characterization that Martin du Gard most closely approaches to Tolstoy. In both novelists we find the assimilation of the mental to the physical: the reduction of mankind to the physical lowest common denominator, the attempt to express personality by the significant physical detail (Karenin's protruding ears; Chasle's squeaky shoes). This is surely what Martin du Gard had in mind when he spoke of

[1] I. Berlin, *The Hedgehog and the Fox*, 2nd ed., London, 1954, p. 20.

Tolstoy's ability to *voir en profondeur*;[1] but it is exactly in characterization that the difference in achievement becomes most evident. Despite all his efforts, Martin du Gard falls short of Tolstoy's ability to create an apparently unlimited number of minor characters. Where he has to rely on invention rather than observation, the results are sometimes unfortunate, as in the case of Gregory. Nor is his canvas, in the earlier volumes of *Les Thibault*, anywhere near so broad as Tolstoy's; and when he does, in *Été 1914*, wish to create vast numbers of minor characters, he generally fails to differentiate them from each other. Except for the prominent few, such as Meynestrel, Alfreda, and Paterson, the revolutionaries remain little more than names.

On the other hand, many of the more important characters in the early volumes are rounded figures in the Tolstoyan tradition. M. Thibault is excellently drawn, dominating the novel until his death (and the parallel between *La Mort du Père* and *Ivan Ilyitch* is an illustration of the closeness of Martin du Gard's best work to that of Tolstoy). Jérôme and Mme de Fontanin, and other characters such as Vécard and Philip, are equally felicitous, lacking neither plausibility nor individuality. Those characters who are to some extent comic, such as Chasle or Mlle de Waize, are less admirable; while Martin du Gard's weakness in portraying women, noticeable in *Devenir*, is never fully remedied: there is a certain colourlessness about Jenny, and a hint of improbability about Rachel and Anne, which renders them less full and rich than Tolstoy's female creations.

The change of plan in *Été 1914* undoubtedly damaged the conception of certain characters. It is not only that the development of Jenny and Mme de Fontanin is somewhat implausible, even allowing for the changed conditions of the war. Of the main characters still alive, only Jacques remains as an entirely unified conception, and this, we may suspect, is only because he remains in essence exactly as intended originally. As a study in the psychology of the rebel, Jacques is finely and sympathetically drawn throughout the novel, and this at a time when the

[1] *Souvenirs*, p. xlvii.

'rebel' or the 'outsider' was not a critical cliché. His entire development follows a credible and logical line, and his death is the natural conclusion of his life. In the case of Daniel, however, we have a feeling of unfulfilled promise, when we contrast his rôle in the first three volumes with his position in the series as a whole. In the original plan it seems unlikely that he was to be maimed in the war; all the signs are that Martin du Gard intended to paint in some depth the portrait of a creative artist. Of this, in the final version, only a few brief scraps of description remain (notably in Chapter XXXI of *Eté 1914*).

The position of Antoine in the novel is also somewhat doubtful. From the earliest volumes he is a privileged character, seen from within as well as from outside; and he suffers from the disadvantage of the privileged character, who tends to be a witness of events rather than a participator in them. The resulting lack of stature is not of prime importance in M. Thibault's lifetime; but after the latter's death there is no dominant character (Philip is clearly inadequate) to hold the different threads of the narrative together. Originally Antoine was intended to become a *grand praticien*, with a family of his own; this transformation might have succeeded in filling the vacuum; but the change of plan caused this conception to be abandoned. *Eté 1914* and *Epilogue* both suffer from the lack of a unifying figure, while Antoine, as a central character, is never entirely adequate.

At the same time, Antoine is undoubtedly in the Tolstoyan manner. Maurois has commented upon the similarity between Antoine and Prince Andrei,[1] and the similarity also extends to Pierre Bezukhov and Levin, especially in *Epilogue*. In many respects *Les Thibault* is a *Bildungsroman* with Antoine as the hero; like Bezukhov and Levin he finally becomes involved in the fate of mankind as a whole, and is thereby enabled, to some extent, to transcend his own self. But where Tolstoy had been able to overcome one of the difficulties of the *Bildungsroman*— the necessary passivity of the hero, who has to learn from his experiences—and had succeeded in incorporating elements from

[1] A. Maurois, *Mémoires*, vol. i, Paris, 1948, p. 332.

it without damaging the unity of his novels, Martin du Gard is unable fully to integrate his final conception of Antoine into the fabric of the novel. (The change in technique in *Epilogue* from third to first person is an indication of his uneasiness.)

Although the desire to emulate Tolstoy was certainly a worthy aspiration, it may also have proved, as Judrin has suggested, unfortunate,[1] since Martin du Gard's abilities were not fully adequate to this grandiose task. If his aims had been less ambitious, they might have met with more widely acclaimed success.

Of other writers whose names have at various times been coupled with Martin du Gard, only one seems indispensable to a study of him: Gide. Rolland was keenly admired by Martin du Gard, but there is a common influence in Tolstoy, and by 1920 he had broadened his conception of the novel to take in more than Rolland. In the early years, as we have seen, Barrès was a stong influence; but one which he outgrew (and may not even have recognized). Duhamel and Romains offer many parallels, particularly in the humanistic attitude of the former and pseudo-scientific temper of the latter. But these parallels are due more to a common literary heritage– that of Naturalism —than to any interacting influences. Such influence as there was, went probably from Martin du Gard to the others, on chronological grounds; both Duhamel and Romains may have been encouraged in their choice of form by the success of *Le Cahier gris* and *Le Pénitencier*.

The relationship with Gide is more important. It was, indeed, one of the most striking literary friendships of the century, and the correspondence between the two, if it ever appears, should prove of outstanding interest. At the same time, it is easy to overestimate the mutual influence, and to make Gide's work the paramount influence upon Martin du Gard, as certain critics, notably Clouard, have done,[2] seems a definite mistake. There can be no doubt that Martin du Gard was impressed by

[1] R. Judrin, in N.N.R.F., 12/58, p. 1078.

[2] H. Clouard, *Histoire de la littérature française contemporaine*, vol. ii, p. 400: '. . . s'il (Martin du Gard) descend de Gide par l'esprit . . .'; 'Toute sa hardie et minutieuse exploration psychologique est gidienne.'

Gide's work, especially *Les Nourritures terrestres*, from which the epigraph to the closing section of *Barois* is taken (i.e. before the two men had met).[1] But we have an express disavowal of Gidean influence:

... pour le détail, pour la conception du roman, pour la composition architecturale (et non symphonique) du plan, pour le choix des sujets, pour la méthode de travail, la technique, nos façons de voir sont irrémédiablement inconciliables ... (..) ... c'est un fait: aucun livre de Gide n'a été pour moi un de ces livres de chevet, sur lesquels on se modèle à la suite d'une longue et lente fréquentation.[2]

This is fully borne out by external evidence. Martin du Gard's enthusiasm for Barrès and Tinan is sufficient to explain his rapturous welcome of the *Nourritures:* Barrès's *Un homme libre* stands behind the *Nourritures* no less than behind Tinan. The treatment of Jérôme and Daniel de Fontanin constitutes a devastating attack upon the Gidean philosophy of egoistic sensuality and *disponibilité*. The methods of work of the two men were at opposite poles: Martin du Gard believed firmly in hard work rather than inspiration, in careful planning rather than spontaneity, and his psychological vision follows Tolstoy, whereas Gide preferred Dostoievski. He also disapproved of much of Gide's work after 1918,[3] and indeed confided to the present writer in 1955 that he thought little of Gide's work would survive, not even the *Journal*. At the time of the composition of *Les Faux-Monnayeurs* there was undoubtedly influence of one writer upon the other; but Gide's first attempt at a major novel—a *roman-somme*—clearly owed more to Martin du Gard than *Les Thibault* did to himself; Martin du Gard's work follows logically from his previous novels, while Gide's does not. In both writers we find a desire for technical virtuosity, and here Gide may have inspired rivalry; in both we find an interest in similar themes: adolescence, sexuality, and the frailty of human

---

[1] Martin du Gard must therefore have had access to one of the only 500 copies of the *Nourritures* which were sold between 1897 and 1917 (cf. K. Mann, *André Gide and the Crisis of Modern Thought*, London, 1948, p. 147).

[2] *Notes sur André Gide*, pp. 1417–18.

[3] E.g. Gide, *Journal 1889–1939*, p. 683 on *Si le grain* . . .; *Notes sur André Gide*, p. 1375 on *Corydon*; ibid., p. 1403 on *Geneviève*, etc.

relationships, while there are also superficial resemblances between characters—Rachel and Lady Griffith; but this indicates a parallel rather than mutual influence. In every case the trait may be traced back in Martin du Gard to a time prior to his close knowledge of Gide's work, and there is in fact no evidence that his contact with Gide caused Martin du Gard to make more than minor alterations to his novel (such as the discussion between Vécard and Antoine after M. Thibault's funeral). There is an essential difference in attitude, which is illustrated by *Confidence africaine*. The abnormal theme might appear to be Gidean, but Martin du Gard's attitude is throughout one of sympathetic comprehension and acceptance—a humanist attitude —radically different from Gide's almost perverse pleasure in the abnormality of a situation.

The question of humanism is cardinal to an understanding of Martin du Gard; indeed, in the last analysis, his work stands or falls with the humanist philosophy. Despite his aim of transparency of style, despite his attempt to remain impartial and objective in his narrative, his entire work rests upon the philosophy of humanism, which we may define as the search for a meaning in life in a world without God.[1] This is indeed one of the fundamental themes of the modern novel, but its implications have rarely been so searchingly examined as by Martin du Gard. For him, death is the primary *donnée* of the human condition, and death inevitably means personal annihilation; man must therefore find a meaning within life, since no escape from death is possible. Man has in fact to act as if there were no death.

This humanism pervades his entire work, but is especially prominent in *Les Thibault*. Its manifestations are to be found in the identification of evil with suffering, so that Antoine in his fight against disease becomes a symbol of Man; or in such details as Martin du Gard's apparently more favourable attitude towards the Fontanins in the first two volumes. This springs

[1] Martin du Gard in fact fully realized the impossibility of absolute objectivity; in a letter to J.-J. Thierry he commented: 'Toute littérature qui vaut quelque chose, dont l'auteur a une personnalité, est *engagée*, même les *Fables* de la Fontaine . . .' (quoted in *N.N.R.F.*, 12/58, p. 1015).

from his belief in the value of the individual and in individual responsibility: the Protestant religion approaches closer to this ideal than the Catholic, so he regards Mme de Fontanin's upbringing of her children as superior to M. Thibault's more rigid methods. Yet his treatment, even of morally objectionable characters, is always charitable; their weaknesses are painted as essentially human ones; and if any character, such as Jérôme, is utterly condemned in the novel, it is not on moral principles but because his attitude to life is inadequate to guarantee happiness either to himself or to others.

The theme of vocation is central to this humanism, which accounts for its importance in the novel, together with the related themes of education, adolescence, and ambition. Antoine's strictures to Jean-Paul in *Epilogue* form Martin du Gard's final message: 'Accepte-toi, avec tes bornes et tes manques. Et applique-toi à te développer, sainement, normalement, sans tricher, dans ta vraie destination . . .';[1] and the lives of Daniel, Jacques, and Antoine himself, can only be judged in the light of this theme. Daniel, prior to the war, seems to have developed a satisfactory attitude towards life, in his life of unbridled egoism and calculated irresponsibility. He embodies the Gidean ideal, and the damage he inflicts on others, such as Rinette, has already been shown in *La Belle Saison*. In *Eté 1914* and *Epilogue* he is no longer able to live divorced from the historical context of the age—'ce merveilleux refuge où il avait eu le privilège de pouvoir installer sa vie';[2] after violent contact with that historical context, he finds himself unable to live at all. His art had depended not upon his spiritual resources but upon his sexual capabilities, and once these are destroyed he cannot face life. His attitude is therefore clearly negative, both morally and practically.

In Jacques's case, we are shown another aspect of the relationship of the individual with society, Jacques never attempts, like Daniel, completely to isolate himself from his fellow men; even his *fugues* are primarily motivated by his inability to make adequate contact with his family and those around him, not by any fundamental misanthropy. But in fact he can never adjust

---

[1] *Epilogue*, p. 951.   [2] *Eté 1914*, p. 276.

himself, even to ordinary social contacts; his egoism is no less thoroughgoing than Daniel's. Not only does he unnecessarily ruin two lives—those of Jenny and Gise—his craving for total ideological independence prevents him from making the best use of his gifts and abilities. His desire for purity largely takes the form, not of spiritual or sexual innocence, but of escape from any type of practical social responsibility—despite his emotional sympathy for the underprivileged. He can never bring himself to abdicate his individuality and submit himself to the will of the collectivity; he is indeed a rebel, not a revolutionary, and his rebellion is caused by his own psychological deficiencies. There is no doubt that Jacques is not intended to be the subject of admiration; his attitude too is inadequate in the face of the more violent aspects of life. When the cataclysm overtakes Europe he cannot accept it, and his death is only another form of escape. Thus pure idealism is not satisfactory; heroism even less so, since it merely leads him to an absurdly undignified end. (Meynestrel offers another illustration of the inadequacy of the revolutionary attitude; although war will, he believes, offer the opportunity for successful revolutionary action, he cannot live without a satisfactory emotional relationship; and when Alfreda leaves him he too takes refuge in virtual suicide.)

This negative conclusion in respect of Daniel and Jacques is, at first sight, reversed in Antoine's case, since his development appears to follow a steadily positive course (with the exception of his worldly attitude immediately prior to the outbreak of war, an episode inserted, no doubt, mainly to serve as an antithesis to Jacques's life in Geneva and to Antoine's own subsequent career). He is, above all, the representative of the humanist philosophy; the keynote is *équilibre* and *sens de la mesure*. In the original plan, we may well believe that he was intended as the successful counterpart to Jacques, achieving full development, a complete sense of integration in and involvement with society. In *Epilogue* he does so: only to die. It is a strange but deliberate parallel that the lives of so many of the characters end in suicide: Jacques, Jérôme, Daniel (who intends suicide), and Antoine.

Yet only in one case does the act of suicide not imply escapism from life: Antoine takes his own life as the supreme method of showing that even in death he has some control over his environment, that only he can decide the exact moment of death. Elsewhere there is no dignity in death. Yet Antoine is destroyed nevertheless. His fate represents Martin du Gard's final conception of life: in the end, whatever man's success within life, death will claim him. In a world without God, no attitude is adequate: the attempt to transcend the self, to find a replacement for religion—and immortality—must always fail. Daniel attempts a life of art and sensuality, Jacques one of revolutionary action, Antoine one of energetic activity and service to the community, Barois a crusade for freedom of thought; in the long run, none succeeds, and the only difference is in the degree of temporary satisfaction. In the privileged conditions of pre-1914 life, Daniel and both Thibaults seem to have found solutions which are adequate in the short run; but once those favourable circumstances have disappeared, only Antoine can adjust his attitude. Finally he too is destroyed, but from outside, not from within. His death is in the stoical tradition; while his diary, intended for Jean-Paul, is a second *Bouteille à la mer*.[1]

There can be no doubt that Martin du Gard's conclusion is one of black pessimism; and this has earned him a good deal of criticism, on the ground that his work represents an arid materialism, that no ray of light is visible in his conception of man. Mme Magny has, for instance, charged him with creating 'un univers sans issue',[2] and has claimed that his world is 'muré dans son tragique intérieur'.[3] Yet this criticism is largely beside the point. His tragic conception of life is not the conclusion, but the premiss of his work; and to disagree with this conception is to pass a moral judgment in his *Weltanschauung*, not an aesthetic judgment upon his artistic achievement. (This would be perfectly legitimate, but it implies assimilating all aesthetic judgments to moral ones, a step which few literary critics are willing to take.) Mme Magny goes on to state that the idea of

---

[1] Cf. G. Monin in *Problèmes du roman*, Brussels, 1945, p. 48.
[2] Magny, op. cit., p. 328.   [3] Ibid., p. 331.

la condition humaine is absent from *Les Thibault*;[1] this again would appear to be misconceived, for it is precisely a vivid perception of the human condition which inspires Martin du Gard's tragic conception of life and therefore his pessimism. The primary themes of his work are metaphysical, as we have seen, and it is this which most clearly differentiates him from writers following more closely in the Naturalist tradition. Pessimism is an integral part of humanism; self-transcendence, *dépasser l'homme*, is by definition impossible. Man must live upon his own moral resources; each individual is both unique and uniquely valuable.

This pessimistic humanism was Martin du Gard's basic attitude throughout his life, since it sprang fundamentally from his lack of religious belief. It was however powerfully reinforced by the effect of the 1914–18 War upon him. Although, when he began *Les Thibault*, he was treating largely the same themes which had interested him before 1914, by the early 1930's he found himself unable to ignore the disaster which had overtaken the Europe of his youth, and, almost alone among modern novelists, he chose to end his major novel with a catastrophe. This is a long way from the naïve belief in progress which some critics have claimed to perceive in his work. He does not believe that the world is bound to improve, but that the only hope for mankind lies in the possibility of its being perfected, in the intelligent employment of man's rational faculties. Antoine's action in spending the last weeks of his life writing advice to Jean-Paul and keeping a record of his own mortal illness for publication, so that it might help future sufferers, illustrates this hope in the future. Ultimately all effort is absurd, but while we are still alive it must be regarded as worth while. Only thus can man attain any final dignity in life. In Martin du Gard we can observe the same search for ethical imperatives in a meaningless world which we later find in Existentialist writers, the quest for an answer to the question, 'A quoi ça rime, la vie?'. He can find no answer, and his pessimism is ultimately absolute; but it would be a bold man who today would prophesy that this pessimism could in no circumstances be justified.

[1] Ibid., p. 327.

It is difficult to assess Martin du Gard's chances of survival as a novelist. It is certain, however, that since the last war his reputation has been in decline, outshone by younger writers whose works seem to have more relevance to the present generation. One criticism has been that his thought has never progressed beyond 1918, or even 1914. In one sense this is true: he was never able (unless he finally succeeded in *Maumort*) to find an adequate post-1918 vehicle for this themes and characters. The modern reader tends to demand a modern setting for the novel, and the idea of a leisurely work in ten or more volumes has been running counter to the popularity of the quick-moving narrative of the novel of adventure or violence. Even a studied realism has tended to give way to fantasy and allegory. Yet basically Martin du Gard's themes are very similar to those of Malraux, Sartre, or Camus: one need only compare Jacques's career and his attempt at a heroic suicide with that of Kyo Gisors or Tchen in *La Condition humaine*, or Mathieu in *Les Chemins de la Liberté*. The theme of the relationship of the individual and the collectivity and the search for a satisfactory replacement for religion is common to both Malraux and Martin du Gard; while Antoine's fight against disease and suffering is closely paralleled by that of Rieux in *La Peste* (it is not for nothing that Camus has shown such sympathetic understanding of Martin du Gard's work in his *Préface*). There is even a parallel between *Barois* and *Les Mandarins:* in both novels we find the same rather arid intellectual atmosphere, the same preoccupation with ideas and their propagation, the same involvement with practical politics. The greatest difference between Martin du Gard and these later writers (apart from his greater pessimism) lies in the vehicle chosen, which in their case is more striking and more immediately relevant to the present historical context.

Les Thibault, in particular *Eté 1914* and *Epilogue*, is not adequate to carry the full burden of Martin du Gard's message and his art. Yet it has qualities which may well, in an era possessed of more leisure—or more perseverance—than our own, ensure its survival as a minor classic; above all its moral coherence as an expression of humanism and its absolute refusal to distort the reality of life, however unpalatable that reality may be. Martin du Gard is not a great thinker, despite the appearance of *Barois*, since all his ideas are no more than second-hand (save in the one sphere of literary technique, where he follows in the tradition of Flaubert and Henry James). His work lacks Proust's depth of psychological analysis; but he has nevertheless created an admirable gallery of characters, and in particular of sexuality is vivid and convincing, without ever descending to obscenity or exhibitionism. His attitude to life makes him a *moraliste* in the finer sense: he portrays the world from a definite moral viewpoint; his patient craftsmanship and the ideal of transparent style made his work immune from facile imitation (he has no obvious mannerisms), and it will always yield value to the perceptive reader. His life and achievement will remain a minor monument in the field of human endeavour.

BIBLIOGRAPHY

1. Works by Martin du Gard

The *Pléiade* edition contains all Martin du Gard's work, with the following exceptions:

L'Une de nous, Paris, 1910.
Noizemont-les-Vierges, Liège, 1928.
Dialogue, Paris, 1930.

Articles

Le Vieux Colombier, in *N.R.F.*, December 1919, pp. 1113-18.
On Gide in *Hommage à André Gide* (special issue of *N.R.F.*, Paris, 1928).
Martin du Gard's Nobel Prize Award speech is printed in: *Les prix Nobel en 1937*, Stockholm, 1938.
Correspondence with Pierre Margaritis and Marcel Lallemand appeared in the special edition of the *N.N.R.F.*, *Hommage à Roger Martin du Gard*, December 1958.

2. Books

R.-M. ALBÉRÈS, *Portrait de notre héros*, Paris, 1945.
G. ALMÉRAS, *La médecine dans Les Thibault* (thesis), Paris, 1946.
B. AMOUDRU, *De Bourget à Gide*, Paris, 1946.
M. ARLAND, *Essais et nouveaux essais critiques*, Paris, 1952.
E. AUERBACH, *Mimesis* (English translation), paperback edition, New York, 1957.
AURIANT, *Fragments*, Brussels, 1942.
J. W. BEACH, *The Twentieth Century Novel*, New York, 1932.
I. BERLIN, *The Hedgehog and the Fox*, London, 1954.
C. BEUCHAT, *Histoire du naturalisme français*, vol. ii, Paris, 1949.
A. BILLY, *La littérature française contemporaine*, Paris, 1928.
—— *L'époque 1900*, Paris, 1951.
C. BO, *Saggi per una letteratura*, 2nd edition, Brescia, 1946.
G. BONNET, *La morale de Félix Le Dantec*, Poitiers, 1930.
C. BORGAL, *Roger Martin du Gard*, Paris, 1957.
J. BRENNER, *Martin du Gard*, Paris, 1961.
P.-J. BRODIN *Les écrivains français de l'entre-deux-guerres*, Montreal, 1942.
—— *Présences contemporaines*, Paris, 1955.
R. CAILLOIS, *Puissances du roman*, Marseille, 1942.

J. CHARPENTIER, *Tours d'horizon*, Ligu... , 1943.

H. CLOUARD, *Histoire de la littérature française du symbolisme à nos jours*, vol. ii, Paris, 1949.

J. COPEAU, *Souvenirs du Vieux-Colombier*, Paris, 1931.

N. CORMEAU, *Physiologie du roman*, Brussels, 1947.

A. CRESSON, *La position actuelle des problèmes philosophiques*, Paris, 1924.
—— *Les courants de la pensée philosophique française*, vol. ii, Paris, 1927.

P. DAIX, *Réflexions sur le méthode de Roger Martin du Gard*, Paris, 1958.

C. DELHORBE, *L'Affaire Dreyfus et les écrivains français*, Paris, 1932.

R. DUMAY, *Mort de la littérature*, Paris, 1950.

J.-E. EHRHARD, *Le roman français depuis Marcel Proust*, Paris, 1933.

E. FAGUET, *Politiques et moralistes du dix-neuvième siècle*, 6th edition, Paris, 1903.

E. M. FRASER, *Le renouveau religieux d'aprés le roman français de 1886 à 1914*, Paris, 1934.

M. FRIEDMAN, *Stream of Consciousness: a Study in Literary Method*, Yale U.P., 1955.

W. M. FROHOCK, *André Malraux and the Tragic Imagination*, Stanford U.P., 1952.

R. GIBSON, *The Quest of Alain-Fournier*, London, 1953.
—— *Martin du Gard*, London, 1961.

A. GIDE, *Divers*, Paris, 1931.
—— *Journal des Faux-Monnayeurs*, (*Œuvres complètes*, vol. xiii), Paris, 1937.
—— *Si le grain ne meurt* (111th edition), Paris, 1947.
—— *Journal 1889–1939*, new edition, Paris, 1951.
—— *Journal 1939–1942*, Paris, 1946.
—— *Journal 1942–1949*, 73rd edition, Paris, 1950.
—— *Littérature engagée*, 13th edition, Paris, 1950.

V. GIRAUD, *Le problème religieux et l'histoire de la littérature française*, Paris, 1938.

H. GMELIN, *Der französische Zyklenroman 1900–1945*, Heidelberg, 1950.

J. GREEN, *Journal vol. i*, Paris, 1938.
—— *Journal vol. iv*, Paris, 1949.

H. GRIMRATH, *Der Weltkrieg im französischen Roman*, Berlin, 1935.

J. A. GUNN, *Modern French Philosophy*, London, 1922.

G. GUSDORF, *La découverte de soi*, Paris, 1948.
—— *Mémoire et personne*, vol. i, Paris, 1951.

M.-F. GUYARD, *La Grande-Bretagne dans le roman français, 1914–1940*, Paris, 1954.

H. HATZFELD, *Trends and Styles in Twentieth Century French Literature* Washington D.C., 1957.

M. Hébert, *Science et religion*, Paris, 1895.
—— *L'évolution de la foi catholique*, Paris, 1905.
—— *Testament spirituel*, Novara, 1914.

E. Heller, *The Ironic German*, London, 1958.

F. W. J. Hemmings, *The Russian Novel in France 1884–1914*, Oxford, 1950.

F. C. Hoffman, *Freudianism and the Literary Mind*, Baton Rouge, 1945.

A. Houtin, *Un prêtre symboliste: Marcel Hébert 1851–1916*, Paris, 1925.

H. James, *The Art of the Novel* (collected prefaces), London, 1935.

M. Jarrett-Kerr, *François Mauriac*, Cambridge, 1954.

E. Knight, *Literature considered as Philosophy*, London, 1957.

M. Kurtz, *Jacques Copeau* (French translation), Paris, 1950.

A.-E. Kurzweil, *La crise de la famille dans le roman français contemporain*, Budapest, 1937.

W. Lacher, *Le réalisme dans le roman contemporain*, (thesis), Geneva, 1940.

J. de Lacretelle, *L'heure qui change*, Geneva, 1941.

P. Lafille, *André Gide romancier*, Paris, 1954.

R. Lalou, *Histoire de la littérature française contemporaine*, vol. i, 8th edition Paris, 1922.
—— ibid., vol. ii, 3rd edition, Paris, 1946.
—— *Roger Martin du Gard*, Paris, 1937.
—— *Le roman français depuis 1900*, Paris, 1947.

M. Laparade, *Réflexions sur quatre médecins de roman*, (thesis), Bordeaux, 1948.

P. Léautaud, *Entretiens avec Robert Mallet*, 7th edition, Paris, 1951.

F. Le Dantec, *Les influences ancestrales*, Paris, 1905.
—— *L'athéisme*, Paris, 1907.

P. Lubbock, *The Craft of Fiction*, new edition, London, 1954.

G. Lukacs, *Studies in European Realism* (English translation), London, 1950.

J. Madaule, *Reconnaissances*, vol. iii, Paris, 1945.

C.-E. Magny, *Histoire de roman français depuis 1918*, vol. i, Paris, 1950.

K. Mann, *André Gide and the Crisis of Modern Thought*, London, 1948.

M. Marchand, *Le complexe pédagogique et didactique d'André Gide*, Oran, 1954.

H. Massis, *Comment Emile Zola composait ses romans*, Paris, 1906.
—— *Romain Rolland contre la France*, Paris, 1915.
—— *Jugements*, vol. ii, Paris, 1924.
—— *Maurras et notre temps*, two vols., Paris 1951.

G. de Maupassant, *Pierre et Jean*, 61st edition, Paris, 1897.

F. Mauriac, *Ecrits intimes*, Geneva, 1953.

P. Mauriac, *La médecine et l'intelligence*, Bordeaux, 1949.

A. Maurois, *Etudes littéraires*, vol. ii, Paris, 1947.
—— *Mémoires*, vol. i, Paris, 1948.

R. Michaud, *Modern Thought and Literature in France*, New York, 1934.

P. Mille, *Le roman français*, Paris, 1930.

C. Moeller, *Littérature du vingtième siècle et christianisme*, two vols., Paris, 1953.

J. Moreau, *L'oeuvre de Félix Le Dantec*, Paris, 1918.

L. Morino, *La Nouvelle Revue Française*, Paris, 1939.

D. Mornet, *Introduction à l'étude des écrivains français d'aujourd'hui*, Paris, 1939.

J. O'Brien, *The Novel of Adolescence in France*, New York, 1937.

H. Peyre, *The Contemporary French Novel*, New York, 1955.

L. Pierre-Quint, *André Gide*, new edition, Paris, 1952.

Ed. J. Prevost, *Problèmes du roman*, Brussels, 1945.

J.-L. Prevost, *Le prêtre, ce héros de roman*, vol. ii, Paris 1953.

E. S. Randall, *The Jewish Character in the French Novel 1870–1914*, Menasha, Wisconsin, 1941.

E. Renan, *Souvenirs d'enfance et de jeunesse*, new edition, Paris, 1947.

H. C. Rice, *Roger Martin du Gard and the World of the Thibaults*, New York, 1941.

—— article on Roger Martin du Gard in *Columbia Dictionary of Modern European Literature*, New York, 1948.

J. Rivière and Alain-Fournier, *Correspondance 1905–1914*, vol. ii, 9th edition, Paris, 1930.

R. Rolland, *Journal des années de guerre*, Paris, 1952.

A. Rousseaux, *Littérature du vingtième siecle*, vol. i, Paris, 1938.

C. Roy, *Descriptions critiques*, Paris, 1949.

J. Sageret, *La révolution philosophique et la science*, Paris, 1924.

J.-P. Sartre, *Les jeux sont faits*, Paris, 1947.

—— *Situations II*, 30th editions, Paris, 1951.

D. Saurat, *Modern French Literature 1870–1940*, London, 1946.

J. Schlumberger, *Eveils*, 5th edition, Paris, 1950.

P.-H. Simon, *L'esprit et l'histoire*, Paris, 1954.

G. Sneyers, *Romanciers d'entre deux guerres*, Brussels, 1941.

R. Soltau, *French Political Thought in the Nineteenth Century*, London, 1931.

P. Souday, *Les livres du temps*, IIIe série, Paris, 1930.

P. H. Spencer, *Politics of Belief in Nineteenth-Century France*, London, 1954.

W. T. Starr, *Romain Rolland and a World at War*, Evanston, Illinois, 1956.

H. Taine, *Histoire de la littérature anglaise*, 5th edition, Paris, 1881.

A. Thibaudet, *Les idées de M. Maurras*, Paris, 1920.

—— *Réflexions sur le roman*, Paris, 1938.

—— *Histoire de la littérature française de 1789 à nos jours*, new edition, Paris, 1947.

J. DE TINAN, *Aimienne*, Paris, 1899.

—— *Penses-tu réussir?*, new edition, Paris, 1921.

TRAN VAN TUNG, *L'école de France*, Hanoi, 1938.

G. TRUC, *Quelques peintres de l'homme contemporain*, Paris, 1926.

D. TYLDEN-WRIGHT, *The Image of France*, London, 1957.

S. ULLMANN, *Style in the French Novel*, Cambridge, 1957.

W. WEIDLÉ, *Les abeilles d'Aristée*, new edition, Paris, 1954.

G. WEILL, *Histoire du mouvement social en France 1852-1924*, 3rd edition, Paris 1924.

A. ZÉVAÈS, *Histoire du socialisme et communisme en France de 1871 à 1947*, Paris, 1947.

3. Articles

G. J. BARBERET, *Books Abroad*, Autumn 1958, pp. 379-81.

M. BEIGBEDER, *N.N.R.F.*, 12/58, pp. 1042-5.

E. BERL, *La Table Ronde*, 10/58, pp. 173-6.

H. BIDOU, *Revue de Paris*, 15/5/40, pp. 331-5.

C. BORGAL, *N.N.R.F.*, 12/58, pp. 1092-8.

J. BRENNER, *N.N.R.F.*, 12/58, pp. 1053-9.

A. CAMUS, *N.N.R.F.*, 10/55, pp. 641-71.

A. CHAMSON, *N.N.R.F.*, 12/58, pp. 997-1002.

J. CHARPENTIER, *Mercure de France*, 15/1/31, pp. 333-7.

J. COCTEAU, *N.N.R.F.*, 12/58, pp. 994-6.

B. CRÉMIEUX, *N.R.F.*, 8/29, pp. 256-62.

J. DELAY, *N.N.R.F.*, 12/58, pp. 976-84.

P. DESCAVES, *Erasme*, 1ᵉ année, 1946, pp. 368-70.

G. DUHAMEL, *Revue de Paris*, 12/52, pp. 5-30.

D. FERNANDEZ, *N.N.R.F.*, 12/58, pp. 1079-91.

R. FERNANDEZ, *N.R.F.*, 1/24, pp. 110-13.

C. FRANCILLON, *N.N.R.F.*, 12/58, pp. 1010-13.

R. FROMENT, *N.N.R.F.*, 12/58, pp. 965-72.

O. GRAUTOFF, *Deutsch-französische Rundschau*, Band II, Heft 7, 1927, pp. 627-43.

J. GROSJEAN, *N.N.R.F.*, 12/58, pp. 1107-16.

J. GUÉHENNO, *N.N.R.F.*, 12/58, pp. 1036-41.

L. GUICHARD, *Revue d'histoire littéraire de la France*, 10/60, pp. 559-62.

T. W. HALL, *French Review*, 12/53, pp. 108-13.

F. HALLENS, *N.N.R.F.*, 12/58, pp. 1099-1106.

P. HERBART, *Le Figaro Littéraire*, 30/8/58, p. 4.

H. Hertz, *Europe*, 15/2/37, pp. 244-6.

R. Ikor, *Europe*, 6/46, pp. 28-47.

R. Jardillier, *Arts et Livres*, No. 7, 1946, pp. 86-101.

M. Jouhandeau, *N.N.R.F.*, 12/58, pp. 1008-9.

R. Judrin, *N.N.R.F.*, 12/58, pp. 1074-8.

R. Kanters, *Cahiers du Sud*, 9/40, pp. 433-5.

L. Kraucher, *Germanisch-Romanische Monatsschrift*, 1/33, pp. 59-70.

J. de Lacretelle, *N.N.R.F.*, 12/58, pp. 973-5.

M. Lallemand, *N.N.R.F.*, 12/58, pp. 1018-28.

R. Lalou, *Revue de Paris*, 15/8/37, pp. 821-44.

—— *Revue de Paris*, 10/58, pp. 60-64.

J. Lambert, *N.N.R.F.*, 12/58, pp. 1003-7.

F. Le Grix, *Revue Hebdomadaire*, 21/7/28, pp. 356-63.

J. Madaule, *Esprit*, 11/40, pp. 52-55.

R. Mallet, *N.N.R.F.*, 12/58, pp. 1046-52.

L. Marcantonato, *Cahiers du Sud*, 1939, pp. 515-21.

Maurice Martin du Gard, *Revue des Deux Mondes*, 1/10/58, pp. 463-74.

H. Massis, *Revue Universelle*, 1/2/38, pp. 354-61.

——(Jaco), *Bulletin des Lettres*, 15/10/52, pp. 333-5.

T. Maulnier, *Revue Universelle*, 1/1/38, p. 118.

M. J. Moore-Rinvolucri .*Modern Languages*, 9/52, pp. 85-89.

P. Morand, *N.N.R.F.*, 12/58, pp. 1060-3.

J. P(aulhan), *N.N.R.F.*, 10/58, pp. 577-9.

G. Picon, *Mercure de France*, 9/58, pp. 5-25.

A. Pizzorusso, *Convivium* XXV, pp. 163-81.

R. de Ribon, *Revue Hebdomadaire*, 3/24, pp. 106-12.

J. Romains, *N.N.R.F.*, 12/58, pp. 985-9.

L. S. Roudiez, *Romanic Review*, XLVIII, pp. 275-86.

A. Rousseaux, *Revue Universelle*, 1/7/28, pp. 109-15.

C. Roy, *Europe*, 12/48, pp. 107-13.

G. Sadoul, *Les Etoiles*, 19/6/45, pp. 1 and 3.

J. Schlumberger, *N.N.R.F.*, 12/58, pp. 1068-73.

J. Tardieu, *N.N.R.F.*, 12/58, pp. 990-3.

J.-J. Thierry, *N.N.R.F.*, 12/58, pp. 1014-17.

G. Truc, *Revue Bleue*, 3/1/25., pp. 14-17

P. Van Tieghem, *N.N.R.F.*, 12/58, pp. 1064-7.

J. Vaudal, *N.R.F.*, 6/40, pp. 847-50.

L. Vermont, *Les Nouvelles Littéraires*, 20/11/37, p. 1.

J. S. Wood, *French Studies*, 4/60, pp. 129-40.

INDEX